FLORIDA STATE
UNIVERSITY LIBRARIES

OCT 2 1995

Tallahassee, Florida

Upper Mississippi River Rafting Steamboats

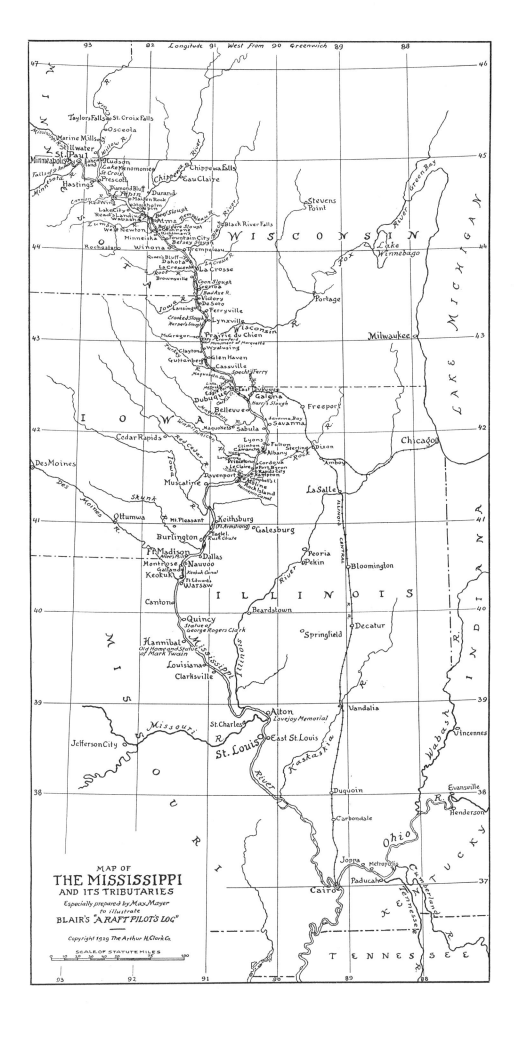

Upper Mississippi River Rafting Steamboats

Edward A. Mueller

OHIO UNIVERSITY PRESS

ATHENS

Ohio University Press, Athens, Ohio 45701
© 1995 by Edward A. Mueller
Printed in the United States of America
All rights reserved

Ohio University Press books are printed on acid-free paper ∞

02 01 00 99 98 97 96 95   5 4 3 2 1

Library of Congress Cataloging-in-Publication Data

Mueller, Edward A.
  Upper Mississippi River rafting steamboats / Edward A. Mueller.
    p.   cm.
  "The written portion of this work centers around the accounts left by Harry G. Dyer"—Pref.
  Includes index.
  ISBN 0-8214-1113-6
  1. Inland water transportation—Mississippi River—History. 2. Steamboats—Mississippi River—History. 3. Mississippi River—Navigation—History. 4. Shipping—Mississippi River—History. 5. Timber—Mississippi River—Rafting—History. I. Dyer, Harry G., d. 1950. II. Title.
HE630.M6M84 1995   94-43491
386′.3′0977—dc20   CIP

Contents

Preface	vii
Rafting on the Mississippi	1
Captain George Winans' Life, Record and Recollections	7
Log of Harry G. Dyer	12
Listing of Upper Mississippi River Rafting Steamboats and Their Owners	31
Building Rafts	33
What It Costs to Run a Raft Boat a Month	35
Raft Pilots	36
Steamboat Cooks	38
Steamboat Hoboes	40
Bell and Whistle Signals	43
Rafting Steamboat Histories	45
Lists	91
Rafting Steamboats	91
Steamboat Nicknames	94
Rafting Pilots and Masters	95
Rock Island Rapids Pilots	97
Engineers	97
Mates	99
Appendix	100
How the Watch is Changed on a Steamboat	100
United States Steamboat Inspectors' Examination for Chief Mate's License	101
Upper Mississippi River Ferries and Ferry Boats	102
Upper Mississippi River Bridges	103
Station Bill on a Rafting Steamboat	104

Steamboats and Masters that Harry G. Dyer
 Worked on or Served   105

Rhyming on the River   106

Mississippi River Distances
 as of the 1880s   107

Mississippi River Distances
 as of the 1940s   108

Index   111

Illustrations follow pages 24, 56, and 88.

Preface

Over fifteen decades ago, the timber resources of the northern midwest states were discovered. It was an era when private enterprise dominated, and entrepreneurs strove to achieve wealth. As a result, the timber resources began to be exploited. The great demand for homes in the middle portion of the country served to absorb all the pine timber that could be logged and transported there. Getting much of this timber to market required the use of timber rafts that floated south along the great Mississippi River and its tributaries to sawmills or to distribution points.

Transportation of this lumber by water evolved into the use of steamboats as the propulsion and steering systems for the large and ever-larger timber rafts during the Civil War and the next five decades.

Printed works have sufficiently dealt with the business aspects of the lumber trades, the lack of foresight in not accomplishing reforestation, and the colorful personalities involved, but little has been written concerning the numerous steamboats and their role in the lumber business.

This brings one to the theme of this book, which is a pictorial and written account of the rafting steamboats and the men who worked them. The rafting steamboats, or "rafters", as they are termed in this book, were for the most part, workboats. Except for a few notable exceptions, these boats were not fancy and certainly not like their larger "packet" relatives. Due to the declining nature of the business in the last decade of the 1800s and the first decade of the 1900s, many rafters were sold and began to appear in other locales with different roles.

The written portion of this work centers around the accounts left by Harry G. Dyer, an old-time rafting steamboat mate, and the life and accomplishments of Captain George Winans, a kingpin in the steamboat transportation business. The assembling and editing the Dyer information, I have produced and set forth the short histories of these rafting steamboats, along with a considerable amount of supplementary information.

Several years ago, I was looking over steamboat materials in the State Historical Society of Wisconsin's Library at Madison, Wisconsin. I found steamboat writings by Harry G. Dyer, a deceased Madison resident, and ascertained that Mr. Dyer had served as a deckhand and mate on many steamboats during the rafting days on the upper Mississippi River. Encouraged by the Society's curator, Charles Brown, in the 1930s and 1940s Mr. Dyer set down descriptive accounts of his rafting career and life on the river as it had been.

After his rafting career was over, Harry Dyer lived in Madison, Wisconsin and worked as a fireman and engineer on the steam heating plant for the State Capital Building. His knowledge of steam engines on rafters stood him in good stead. He married and "swallowed the anchor" completely. As a sideline he built a model of a typical raft and rowboat (the *SATELLITE*), as well as models of several logging tools which were on display at the State Historical Society Museum for many years. However, in the 1940s, Mr. Dyer retrieved his model and its present whereabouts, if any, are unknown.

I spent a considerable amount of time, aided by my brother, John Mueller, attempting to locate relatives of Mr. Dyer, but this endeavor was unsuccessful. Mr. Dyer died in 1950 and is interred in Forest Hill Cemetery in Madison, Wisconsin. His wife preceeded him in death.

As the reader will gather from Mr. Dyer's accounts, he was a lover of the river and the rafting steamboat life. He was very proud to be called a steamboat man and, as time went on, was rather overwhelmed by the nostalgic aspects of his career on the river.

I made copies of Dyer's accounts (most of which were in his handwriting) and then set aside for several years while I pursued other steamboat projects. However, the thought of trying to produce a worthwhile record of those bygone days concentrating on Dyer's material persisted. Finally, I decided to produce this written and pictorial record.

The Murphy Library at the University of Wisconsin-LaCrosse has a collection of thousands of images of steamboats, many of them rafters. The Library was extremely cooperative in making its photo files accessible, and from them the great majority of photos used in this work were obtained. I secured other photos from the State Historical Society of Wisconsin, the Putnam Museum of History and Natural Science at Davenport, Iowa, the Winona (Minnesota) Historical Society, the Sons and Daughters of Pioneer Rivermen, and my own collection. I pursued further research at the Minnesota Historical Society, the Buffalo Bill Museum at LeClaire, the Milwaukee County Public Library, and the Jacksonville, Florida Public Library.

I commissioned original steamboat paintings and renderings for this book. Jacksonville artist William Trotter produced definitive paintings of the *E. RUTLEDGE* and the *F. C. A. DENKMANN*. Likewise, Jacksonville delineator Mike Stevens produced four black and white renderings; the *PAULINE, F. WEYERHAEUSER, NORTH STAR,* and the *OTTUMWA BELLE* the latter as she passed McGregor, Iowa on the last rafting trip. Don Ingram sketched several of the rafter personages.

In 1928, Charles Edward Russell wrote *A Raftin' on the Mississippi*, an interesting, factual narrative of rafting days written in a novelistic style. In 1930, Captain Walter Blair published his account of rafting steamboat days, *A Raft Pilot's Log,* a work which remains a classic tale of rafting times and serves as an excellent record that should be treasured. Both books have long been out of print and are becoming collectors' items. These books were, and are, of significant value and certainly of great interest in this field.

Many people have been of great help in preparing this book. Mrs. Ann Peterson provided essential written information that could not otherwise be readily obtained. Her untimely passing left a marked void in the lives of her family, friends, and fellow steamboat buffs. J. W. "Woody" Rutter provided significant encouragement and went out of his way to foster this project. Don Fuetsch of Cassville, Wisconsin has reams of background steamboat material which I reviewed. Marie Dorsch, archivist of the Winona County Historical Society, Winona, Minnesota, and Scott Rolling of the Putnam Museum of History and Natural Science, Davenport, Iowa, helped locate scarce photos. Roger Osborne and Jerry Enzler of the National Rivers Hall of Fame at Dubuque, Iowa were helpful. Denise Birmingham provided photos of the rafter *WABASH*'s bell, now at an estate in Coconut Grove, Florida. John Anfinson of the St. Paul U.S. Army Corps of Engineers provided key maps of the upper river. Joseph Dobler of Newport Beach, California provided information and photos from his grandfather's rafting career.

However, were it not for the unflagging efforts of Ralph DuPae in collecting steamboat photos over the years, and Ed Hill's curatorial and administrative talents in preserving and duplicating the photos at the Murphy Library, this book would not have been possible. Sincere thanks are especially tendered to Ralph and Ed. Steamboat buffs everywhere owe a tremendous debt to Captain Fred Way, Jr. and George Merrick for their collecting and writing of steamboat histories. Details are covered elsewhere concerning their work.

I also wish to thank those people who helped in the publication mechanics; Cathy Scott did the majority of the word processing, Bob Walter and Bernadette Gatos at Morales and Shumer Engineers, (where I am Vice President) especially helped on the computer aspects due to my propensity of "losing" text. The kindness of Eduardo Morales and Robert Shumer in giving me permission to use the facilities of the firm was greatly appreciated.

I wish to express my pleasure in having this book published by the Ohio University Press.

Rafting on the Mississippi

How Boating Men Handled Logs and Lumber During the Growth of Steam and Before Gas Power Appeared

HARRY G. DYER

Note: Some of this material was published in February 1924 in *Boating* magazine, and emphasizes Captain George Winans' career. Mr. Dyer knew and worked for Captain Winans and a considerable number of Captain Winans' experiences on the river were published in the *Burlington Iowa Saturday Evening Post* newspaper at various times in the 1910s and early 1920s. Mr. Dyer also wrote a more detailed account in 1945 that was not published. The author has combined the two works into a single account and has added a few items of background information.

Mr. Dyer states, "I have no way of finding out when the first raft went down the Mississippi River. In 1838, a water power sawmill was built at St. Croix Falls, Wisconsin, and in 1840, they were rafting lumber to down river points as far as St. Louis, Missouri.

"The first record I have of logs being rafted down the river [was] in 1844 when four log rafts in charge of Stephen B. Hanks left Stillwater, Minnesota for Clinton, Iowa. Captain Hanks, who was a cousin of Abraham Lincoln, had as pilots, besides himself, Severe Bruce, William Ganley, and Jas. McPhail, better known as "Big Sandy" McPhail. At first all the rafts were lumber. The rafting of logs came later. Lumber was rafted in "cribs." Initially a crib of lumber was sixteen feet square and from eighteen to twenty-six inches deep. Later on, the length of the crib was doubled, making it sixteen x thirty-two feet.

"The material for the frame of a crib was twenty planks, two inches thick, ten inches wide and sixteen feet long; and eighteen-inch round grub pins, hard wood thirty-six inches long, two inches diameter. A two-inch hole is bored in each plank of the frame eight inches from the end. Now, two of the planks are placed end-to-end on the rafting table where the crib is. The two planks make the sides of the bottom frame, two planks make the opposite side of the frame. The grub pins are made in a lathe from small saplings, generally furnished by nearby farmers. A 'head' is left on each pin by the lathe. The end and center planks are also bored to match the sides. Now a grub pin is put in each hole in the side plank with the head of the pin on the underside. The center and end planks are then dropped on the pins, and the frame of the crib is now setting on the rafting table and ready for the lumber.

"The lumber is brought into the rafting shed by movable chains and is picked up by the handlers, laid on the crib frame like a floor. The second course is laid the opposite way and so on until the crib is completed. Now the ends of the grub pins are ten or twelve inches above the top of the lumber. A plank with holes bored exactly the same as those in the bottom plank lines up the pins and a tool called a "witch" presses this cleat down and pulls the pins up. A man with a sharp axe cuts a notch in the side of the pin, and he drives in a short, hard wood wedge. When each pin has been pulled up and wedged, the rafting table is tilted and the crib slides into the river.

"Now the deck load is put on. One crib may have fifty or seventy-five bunches of shingles, another, bundles of lath or bundles of pickets or perhaps three or four thousand feet of dry lumber, but each crib is deck loaded. The reason will be told later on. The cribs are coupled end to end with coupling planks to form a string, and the coupled strings side by side form a raft. Thus, a 16-44 could mean a lumber raft sixteen strings wide and forty-four cribs long.

"The early floating rafts were from ten to fifteen cribs long and eight or ten strings wide. An oar fifty feet long was hung in the center of each string both on the bow and stern, and a big, husky lumber-jack stationed at each oar. The oars were not used as a means of propulsion but merely to keep the raft in the channel. Pulling an oar was rather strenuous work. When the order or signal came from the pilot, each man would grasp the end of his oar stem and throw it up to about the level of his eyes and walk across his string usually five steps, pushing the oar, so it was really pushing an oar instead of pulling it. It was a novel sight to see a floating raft make a crossing. Both the bow and the stern crews were pulling the same way to keep the raft up under the reef and the oar blades would strike the water almost exactly at the same time.

"The cook shanty was located about the middle of the raft and the cook played quite an important part in keeping a crew on the boat and a pilot that employed a dirty, or no good cook always had trouble in getting and keeping men. The men were generally paid by the trip and fare back up the river on a packet.

"We now come to the log part of the rafting business. The first St. Croix River logs left Stillwater, Minnesota in 1845. [Legend has it that] many logs broke loose at Marine Mills, Wisconsin, and floated down to Stillwater and only stopped there because there was no current to carry them any further. There is no current in the St. Croix River from Stillwater to its mouth at Prescott, Wisconsin. These logs were sold to St. Louis parties and were rafted at Stillwater and floated to St. Louis.

"Logs were also rafted in strings sixteen feet wide and about three hundred feet long. Two booms made of square timber, a head block connected them at the front and formed a "pocket" into which the logs were floated loose. The first tier was straightened out with the front end against the head block. A pole two or three inches in diameter and sixteen feet long was laid across each end of the tier and a 1¼ inch hole was bored in each log eight inches deep on each side of the pole. Now, a strip of hard wood, generally oak, about ¼ inch thick, one inch wide, and sixteen inches long, called a lockdown, was placed over the binder (the pole described above), with the end in the holes and a hard wood plug six inches long, 1½ inches square was driven in each hole. This was called the plug and lockdown method. The logs were of different lengths but the front ends were against the head block so it was easy to 'break joints' with the logs in the next tier. Had the logs been all the same length, it would have been very hard to keep the raft stiff enough to handle it when it was completed.

"About 1878 they commenced to use the brailing method of rafting logs. At the rafting works a stationary boom or form was built of square timber bolted together and closed at one end. The logs were placed in tiers inside this form end to end. The outside logs on each side were lapped about two feet and at the center of the lap a two-inch auger hole was bored in each log eight inches deep. A piece of new one-inch rope was cut to reach to the bottom of the holes and a hard wood plug two inches square was driven in the holes beside the rope. Two men, working one each side of the brail did this work while the rest of the rafting crew were 'tailing in' the logs. The longest logs were picked for the outside or boom logs to save boring and when the brail had been built to the desired length, a header made of logs securely fastened together was placed across each end of the brail, then the lower end of the form was opened and the brail of logs was 'dropped out' and another brail started.

"At Beef Slough where the Chippewa River logs were rafted, the brails were forty-five feet wide and five hundred feet long and six brails made a raft. At the Stillwater works on the St. Croix River, the brails were sixty feet wide and four brails made a raft. Later on, the Beef Slough brails were made 600 and 650 feet long. Beef Slough leaves the Chippewa River at Round Hill nine miles above the mouth of the river, follows down the Wisconsin bluffs about twelve miles and comes into the Mississippi just above the town of Alma, Wisconsin. The rafting works were near the foot of the Slough. Here the logs were sorted, scaled and rafted.

"The logs were sorted by their owners' names. Each log had two marks—one called the bark mark cut in the side of the log deep enough to show when the bark came off. This mark was put on with a sharp axe as the log was cut and lay in the woods. The end mark was put on both ends of the logs with a stamping hammer four times. When the log was in the water, the bark mark might be on the under side but two of the end marks would be in sight. The letters or figures of the end mark were raised and stamped into the wood. These marks showed the ownership of the log and were registered in the office of the Surveyor General in St. Paul, Minnesota and also in Chippewa Falls, Wisconsin.

"Beef Slough at the start of the rafting season would be filled with logs from bank to bank, a distance of about seven hundred feet. About the center of the slough a strip of water was kept open, called the race. Bridges across the race were where the sorters were stationed, each man with a pike pole. As the logs came down the race, they were switched to either side. Each pocket held a certain mark. In a brailing crew, there were six brailers and four boom men. In starting a brail, logs to form the bow boom were put in place. To make the bow of the brail, two sixteen- or eighteen-foot logs were placed end to end with a lap log across the joint. These logs were fastened together. A hole two inches in diameter, eight inches deep, was bored in each log, and a piece of brail rope one inch in diameter driven in each hole opposite and an oak plug two inches square and eight inches long driven in beside the holes. The logs are now 'tailed in,'; the forty-five-foot space is filled.

"The first log in the first tier and the first log in the second tier are lapped about two feet and again the two plugs and piece of rope are used. The two outside logs in a brail are boom sticks and are the only ones that are fastened together. The boomers are supposed to keep ahead of the brailers, and when the brail is completed, it will be about five hundred feet long and forty-five feet wide and there will be an average of thirty-six to forty boom sticks on each side. About every seventy-five feet of the brail, a wire cable, ½ inch, was put across it and fastened to keep the logs from spreading.

"As soon as the brail was six hundred feet long, the stem boom was put on, the pocket was opened, and the brail floated out into the main river. Two men in a skiff in which a line 1,200 feet long, 1¼ inches in diameter was coiled, were now in charge. By means of the line, they would land the brail a mile or two below the 'works' to wait until two more came through the 'works.' These were placed alongside the first brail, and it was now a half raft or a three-brail piece. A full raft was six brails. The reason for this was that on its way down the river, the raft had to be split lengthwise at the bridges. The draw spans were too narrow for the full raft. A six-brail raft was 600 feet long and 275 feet wide and contained from 800,000 to 1,000,000 board feet of timber.

"In 1889 the rafting works were moved from Beef Slough to West Newton Slough, a little further down the river and on the opposite or Minnesota side. The head of Beef Slough was silted up and the Federal government seemed reluctant to carry out needed improvements to keep it in operation. It was impossible to get logs into Beef Slough. [However, in order to use West Newton, it was necessary to switch logs into the head of the slough.]

"A sheer or fin boom was used for this purpose, and it was made of square timbers to make a surface three feet wide on top and twenty inches deep. It was made in links each about fifty feet long and coupled together with an iron link and pin. The fins were made of plank eighteen inches wide and sixteen feet long. A fin was connected to each link of the boom and connected by a ½ inch rope wire. For every three links of the boom a crank windlass was bolted to the boom and the cable for three links was attached to the windlass. When the boom was opened, the fins lay alongside and against the boom. The lower or downstream end was not fast to the shore. To close, the fins were pulled up to right angles with the boom by the windlasses, a man to each windlass. Then the current of the river pushing against the fins gradually forced the boom up and across the river. When the boom was closed, the lower or open end was three or four hundred feet below where it was fast to the shore, forming a slant so the logs would not stop when they hit the boom, but go right along into West Newton.

"[As a sidelight], one afternoon the blacksmith at the Beef Slough rafting works happened to have a little spare time and he took a ½-inch iron rod and made a boom chain [shaped like a figure eight]. He had just gotten it complete when one of the 'brass collars' came along and said, 'What are you making, Bill?' The blacksmith said, 'Nothing much,' but the 'big man' insisted on seeing it. Then Bill said, 'You could have a plug made to fit those rings and you would save all that manila rope you now use in booming.' But the big man said, 'Forget it. They would drown them faster than you could make them.' But in a very short time a patent was granted on the boom chain and thousands of them were made and a great many of them were used hundreds of times. Did it help the blacksmith? No. He only got the idea and made the chain, but the 'big man' got every cent of the royalty. He had the patent.

"At the start of the rafting business, the rafts were floated down the river and the speed depended on the stage of the water, varying from 2½ to 4 miles per hour. Some of the rafts were towed through Lake Pepin by steamboats, but from the foot of the lake, the current of the river supplied the motive power.

"On the 12th day of September 1863, Captain George Winans started the first raft to be towed by a boat below Lake Pepin. He started from Read's Landing, Minnesota, with a lumber raft for Hannibal, Missouri, and towed by the steamer, *UNION*, but owing to a breakdown of the boat's machinery, he only got a few miles below the starting point, but he satisfied himself and others that it could be done and a year later, on the 4th day of September 1864, Captain Cyrus Bradley, with the same *UNION*, left Read's Landing with a log raft for W. J. Young & Company, Clinton, Iowa, and delivered it in good condition in two days less time than usually taken for a floating raft. This trip revolutionized the rafting business. In 1865 Captain Bradley brought out the *MINNIE WILL* and from that time on, boat after boat was built for the rafting trade until in 1886 at least seventy-five boats were in the rafting business between St. Louis, Missouri, and Stillwater, Minnesota.

"Among the earliest floating pilots were James McPhail, William Ganley, Big Joe Perro, George Winans, George and Pembroke Herold, Asa Woodward, Thomas Forbush, Robert Erwin, Stephen Hanks, Charles Rhoades, Jerry Turner, David Hanks, and many others.

"The early raft boats were all small sidewheel-geared boats of from fifty to seventy-five tons; boats such as the *ANNIE GIRDON, MINNIE WILL, L.W. BARDEN, CHAMPION, BUCKEYE, L.W. CRANE,* and *JULIA HADLEY* being in this class. These small sidewheelers did but little to increase the speed of the raft, but helped keep it in the channel, did away with the stern oars, and furnished the means for transportation of the crew back up the river. The oars were used only to keep the raft in the channel, not to increase its speed. The engines were connected to a core wheel about the middle of the boat, instead of to the wheel shaft. In this way, there was no 'slow down' of the wheels when the engine passed the center of the stroke.

"In the early 70s, the building of sternwheel boats began and also an increase of size until there were some of over two hundred tons burden; the *F. WEYERHAEUSER, THISTLE, BLUE LODGE, KIT CARSON,* and *J. W. VAN SANT* being two hundred tons or over. One of the smallest, if not the smallest raft boat, was the *CHAMPION* owned by the Knapp, Stout and Company and measuring less than forty tons. With the coming of the raft boat came the steamboat raft pilot and then the struggle to see who could make the quickest trip, run the darkest night, who could take down the largest raft and make the most money for the owners.

"When the lumber companies owned the boats, the captain was not responsible for the raft while it was underway and he had nothing to say about how much deck load should be put on a crib. When the captains began to buy and build the steamboats, things were changed. A captain went to a lumberman and signed a contract to tow his lumber for a certain price per thousand. The lumberman said he would have a little dry lumber for a few cribs. The captain said that would be fine, but he soon found four or five thousand feet of dry lumber on each of fifteen or twenty cribs and he did not get a cent for towing that dry lumber! Also, he found that the lumbermen knew exactly how many shingles, lath, pickets, etc., were on each raft, and he, the captain, was responsible for every board, bunch, and bundle until the raft was delivered at its destination, and any shortage be paid for at full market price.

"I have known pilots who have lost half their profits by paying for losses for which they were in no way responsible. The Knapp, Stout Company, when they owned their own boats, allowed their captains seventy-five cents a thousand feet for expenses and the company stood for the losses, but after they sold their boats, they paid sixty-three cents per thousand and the captain paid the losses, and the captain did not get a cent for the deck load.

"New pilots kept coming to take the place of the older ones, some of the older pilots bought or built a boat and began towing by contract, but most of the boats were owned by the various sawmill and lumber companies along the river and the pilots hired by the month or season. The captain of a raft boat was always first pilot and stood a regular watch at the wheel.

"In the list of noted raft boats pilots, we find Cyprian Buisson, John Hoy, Jerome Short, Otis McGinley, Stephen Withrow, William Dobler, Andrew Luken, Peter O'Rourke, Ira Fuller, George

Winans, and George Tromley, Jr., and I think they would all admit that Captain Cyp Buisson was second to none. Each of these men was a master in getting a raft down the river. Each one had his own method of running the bridges and bad bends, and the man with weak nerves had no business in the pilot house of a raft boat.

"With the coming of the electric searchlight, the pilot's work was made much easier. Then, instead of having to strain his eyes to keep on his marks, he would signal to the engineer to start the electric light engine and in a minute or two a broad ray of light would spread over raft and river. The St. Louis and St. Paul packet, *GEM CITY,* was the first boat on the upper Mississippi to have an electric searchlight. The rafter *SAM ATLEE* was the first raft boat to have the light. This was in 1881. The *B. HERSHEY* and the *ARTEMUS LAMB* came next and in a very short time, every raft boat on the river had an electric searchlight.

"Each pilot had his own way of running the bridges and that was where much of the time was gained or lost in making the trip. The raft was always made to split lengthwise through the center. This was necessary in order to get through the many bridges that spanned the river. At some of the bridges, it was necessary to land half of the raft above the bridge, take the other half through and land below and go back and get the other half. At some of the bridges the raft could be 'double headed'; that is, put one half ahead of the other as at Clinton, Iowa. Another way was to 'make a fly.' Split a mile or so above the bridge and let one half float while the boat towed the other half through the bridge. Then let go and go back and get the first half, tow through the bridge and couple up and go on. Another way was to 'split on the pier.' Risky and only done by the 'star' pilots. The two halves of the raft would be spread apart at the bow to allow a sixteen-foot log to be fastened crosswise between the two halves, holding them sixteen feet apart. The boat was then changed over to the center of one half. When the cross log at the bow struck the bridge pier, the log would break loose and allow one half of the raft to go each side of the pier, the half to which the boat was attached going through the draw span.

"In 1890 Captain George Winans started the use of the bow boat. Up to this time, the rafts were about 550 feet long and 250 feet wide. Captain Winans owned the *JULIA* and was towing lumber from Read's Landing, Minnesota, to St. Louis, Missouri. In 1890 he built a small boat called the *SATELLITE.* He placed this boat crosswise on the bow of his raft and the raft was made twice as long and one-half as wide as formerly. The bow boat was securely fastened and an electric wire was run from the pilot house of the *JULIA* on the stern of the raft to an electric bell in the engine room of the *SATELLITE* on the bow. If the pilot wanted the bow of the raft to go to the left, he would ring the bell once, and the engineer on the bow boat would 'come ahead' and gradually push the bow of the raft to the left until the bell was rung to stop. If the bell was rung twice, the engines were reversed and the bow of the raft pulled toward the right.

"The bow boat was the beginning of the end of the rafting business on the upper Mississippi. Before the bow boat came into use, a lumber raft contained from two to two and a half million feet of sawed lumber and a log raft from five hundred thousand to one million feet. In July 1901, Captain Winans with the *SATURN* and the bow boat *PATHFINDER* left Read's Landing, Minnesota, with a lumber raft sixteen strings wide and forty-four cribs longs, making a raft 256 feet wide and 1,408 feet long that contained 9,152,000 feet of sawed lumber in the crib. Every crib in the raft with the exception of the first two tiers across the bow and stern was deck loaded. Shingles, lath, pickets, craft stuff, stock boards, etc., were placed on each crib, and making easily another million feet.

"This was the largest raft ever taken down the Mississippi River. Captain Winans was owner and master of the *SATURN* and on this trip, George Winans, captain; Peter O'Rourke, pilot; Levi King, chief engineer; Levi King, Jr., second engineer; Harry Dyer, mate; Earl Winans, clerk and captain of the bow boat; and Mrs. Ella Tesson, steward, comprised the crew. Most of the lumber was consigned to the Knapp, Stout Lumber Company, St. Louis, Missouri and was delivered in twelve days from the time of leaving Read's Landing. There were 704 cribs in the raft, each containing about 13,000 feet of lumber, and to ship by rail would have required at least 800 cars for the lumber and 100 more for the deck load.

"At first it was thought that the bow boat could not be used on a log raft thinking that the raft could not be kept stiff enough to stand the working of the bow boat, but it was tried and found that it could be done and in a short time fifteen of the log boats were towing rafts from 950 to 1,200 feet long, and in 1897 Captain Otis McGinley with the steamer *F. C. A. DENKMANN,* took a log raft 1,550 feet long from the West Newton, Minnesota to Rock Island, Illinois. Is it any wonder with such rafts as this going down the river that the pine timber in Northern Wisconsin and Minnesota soon disappeared?

"Logging on the Chippewa River and its tributaries ended in 1905 with 25,365,875,930 board feet raft out; on the St. Croix River in 1914 with 12,444,281,720 feet. These figures are from the Surveyor General's office in St. Paul.

"Never did men have the situation in their own hands to equal the raft pilots on the upper Mississippi. It took a cool-headed, nervy man to be a raft pilot and he could not learn the river and how to handle a raft in one year, or in two, or three years. Before the bow boat came into the work, the rafting season began with the opening of navigation and closed about November 1st. Many of the lumber companies had three or four boats towing logs to their mills. With the advent of the bow boat and the long raft or double-header [one common raft coupled ahead of another] great changes were made. Each pilot tried to see who could take the largest raft and make the quickest trip. There was generally a good stage of water in the spring and these big rafts and quick trips soon filled up the mill landings. The logs were then temporarily laid up in some slough or bayou as near their final destination as possible.

"Lansing Bay and Lynxville Bay would be filled and many others nearer the mills. Then one or two boats of each company would be laid up and enough boats kept in service to 'drop the logs in' from the bays to keep the mills supplied. Heretofore, many of the pilots were hired for the season, now they were hired by the month and when their boat was laid up their wages laid up also. In 1897 Captain William Dobler, with the *BART E. LINEHAN*, made eight round trips from the West Newton Rafting works to Quincy, Illinois, in sixty-four days. I don't think this record was ever equaled.

"The quickest trip I ever knew of was made in 1884 by the *MENOMONIE*, Captain Stephen Withrow. The *MENOMONIE* left Read's Landing, Minnesota, on Monday morning just as the breakfast bell was ringing with twelve strings of lumber twenty-four cribs long. The following Sunday at noon she had delivered her raft in Alton Slough and was lying at the levee at Alton, Illinois. The raft was consigned to Knapp, Stout and Company, St. Louis, Missouri and enough time was spent in putting the raft in Alton Slough to have delivered it in St. Louis. The raft was not landed from the time it left Read's Landing until it was landed at Piasa Island above Alton to split to deliver. At the bridges five strings would be floated through with oars as in floating days, the boat taking the other seven strings. At the Rock Island bridge, D. F. Dorrance, the rapids pilot, put the full raft through the wide span at the right of the draw span and Captain Withrow did the same thing at Louisiana bridge.

"Now to close, a few words about that good old pilot, Captain Stephen B. Hanks. He was one of the first pilots on the river, began running logs from Stillwater, Minnesota in 1842 and was a pilot on the upper Mississippi for fifty years. He was a cousin of Abraham Lincoln. He lived at Albany, Illinois, for a long time and retired from active work in 1892.

"When the last raft to go down the Mississippi was passing Albany, Captain Walter Hunter of the *OTTUMWA BELLE*, who was in charge of the raft, sent a skiff ashore and got Captain Hanks and took him to Fort Madison, Iowa, so he was on practically the first and last raft to go down the river. The last log raft went down the Mississippi in 1914. The last lumber raft went down the river in 1915, towed by the *OTTUMWA BELLE* and the bow boat *PATHFINDER*. Captain Stephen B. Hanks died at Albany, Illinois, in 1917 (October 7), aged ninety-six years.

"A grand total of logs rafted down the river was 46,974,220,170 board feet."

Captain George Winans' Life, Record and Recollections

George O. Winans made an indelible mark in the rafting trade on the upper Mississippi River. Born on its banks, he lived eighty-seven years on or near it, making and losing fortunes in doing so. Harry Dyer thought, "he was the best all around steamboat man among the masters and pilots of the upper Mississippi River. He was a fine man to work for, a good pilot, and absolutely fearless. I heard a pilot say one time, 'the devil couldn't scare George Winans even if his tail was afire.' When he knew he was right no argument would change him. And when he found he was being imposed on or someone was taking some of his property, no one could put up a harder fight. One reason he was a good pilot was that he never got excited."

He was born at Camanche, Iowa on January 8, 1839. His first encounter with the river was when he was pushed off the steamboat *AMARANTH* in 1843 when only four years old and fished out with a pole. Some cattle on board had gotten too close and George was crowded overboard. He attended the Camanche village school and later on McCaroll Academy at McCaroll, Illinois, thus achieving a better education than most of his river contemporaries.

Knowing that George aspired to a life on the river, his brother, a rafting pilot, gave him a raftsman's job at age sixteen. He manned one of the large sweeps that helped steer the rafts. In 1856 he went to Stillwater on the steamboat *EXCELSOR*. He landed a raft at Burlington, Iowa, in 1856. He piloted his first raft from Read's Landing to Dubuque for Knapp, Stout and Company, November 1, 1857.

Winans moved to Chippewa Falls, Wisconsin, in 1862 and quite possibly married at this time. His wife was about five years younger than he was, having been born in 1844.

For the next several years he was employed in the lumber and rafting trade. He is generally given the credit for first using a steamboat to run a raft. Winans tells the story;

"In 1863 [I] was in the employ of Pound Halbert & Co. of Chippewa Falls, Wisconsin, who were large manufacturers of rafted lumber that found a market at various points along the Mississippi River.

"In August [1863] the Chippewa River became so low that lumber rafts drawing but twelve inches could not navigate and three such rafts were tied up near Rumsey Landing. With no prospect of better water [I] was directed to take men and supplies to the stranded rafts and reraft them, making them but eight courses [ten inches] deep.

"This was done, the result being four rafts out of three, each drawing but ten inches. In this shape, they were run successfully to Read's Landing at the mouth of the Chippewa. Coupling the four rafts with two owned by Carson and Rand made a tow of 108 cribs ready to start on the 10th day of September.

"Supplies were placed on board, a crew engaged and an early start on the 11th was planned. We did not start, simply because we did not have a crew. The men had discovered that there weren't any extra men in town and when I sent [someone] to the Landing to investigate, I was informed that it would take $4.00 per day to secure their valuable company for the trip. As the regular wages had been but seventy-five cents per day, up to that time, we did not negotiate.

"During the winter of 1862-63, Jos. W. Harding and Seth Scott had built a smaller, geared, side wheel boat at Durand, Wisconsin, proposing to operate her on the Chippewa River. The boat was named *UNION* and owing to a mistake in design, drew eighteen inches of water; as there was but fourteen inches in the channel of the Chippewa, by July 1st the *UNION* could not navigate.

"Her owners took her to Read's Landing and did such odd jobs as they could find on the Mississippi. She was idle on the day my speculative crew struck. As the subject of running rafts with a boat had been discussed for two or three years, whenever a bunch of pilots got together, it occurred to me that the present would be a good time to try it. Finding that I could get five men to go, I boarded the *UNION* and soon made a bargain with Seth Scott for the services of himself and boat for $7.00 per day.

"We got to the raft with the boat and five men a little after noon and by evening had a temporary arrangement made by which we could handle the boat behind the raft.

"Owing to the low water, there was no probability of another raft starting for a month and the gentlemen on strike got so uneasy that they sent word that evening that they would go for $1.00 per day.

"Not feeling quite sure of the boat proposition, I agreed, and before the next day's close, I was very glad that I had done so.

"Early on the morning of the 12th of September 1863, the first raft to be towed by a boat, below Lake Pepin, left the shore opposite Read's Landing, in tow of the steamer *UNION* of 28-59/100 tons burthen—Geo. Winans, Pilot, Seth Scott, Engineer and Louie Webber, Cook.

"Everything started out fine. I had a double crew on the bow and the boat did much more than I had expected, but I soon discovered that our apparatus for handling the boat was not sufficient and it broke down before we were out of sight of Wabasha. Shipping up the stern oars and sending part of the crew back, we floated until we made repairs. At Tepeotee, however, it was wrecked again and before the crew could get back, the stern swung down and the boat went aground. Her wheels were too large and struck the bottom and before the engine could be stopped, the pinion stripped more than half the wood teeth out of her core wheel. We had no extra teeth aboard and Winona was the nearest point at which we could get them. This meant a delay of at least three days, the season getting late, and two strings of lumber to be delivered at Hannibal, Missouri.

"We got the boat off the sand, lashed her alongside, and went back to the old, inglorious method of floating. The *UNION* was left at Winona and Seth Scott remained and made repairs and then ran her back to Read's Landing while the raft continued on in the same old way.

"Items in my expense account show the experiment cost the Lumber Company $86.00. It also confirmed my long entertained belief in the ultimate success of the raft towing steamboat.

"The water was so low that the raft had to be divided into six pieces to get over the Rock Island rapids, and four day's time was consumed. Before reaching the Des Moines rapids, more than half the raft had been sold, but it required, largely because of bad weather, six days to pass those rapids.

"Landing below Keokuk we cut out lumber to go to Warsaw and in doing so, one crib got away and grounded on a sand bar near Alexandria. Running between Warsaw and Keokuk was the *EAGLE*, a small side wheel packet built and owned by the Leyhe Bros. of Warsaw. I engaged the *EAGLE* to pull off and tow the grounded crib of lumber to Warsaw and also to tow the balance of the raft to Hannibal, Missouri—its destination. Starting on the morning of the 8th of November, the raft was landed at Hannibal the same evening and the second raft had been towed by a steam boat.

"[Winans'] expense account showed it cost the Lumber Company $50.00 for the boat and crew, consisting of one master, one engineer, and one fireman. [I] was the pilot and was receiving $1,200.00 for the season.

"During the season of 1864 the water in the Mississippi River was still lower and the low water mark established at Cairo that year is still the zero mark for all the Upper Mississippi River gauges. The steamer *UNION* was still owned by Harding and Scott and still looking for work, as the Chippewa was again too low for her to navigate. Arriving at Read's Landing on September 4th, I was met by Mr. Scott who said he was engaged to tow a raft for Cy (Cyrus) Bradley and wanted to get two oar stems off our lumber as Bradley had sent word to him that he wanted them to rig up winches with which to handle the boat. He said the tow was then in sight below Lake City, and he was to meet them in time to get the boat harnessed in by the time the tow got through. We went over to the lumber, opposite Read's Landing, and I sold him two oars for fifty cents, as my old expense book shows. I could see the tow in charge of, I think, the *MINNESOTA*, but of that I am not sure. I started up the Chippewa before the *UNION* got out of the Lake, but returning two days later I was told she passed all right.

"I started a floating raft a day or two later and

met the *UNION* at Clayton on her way back, and later understood she delivered her raft at Clinton without mishap in two days less time than was usually required for the floating trip. That was the first raft that went through to its destination towed by a steam boat; but it was not towed by that boat from Stillwater. The *UNION* would have required four days to tow through both lakes.

"The *UNION* had been sold before Bradley got back from his first trip and came into the management of [myself], who made two trips with her in 1864, and used her continuously until the close of the season of 1867, when she was cut down by the ice and later sold to Captain E. E. Heerman.

"After the trip with the *UNION*, Bradley made a trip with the side wheel steamer *ACTIVE* and in 1865 brought out the *MINNIE WILL*, named after a niece of his. From 1865 the pace never faltered and boats multiplied. Any intimation that Bradley was considered a dreamer because he advocated the towing of rafts by steamboat is not based on the facts. It was a common subject of discussion and every one believed in it. Why shouldn't they? For years rafts had been towed through the lakes successfully, and the principle was the same.

"[I] have a model of a boat, whittled out in 1862, showing what my idea of the coming boat was, and very glad that [I] did not have the money necessary to build it, as it would have been a lamentable failure.

"Mr. T. B. Wilson, of Knapp, Stout & Co. was an enthusiastic believer in the idea as early as 1862, and Judge Cady, the same year, offered to furnish half the money to build one if John Newcomb and [I] would furnish the other half.

"If I have not called any of the old timers 'Captain' it is because at the time of which I write there were no captains, of record. There were, however, a large number of hard-headed, hard-working men who, every day of their lives, displayed a skill that was never equalled by a like number of men in any walk of life."

The Winans had a son, Francis, affectionately termed "Frankie," who was born in 1866. He died as a toddler in February 1869. A daughter, Winifred, was born in December 1868 at Chippewa Falls. Later on a son, Earl Francis, was born. He was to have an association with the river also, but was not the stalwart on the waters that his father was.

In just a few short years, George Winans had successfully picked up the knack of running large rafts. In 1869 from August 17–30 he ran a large lumber raft, fifteen strings by sixteen cribs long from Read's Landing to St. Louis. It had 3,400,000 board feet of lumber and spread out over 3.1 acres. The side wheeled *BUCKEYE* was the tow boat and no bow boat was used, some dozen or so men instead manned the bow oars. A surviving photo shows the tent-like wooden shelters the men built to ward off the sun and a covered cooking area that was in the center of the raft. On this trip, E. C. Bill was master of the *BUCKEYE*, his son, F. A. Bill, was clerk and the owners were Bill and Champion. The deck load consisted of 412,000 lath, 75,000 shingles and 33,000 pickets. This was the largest raft to this time.

Harry Dyer relates an incident concerning George Winans. "Captain George Winans was coming up the Mississippi River in about the year 1870 with his steamboat *JULIA* and towing a barge loaded with coal. He had delivered a log raft at St. Louis and was returning to Stillwater. When he reached a locality just below Burlington, Iowa he found Captain Ira H. Short there with his craft, the *MOUNTAIN BELLE*. Captain Short had got his log raft stuck on a sandbar and was vainly trying to extricate it.

"When Captain Winans stopped to inquire about his trouble Captain Short, who was a man of an imperious nature, said, 'George, I'll have to commandeer that barge of coal!' He feared that he would run out of coal before he got the raft off the bar.

"His words and his attitude so irritated Captain Winans that he yelled in reply, 'No _____, you ain't going to commandeer my barge of coal! And if you try to do it, _____ there will be trouble! I licked the whole Short family once and, by God, I can do it again if you say so!'

"Then he proceeded on his way.

"As boys, George and Ira were playmates. The Shorts lived in Albany, Illinois, and George across the Mississippi at Camanche, Iowa. On one occasion, George gave Ira a licking, and Ira's two brothers entering the fight, he licked them also. Hence the above reminder.

"Short as a steamboat captain was a man who always demanded, 'I want this and that; you do this and so.' Winans, when imposed upon or given orders he resented, was apt to say, 'Who says so?'"

Winans owned many rafting vessels in his time. Perhaps he was seeking the ultimate rafter. He owned the *IOWA CITY, JULIA, SATURN* (1st), *SATURN* (2nd), *SILAS WRIGHT, SATELLITE* (1st), *SATELLITE* (2nd), *MAY LIBBY, PATHFINDER, FRANK, DAN THAYER, ST. CROIX, ZALUS DAVIS, NEPTUNE, JOHN H. DOUG-*

LASS, C. W. COWLES, ADMIRAL, MARS, SAM ATLEE and, as he said, "perhaps some others." In addition to serving on the above as master and pilot, he also served as master and pilot on the *BUCKEYE, J. W. VAN SANT, UNION, LONE STAR, MOUNTAIN BELLE, JAMES MEANS, PEARL, CHIPPEWA FALLS, ALVIRA, WYMAN X, J. W. WHITNEY, J. H. WILSON, CITY OF WINONA* "and some others I cannot recall at this time."

Winans also indicated that the second steamboat to tow a raft was the *TIGER*, built at Minneapolis and commanded by Jack Chapman. The first vessel built expressly for a bowboat was the *EMMA*, which was owned by C. Lamb and Sons. Winans says, "She was not a success because the pilot [now living] said she was not. The first bowboat to succeed was the *LOTUS*, built by Tom Roundy for A. B. Youmans of Winona."

In 1888 Winans ran for election in his Waukesha area on the Democratic party ticket for a term in the Wisconsin state legislature. He won, receiving 2,382 votes against 1,642 votes for the Republican candidate, M. L. Snyder. A third party candidate, George McKerrow, running on the Prohibitionist ticket garnered only 140 votes. Details of Winans' service in the Assembly for a two-year term (1889–1890) are not known, but he did not stand for re-election. Supposedly, he went to California in 1890 for a brief spell. [I have been unable to positively confirm this.]

Captain Winans could deal harshly with one who did not measure up to his standards. In October 1904, he berated Elmer McCraney of Lansing, Iowa. "In common with people generally, I have always known you as a treacherous sneak but didn't know how complete a stinker you could make of yourself until I learned of your action regarding the raft I brought to Dubuque. I am rather old to plan much but think I will live long enough to play even with you. As a starter, I will say that if you run the Joyce logs, another year, you will do it for $800 per raft. Yours with contempt, Geo. Winans" (Copy of October 12, 1904 letter furnished by the Dubuque County Historical Society, thanks are tendered).

Harry Dyer relates another occurrence of Winans' character. Because Winans had a better education than most of his contemporaries, he was often chosen to present the viewpoints of steamboat people to the Washington bureaucracy. At this time, the U.S. Steamboat Inspection Service was under the jurisdiction of the U.S. Treasury Department instead of the Department of Commerce. "Once Captain Winans went to Washington to bring some important matters to the attention of the U.S. Steamboat Inspectors. John C. Dumont, a pompous old military officer with no knowledge at all of steamboats, was the chairman of the Board. Captain Winans presented his recommendations to the body in considerable detail. They listened to him but refused to take any action. The Captain presented additional arguments but was unable to move the members. They turned down all of his recommendations.

"Then the captain became very angry and said, 'All of the railroads built on both banks of the Mississippi River are not as detrimental to steamboats as is this board of steamboat inspectors.' General Dumont in reply said, 'I consider this statement an insult to this board.' And Captain Winans fired this parting shot, 'Consider it what you damn please, it's the truth.' Then he picked up his grip and left, his short stubby beard probably standing out straight from his chin as it did when he was very angry."

Captain Winans indicated that the fastest floating trip with a raft was made by Tom Forbush, nine days and two hours from Read's Landing to St. Louis. The fastest boating trip was made by the *CITY OF WINONA* and the *LOTUS* (as her bowboat), four days and one hour from Beef Slough to Hannibal.

After he left the river, Captain Winans summed up his achievements; "I have taken 975,000,000 feet of lumber to various points on the Mississippi River that I have a record of, and a large quantity of lumber and logs of which I have no record. [I] fitted up a raft at Stillwater on the 4th of July, 1858, and had to stop work because of snow and ice."

Fred A. Bill, a dedicated riverman, helped carry on the publicizing and recording of the rafting people in George Merrick's columns in the Burlington, Iowa *Saturday Evening Post*. He summed up Winans' achievements at the time of his death as follows; "The passing of this venerable man removes one of the most picturesque, active and best known navigators on the upper Mississippi . . . A complete history of the career of this remarkable man would make a huge volume, and we do not mean 'maybe' when we say it!" Bill continues, "This man knew the river as the ordinary person knows the inside of his own house. He knew it up and down and crosswise and beneath the surface of the water. No night was too dark and no storm too hard to drive him to the bank if he took a notion to run. While he thus knew the river and his knowledge was coupled with unusual skill, very few men participated in more disastrous accidents than he. These, he would always admit, were generally the result of carelessness and would often occur in what was termed 'good river' and not in close places. Being a 'fiend' for work, he stood long watches and acquired the habit of getting 'forty winks' when the opportunity presented in a good piece of river, and timing himself to wake up at the proper time. Sometimes his mental alarm clock failed to work by a few seconds and the nap was a little too long, for which he generally paid dearly.

"From about 1901 to the end of the logging business in 1916, he had the contract to drop all the logs from the St. Paul boom to Prescott. During this period, and since, St. Paul was his home.

"Industrious; he worked hard and made and lost fortunes in his chosen calling. Honest, reliable, upright in all his dealings with his employees and employers and respected by them all, we shall not look upon his like again."

Winans' wife died in 1912 and his son, Earl Francis, lived at Prescott, which might be the reasons he gave up his Waukesha home and moved to St. Paul where he lived in several hotels. His daughter possibly took care of her mother while she was living and after her death was employed as a librarian at a teachers' college in Eau Claire.

In conclusion, the rafting highlight of his life occurred in June 1901, when with his SATURN (1st) as the towboat and the PATHFINDER as the bowboat, he delivered a raft sixteen strings wide, forty-four cribs long. This raft was 256 feet wide, 1,450 feet long and twenty-six inches deep and contained 8,431,483 feet of lumber. The raft was deck loaded with shingles, lath, dry lumber, square timber, etc., to make another million feet. It took ten days to go from Stillwater to St. Louis.

This SATURN was built according to Winans' idea of what a rafter should be. Her boilers faced aft instead of forward and thus saved carrying of coal from the deck room to the fire box. Her pilot house was forward of her smoke stacks and flush with the end of the hurricane roof. In "hitching in" to a raft, the pilot could see just how far the stem of his boat was from the stern of the raft. Everything worked exactly as he thought it would.

Captain Winans died on January 22, 1926 at his St. Paul home, the Seymour Hotel. He was eighty-seven years old. He was interred in the family plot at the Prairie Home cemetery in Waukesha next to his wife and young son. His daughter, Winifred, died in February 1952. She was cremated and her remains were interred in May 1952.

Log of Harry G. Dyer

Steamboatman, Upper Mississippi

1881-1902

Note: Mr. Dyer kept a record of his experiences during his rafting days. The author sets this forth below, largely in Dyer's original text. Slight editing has been done, names of steamboats have been capitalized and some material on the salvage of the *BART E. LINEHAN* has been added from another work of Dyer's. Headings for each year have been added by the author.

1881—The Beginning

At nine o'clock A.M., June 5, 1881, the steamer *RUBY*, a small sidewheel boat built at DeSoto, Wisconsin during the winter of 1880-81, pulled out from that village bound for Stillwater, Minnesota to enter the rafting trade. The *RUBY* was owned by two DeSoto men, Capt. Albert H. Marcham and Henry Gardner. She had been chartered to James Hawes of Red Wing, Minnesota to tow logs from Stillwater to the Belcher sawmill at Red Wing. Her officers were A. H. Marcham, master; Henry Gardner, engineer; George Harrell, pilot. One of her deck crew was a seventeen-year-old boy, Harry G. Dyer, starting what was to be a twenty-two-year term as a steamboatman. At that time the raftboat fleet consisted of about seventy-five boats, most of them owned by the big lumber companies.

The *RUBY* arrived at Stillwater, June 6, 1881, at nine o'clock A.M., and the rest of the day was put in getting the kit aboard. I found I was entered on the crew list as "linesman", salary $30 a month and board. Our work started the next day when we towed a "boom" to Lakeland, nine miles below Stillwater. A boom was a lot of extra long logs chained together end to end. It was then run around a big bunch of logs and the ends of the boom brought together, making a bag to hold the logs. In this way of towing, the steamboat was ahead of the tow and it was only used for towing short distances. We delivered the boom at the Lakeland mill and were back in Stillwater at seven o'clock P.M.

The next day was something different. We were to take a raft to Red Wing and the raft had to be lined up. The raft was 500 feet long and 120 feet wide. Sixteen cross lines, eight A lines, two corner lines and a check line completed the kit. The cross lines were one inch thick and 130 feet long, the A lines one inch thick and 225 feet long and the check line 1 and ¾ inches thick and 1,200 feet long. The cross lines and A lines kept the raft stiff and straight and the check line was used only in landing the raft.

Our towing to Red Wing only lasted a few weeks. Mr. Hawes had some trouble with the owners of the boat and they canceled his contract. But the *RUBY* never stopped going. In less than twenty-four hours she was under contract to Gillispie and Hayes, Stillwater steamboatmen, and though they owned three boats, the *IDA FULTON, NINA,* and the *MARK BRADLEY,* they had more work than they could do. The first work we had with them was taking a raft to LaCrosse for the John Paul Co., then a raft to McGregor, Iowa, for Fleming Bros., then one to Sabula, Iowa.

On the Sabula trip I got my first experience in a breakup. Fifteen miles above DeSoto, Wisconsin, there are two channels. A raft channel, used only in high water, goes down the Minnesota shore from Brownsville, Minnesota to Genoa, Wisconsin and Coon Slough down the Wisconsin side, used in low water. There are two very sharp bends in this channel, one called the "Devil's Elbow." On the trip to Sabula, we had to run this channel and coming around the "Elbow" we made connection with the head of the island on the right-hand side and in a very few minutes our raft was a lot of loose logs and it took a week to gather them up and re-raft them.

Our next trip was to Port Byron, Illinois and on that trip we got stuck trying to run the low water channel at Clinton, Iowa. All of this bad luck was caused by blunders of our pilot. George Harrell was an old-time floating pilot and was never classed as a No. 1 raft pilot, but in 1881 the rafting business was booming and good pilots were hard to find.

In August 1881 the first electric searchlight appeared on the Upper Mississippi. The steamer *GEM CITY*, a big sidewheel packet built for the St. Louis-St. Paul trade, and out in August 1881, was the first boat on the upper river to have an electric searchlight.

The rafter *SAM ATLEE* was the first raft boat to have an electric searchlight. The *ATLEE* came out a new boat in September 1881. In the spring of 1882 two more raft boats, the *ARTEMUS LAMB* and the *B. HERSHEY*, were equipped and in a year or two more every raft boat on the river had an electric light and it was surely a great thing for the pilots.

As a general thing all the raft boats carried a double crew and ran day and night. The *RUBY* was an exception; we carried a single crew and "went to the bank." The pilots of *all* Mississippi steamboats handle their boats from marks on the shore and on a dark night it was a constant strain on their eyes to find those marks. On every crossing, that is, when the channel changes from one side of the valley to the other, they had one or two marks, one at the head and one at the foot of the crossing. It might be a tree, a corner of a home, the steeple of a church, but if the boats were on their marks, they were right in the channel. When the searchlight came, all the pilot had to do when he came to a bad bend or a tight place was to ring a bell in the engine room, and the engineer started the dynamo and the channel was lit up for a mile ahead of him. The light also did away with all the danger at the bridges.

Many a dark night I have put six or eight lanterns in a skiff and pulled ahead of the raft and hung one at the foot of a crossing, the head of an island, or a "shoulder." As the boat and raft came along, my partner in the other skiff would pick them up. Then he would go ahead and hang them out and I would pick them up.

On the 18th of October 1881, the *RUBY* laid up for the winter at DeSoto, her home port, and I shipped ashore with $104.35 in my pocket and considered myself a steamboatman and raftsman, first class.

The season was getting short but a few days later I shipped out on the steamer *ALFRED TOLL* with Captain Abe Looney and picked up $35.00 more before navigation closed. That ended my first year as a steamboatman.

1882—On the *SILVER WAVE, JIM WATSON, MOLINE,* and *ISAAC STAPLES*

April 19, 1882, after going to school all winter, I shipped on the steamer *SILVER WAVE*. Jerome E. Short, captain; George Harrell, pilot; John Burns, mate. Our first raft was a trip from Lansing, Iowa to Muscatine, Iowa. During the summer, when the rafting works are running full force, the logs are coming so fast that the mills can't take care of them, so the boats store them in some of the bays along the river and the bay at Lansing, Iowa was one of the best for this purpose and sometimes would have fifty rafts "laid up." Some of them would be there all winter and taken out in late spring.

Our first raft was rafted in June 1881 and did not get to Muscatine until April 1882. Jerome Short, or "Lome" as he was known by his friends, was a *star* pilot. Our raft was owned by the Musser Lumber Co., Muscatine, Iowa. At that point was the mill of the Hershey Lumber Co., owners of the towboat *B. HERSHEY*. And her captain, Cyprian Buisson, was another *star* pilot. The captain of a raftboat always stood a watch at the wheel.

It was always a race between these two pilots although the *HERSHEY* was a more powerful boat than the rival *SILVER WAVE*. When the *HERSHEY* delivered a raft at the Hershey mill, the *SILVER WAVE* was generally in sight with one for the Musser mill. The *SILVER WAVE* was owned by the Van Sant and Musser Transportation Co. Unlike my first boat, the *SILVER WAVE* carried a double crew and the only time we went to the bank was for coal or to deliver a raft.

About the 15th of June we towed a crockery barge

from Fairport, Iowa [called "Jugtown" by rivermen] to Alma, Wisconsin. Situated at Jugtown were four or five potteries and their owners would load this barge with jars, jugs, crocks, flower pots, etc., and then hire some boat to tow it up the river and then float back, stop at the different towns, and sell their pottery.

On this trip the owner of the crockery, a Mr. Womacks, and our second pilot got to be very good friends. At Jefferson City, Missouri, the *JIM WATSON* was for sale. By much explaining, arguing, and such, our second pilot, George Harrell, got Womacks to consent to buy the *WATSON*. In the meantime I was "running line" on the *SILVER WAVE*, but they got me to go to Jefferson City with Womacks and examine the hull of the *WATSON* before they bought her. Womacks was to furnish the cash and Harrell to be captain. I believe the reason he could not go to Jeff City was because he had to get someone to take his place on the *WAVE*. But he finally got there and they bought the *JIM WATSON*. She was a good towboat but in need of repair.

They took her to Rock Island, pulled her out on the ways and had some work done on her hull and in a few days she was back in service and bound for LaCrosse. There she had to have a raft kit. Lines, tools, peavies, augers and pike poles, etc. Capt. Harrell had told Womacks that he had hired Antoine LaRoque for second pilot. Antoine was second pilot on the *B. HERSHEY* and a first class pilot and he stayed on the *HERSHEY*, and Harrell hired two old floating pilots, Jim Butts and Jack Chiser. We got a raft for Montrose, Iowa. When we got to DeSoto I got off with an injury to my hand and glad that I did, for inside of three months the *WATSON* was in the U.S. marshal's hands and Harrell's bubble had burst.

As soon as my hand got well I shipped on the *RUBY* again and went to Stillwater. It was harvest time and wages always came up, but not on the *RUBY*. So in a few days I was on the steamer *MOLINE* with Captain Isaiah Wasson, Jerome Ruby, Sam Nimrick, and Dan Dawley, engineers and Tom Cody, mate. The *MOLINE* was owned by Dimmock, Gould and Co. of Moline, Ill. I made two or three trips on the *MOLINE*, but Mr. Cody was a joke as a mate. If you were a "booze fighter" you were O.K. with Cody. If not, you could do all the work while Cody's boys were in their bunks, so I got off at LeClaire one morning and that afternoon shipped on the *ISAAC STAPLES* with Captain Vincent Peel, Jacob Ressor, pilot, Otis McGinley, mate, and Charles Reese, engineer.

Capt. Peel was a fine Christian man and a fine man to work for. He wasn't a raft pilot and in a short time the mate, Mr. McGinley, was promoted to pilot, and Harry Bell came aboard as mate. "Shorty" Bell, as he was called by steamboatmen, was a good man and good mate and eventually married Capt. Peel's daughter, Mary. On the 18th of April 1889, at ten o'clock P.M., the steamer *EVERETT*, owned by Capt. Peel, was caught in a storm a short distance below Oquaka, Illinois, and capsized and Captain Peel, his daughter, Mrs. Bell, and her little daughter, Vera, a nurse girl in charge of the child, and George Howard, the cook, were drowned. But I have got off my story.

While on the *ISAAC STAPLES* I met an "old timer," an ex-pugilist and riverman, Steve O'Donnell, and he told me the story of the fight (riot) on the *DUBUQUE* and he ought to have known, for he was a participant. On the 15th of October 1882, as the season was nearing the end (and my bank account was much less than the year before) I got off the *ISAAC STAPLES* at Montrose, Iowa. Due to my trip to Jefferson City in June and so much jumping from one boat to another, I was about $75.00 short of 1881.

I started for the Lower River and at Memphis, Tennessee, I shipped on the *SAM ROBERTS*, a towboat owned in Evansville, Indiana and engaged in towing grain to New Orleans.

1883—Trouble in Getting Paid, Shipping on the *BELLA MAC*, *A. T. JENKS* and *MENOMONIE*

In February 1883, I was on the steamer *POLAR STAR* up the river with a tow of barges of logs for St. Louis. One night about midnight, just above Columbus, Kentucky, the *POLAR STAR* exploded her boilers killing six men, the second mate, two firemen, and three coal passers. All that saved me was that I was out on the head of the tow sounding water, but I lost everything I had but the clothes I had on.

Back at Cairo I went back on the *SAM ROBERTS* and made another trip to New Orleans with eight barges of shelled corn to be shipped to Liverpool, England, and we had to lay at New Orleans eight days while our barges were unloaded.

On our way up the river we stopped at Helena, Arkansas and loaded four of our barges with white ash lumber for the International Harvester Co., Chicago, Illinois. We took it to St. Louis from where it was shipped to Chicago by rail. We were at Helena ten days loading and got to St. Louis May 12, 1883. I told the mate at Cairo on our way up that I was getting off at St. Louis as I did not want to go back down river. We landed at St. Louis at six o'clock P.M. and the next morning the mate asked me to stay until the barges were delivered. I did and after supper I went to the clerk to get my money. He said he couldn't pay me as the boat was in the hands of the U.S. marshal. The two pilots had tied her up.

We were taken to the marshal's office the next morning and our claims sworn in. The boat was lying at Carondelet, a suburb of St. Louis. We all went back and I went to see the clerk, Mr. Chas. Hudson. I asked him if they were going to sell the boat and he said, "yes, she was advertised for sale, Nov. 16, 1883." I asked him if he was going to "pay the crew off" and he said, "No, we will pay the crew when we sell the boat." I gave him my address, 422 South Second St., St. Louis, Missouri. He asked me how long I had been on the river and I told him long enough to learn a little marine law and he said, "Well, I will pay you now," and he did. I asked him how about my fare back to Memphis and he said he wasn't paying any fares. I told him he was going to pay mine from St. Louis to Memphis or to LaCrosse, Wisconsin, which was a little less and I went to see the U.S. marshal and stated my case. He said, "Come on," and we went out and caught a street car for Carondelet, nine miles from St. Louis, where he went aboard the *ROBERTS* and told Mr. Hudson to pay my fare to LaCrosse or Memphis and that was all he said.

Mr. Hudson and I went up to the Diamond Jo Line ticket office at St. Louis and he bought me a ticket to LaCrosse, cabin fare without meals or berth. I asked him what I was going to do for "eats" and "sleeps" and he said you have got money. Another trip with the marshal to Carondelet and he said, "Mr. Hudson you told him you would settle this boat's affairs satisfactorily, now you do it or I will send one of my men to do it for you. Either buy this man a full cabin fare ticket on that [boat] or a railroad ticket." Hudson bought the ticket and I left St. Louis May 15, 1883, the day I was nineteen years old, on the steamer *LIBBIE CONGER* bound home. The year 1882 wasn't so good financially, but it was rich in experience. I was now a full-fledged towboat man.

I got home from the Lower River May 19, 1883 on the good steamer *LIBBIE CONGER*, Capt. James Corbett. Four days out from St. Louis and on the 24th of May I hired on the *BELLA MAC* where my old friend George Harrell from the *RUBY* and the *JIM WATSON* was second pilot. The *BELLA MAC* was called *BELLA DANGER* by steamboat men because she was so unlucky. In May 1882, she exploded her boilers at Twin Islands near Brownsville, Minnesota, killing nine men.

She was rebuilt and in 1885 she burned at the levee at LaCrosse. In 1886 she was snagged and sunk near West Newton, Minnesota. She was raised and repaired and in 1901, she sunk again, at the mouth of Horse Creek near St. Louis. This time she went out of sight and was a total loss.

The second trip I made on her, we got orders to take a half raft out of Bullet Chute just below Genoa, Wisconsin that had been laid up there. Well, we lined it up and Capt. Short said, "Harry, go up and let her go." The mate said, "I'll tell you what she will do, she will hit that bar at the foot of the chute and swing around and break in two." Capt. Short said, "Well, that's what they got." It seems Capt. Short told the owners, McDonald Bros. that there wasn't enough water in Bullet Chute to take the raft out, but they thought there was. Well, I did as I was told—"let her go"—and she swung around and broke in two. Well, we got the raft picked up and re-rafted and started down river and in Crooked Slough just above Lynxville, Wisconsin we had more bad luck. The water was low and we had to "double trip" Crooked Slough, that is, take half of the raft, go through the slough, and land there, go back and get the other half. The first half went through all right, but our luck slipped and the other half hit the head of the Island and there was another big break up and we were at Lynxville six days re-rafting. On the last day the engineer discovered that our wheel shaft was cracked. That meant the boat would have to go back to LaCrosse and send to Chicago for another shaft.

I went home and stayed a few days and shipped on the steamer *A. T. JENKS* with Capt. James Newcomb and mate Frank Clemmons and he was one of the best. The *A. T. JENKS* was owned by Durant and Wheeler of Stillwater, Minnesota. This company was noted among steamboat men as paying less wages and giving their crews less to eat than anyone else in the business. In fact, the Durant and Wheeler line was called the "Bread and Water" line, but I made two trips on the *JENKS* and then, while going up the river near Read's Landing, Minnesota, we broke a hog chain. That is an iron rod running fore and aft over braces to strengthen the boat. This meant the boat would have to go on the ways for repairs. Of course, with Durant and Wheeler, the first thing was to pay off the crew. I was paid off at Read's Landing at nine o'clock in the morning and before noon I had shipped on the *MENOMONIE,* Capt. Stephen Withrow; pilot, William Dobler; mate, Owen Corcoran. The *MENOMONIE* was owned by the Knapp Stout Co. and was towing lumber from Read's Landing to St. Louis, Missouri.

The Knapp Stout Co. were fine people to work for, paid top wages, furnished their boats well and best of all, their boats "went to the bank" at twelve o'clock Saturday night and laid until Sunday night at twelve. Captain Withrow and Mr. Dobler were both "star" pilots. Steamboat men used to say that anyone who can follow Steve Withrow down the river is a pilot. Our chief engineer was Tyler Rowe, second engineer, Billy Shaw. Mr. and Mrs. Harvey Black had charge of the kitchen and they sure knew their business. I laid the *MENOMONIE* up in the winter quarters in New Boston Bay twenty-five miles below Muscatine, Iowa. When I was paid off, my fare was handed to me at Read's Landing, Minnesota, and I didn't have to have the U.S. marshal get it for me. Another nice thing, I was hired to go back on the boat in the spring.

Down below again and in the coal trade that winter, 1883, between Pittsburgh, Pennsylvania and New Orleans. Two trips on the *W. W. O'NEIL* and one trip on the *ALICE BROWN* and the winter was passed and gone. We had to lay the *ALICE BROWN* up at Paducah, Kentucky, March 15, 1884, on account of low water on the upper Ohio and March 17, I was in New Boston, Illinois, ready to go back on the *MENOMONIE.*

1884—A Fast Trip for the *MENOMONIE*

We left New Boston, Illinois, about March 15 with a lumber raft for St. Louis, Missouri. Captain Withrow was back again, but for second pilot we had R. N. Cassidy. Tyler Rowe was chief engineer and John Warren, second and Henry Seyford, mate. The Knapp Stout Company's boats always carried ten men in their deck crew, eight raftsmen and two linesmen. The linesmen were paid twenty-five cents a day extra for pulling the skiff, that means every time the skiff went ashore for orders, telegrams, supplies, etc. All went well until we got to St. Louis. The Knapp Stout landing . . . at St. Louis [was] just below the water works and the current was very swift and for that reason the checkline, that is, the line used to land the raft, was made fast to the piling on the shore, and the balance of the line, about 1,200 feet of rope 1¾ inches in diameter, was coiled in the skiff. The company had their own man to handle check lines.

As soon as the stern of the raft was below the water works point, the skiff and three men would shoot out to the raft and carry the bight of the line to the check works. In a very few seconds, the "strain" was on the line. The *MENOMONIE* was backing full stroke, the line was new and before the strain was on, floated on top of the water. One of the wheel arms caught the line. First, the line slipped off the end of the wheel and out came the cam rods. Then the *MENOMONIE* was helpless. Then the check line parted. Out went another line, then another. When we finally got the raft landed it was 2,500 feet below the Knapp Stout Landing. It took six days to get it back. The *MENOMONIE* was anchored above the landing. Two check lines were run down to the raft and the other end went to the *MENOMONIE*'s capstan, then two St. Louis tugs were hired and put on the bow to push. We got the raft back where it belonged, but it took six days.

In June of this year the *MENOMONIE* made the fastest trip ever made with a raft from Read's Landing to St. Louis. The raft was a lumber raft, 512 feet long, 1,912 feet wide, twenty-six inches deep and contained about three million feet of pine lumber. Now a little explanation. All Mississippi rafts were arranged to split lengthwise in the center. This was necessary in order to get through the many bridges. Then the raft was called the right-hand "piece" and the left-hand "piece." At a bridge the boat was moved over to the center of one of the pieces and this other piece was landed by means of the checkline. The boat then went through the bridge and landed and went back and got the other piece, took it through the bridge and coupled up and went about her business. This was called "double tripping a bridge."

All the lumber in this raft was sawed at the Knapp Stout Co. Mill on the Chippewa River. The lumber was put in cribs at the mills. A crib of lumber was sixteen feet long, sixteen feet wide and twenty-two to twenty-six inches deep. The cribs were made of two-inch plank sixteen feet long and ten inches wide, held in place by round hardwood pins two inches in diameter and three feet long. This frame made the base of the crib, and the lumber came into the rafting shed from the mill and was picked up and laid on the frame of the crib. Generally, four men worked on a crib. The next layer or tier, the boards or planks were laid the other way of the frame, the direction changed with each tier. When the proper number of tiers had been laid, the pins were sticking up ten or twelve inches above the lumber. Then a duplicate frame was put on top, three holes were bored in the top plank and the plank dropped on the pins. Then with a tool called a "witch" each pin was pulled up, a notch was cut in the pin with a sharp axe, and a hard wooden wedge driven in the notch. Then the crib was slid into the river. When the cribs were coupled together, end to end, it made a strip ten, twenty, thirty or forty cribs long and when the strings were coupled side by side, it made a piece or half, and two halves or pieces made a raft.

The rafts that came down the Chippewa were generally ten cribs long and five strings wide. On each end of each string was a large oar fifty feet long. The oar stem was thirty-eight feet long and the oar blade twelve feet long and twelve inches wide and a husky lumberjack was at each oar. The oars were used only to keep the raft in the channel. At Read's Landing at the mouth of the Chippewa River, the Chippewa rafts were made into Mississippi River rafts. The oars on the raft were always left there and never taken back up river, but were used to build check works, for spring poles, and for fuel.

I let the line go on that raft at Read's Landing just as the breakfast bell rang one Monday morning and the following Sunday noon we had delivered our raft in Alton Slough and were laying at the levee at Alton, Illinois. In the time it took up to deliver, we could easily have gone into St. Louis. We left Read's at just 6 A.M. Monday and got to Winona about two o'clock P.M. and at that time we had an oar shipped up on each end of the right hand five strings. Our boat carried a crew of ten men, a man to an oar. At the Winona bridge Pilot Cassidy took charge of the five string piece. Captain Withrow with the boat had the seven strings. By backing the boat, the floating piece was soon ahead and pointed for the draw span. She went through very nicely, Captain Withrow swung in behind us and came through, towed alongside of us. We coupled up, moved the boat back to the center and all was done. We had gone through Winona bridge in thirty-seven minutes. It would have taken two hours to have doubled tripped it.

At LaCrosse, the same thing was done, while at Dubuque the boat "made a fly", letting six strings float while the other section went through the bridge.

The Sabula bridge forty-five miles below Dubuque was "double-headed," one piece being put ahead of the other and then running through the draw. At the Clinton bridge the double-head was again used, but the raft was dropped through the span on the Illinois side of the river.

Three days after starting, we were at LeClaire, Iowa. So far our raft had not stopped a minute. At LeClaire Rapids, pilot D. J. Dorrance came aboard. We expected to split for the Rock Island bridge, but before we got to Moline chain, Dorrance said, "Steve, I'll put her through the wide hole if you want me to." The old man said, "Yes, and you'll knock hell out of her." Dorrance said, "No, I won't break a board. If I do I won't charge you for the trip." "All right," the old man said, "go down to the bow, boys." This meant that Dorrance was going to try and put the full raft through the wide span to the right of the draw. He did and when the raft was about ¾ through, let it go, went through the draw with the boat and picked up the raft below the bridge, gaining two or three hours.

The next bridge was at Burlington, Iowa, then Quincy, Illinois, then Hannibal, Missouri, and then the last one at Louisiana, Missouri. There Captain Steven intended to make a "fly split" and put one piece through the span and let it go, pick up the other piece, go through the draw, and couple up, but all at once he said, "If Dorrance could put her through the wide hole at Rock Island I can do it here. Go down to the bow, boys." This meant go down to the oars on the bow. No part of that raft stopped a minute from the time we left Read's Landing until we landed at Piasa Island, just above Alton, and split to deliver the raft. That was because we had star pilots and a fine crew that knew their business.

Back of the engine room on a steamboat was what was called the "bull pen" or blacksmith shop. The anvil, forge, vise, bench, etc., were kept there, also the rudder arms were in this space. A lattice work partition was between it and the engine room. Sometimes when we were going up river and the "old man" was on watch at the wheel, some of the boys would go back in the "pen" and hold onto the rudder arms so that he couldn't move, then in a minute the whistle in the speaking tube to the pilot house would blow and then, "Tyle, drive those devils out of the 'bull pen.'" Our chief engineer, Mr. Rowe, only had one eye, but when we saw that eye come round the end of the lattice work, we knew he had a monkey wrench in his hand and could throw it, so we disappeared.

On a steamboat, the captain was always called the "old man" although he might be thirty years younger than the second pilot. Fourth of July, we were going up the river and we had to celebrate. We had two anvils on the boat and we took them out on the forecastle. The anvils each had a hole two inches square and two inches deep in the bottom. We filled the holes with powder. The firemen took their slash bars and got up alongside the boilers, one on each side. When all was ready I touched off the powder with a red hot iron and the firemen raised the safety valves. We were right in front of McGregor, Iowa, and from the roar and the clouds of steam people thought the *MENOMONIE* had blown up, but she hadn't.

I stayed on the *MENOMONIE* until October 1, 1884, over six months, and laid her to rest, but in less than a week I had shipped again, this time on the steamer *ED DURANT, JR.*, owned by Durant and Wheeler of Stillwater, Minnesota. Captain A. R. Withrow; pilot Orrin Thompson; chief engineer George Griffin; second engineer John Bear; and mate Frank Clemmons. A very different crew from the *MENOMONIE*'s. Though the captains were brothers, no one would have known it from their looks or their work. Clemmons was a *good* mate. I made two trips and we were in Stillwater getting a raft ready for Hannibal, Missouri. Clemmons had quit. Captain R. J. Wheeler was there overseeing and I asked him if we were going to get any more money this trip and he said he hadn't heard of it. I told him I was done then and started for the boat to get my money, but Captain Withrow said, "Captain Wheeler, I don't know what I'll do, he is the only man I've got that knows anything about the work." "Well," Wheeler says, "pay him $35 then." They called me back and Wheeler said, "Your wages are $40" and I told him they would be $50 if I stayed. It was like pulling a tooth, but he said, "Your wages will be $50."

I stayed on the *DURANT* until we got to DeSoto and got off. Withrow wouldn't pay me and the U.S. marshal at Dubuque told him he must and also for every day he kept my money and my board for the time. I went down below that winter to St. Louis and shipped on a coal boat.

1885—The *DAN THAYER* and *CLYDE* Race

After putting in about three months on the towboat *SMOKY CITY* towing coal from Pittsburgh to New Orleans, we were forced to lay up in the "Duck's Nest" at the mouth of the Tennessee River at Paducah, Kentucky, March 30, 1885. Low water in the Ohio River was the cause of the lay up. I went over to St. Louis and soon shipped on the *BART E. LINEHAN*, a Knapp Stout boat, William Slocumb, master; Jack Bradley, second pilot; William Eagan, chief engineer; Bob Scritchfield, second engineer; and George Langdon, mate.

Our work was to meet the other Knapp Stout boats, the *LOUISVILLE*, *HELEN MAR*, and *MENOMONIE*, take their rafts, and go to St. Louis while they went back after another. Captain Slocumb had more experience on the "lower end" and was better acquainted with the St. Louis landing than the other Knapp Stout pilots. Mr. Langdon wasn't a mate, he just thought he was. He wouldn't ship a steamboat man if he could get anyone else. At one time we had a crew of two "rivermen," my partner, Dick White, and myself, and five men out of a St. Louis rolling mill. Nice crew, all friends of the mate, but when he tried to make Dick and I do their work, he had trouble.

One trip we had to take four strings of lumber down to Crystal City, Missouri, where there was a big plate glass factory a short distance up Crystal. We delivered the lumber and were "taking off the kit." I was coiling down the check line and Langdon came along and said, "When you get that check line coiled down, straighten up those breast lines." When I got the check line coiled down, Dick said, "Let's go up to the glass factory a few minutes," that he knew some fellows up there. The captain and clerk had gone up, so we went. When we got back, I went back on the guards and was washing out one of the skiffs that was pulled up on the guards. Langdon was sitting on the bits on the forecastle and motioned to me to come out there. I went out and he said, "I told you to coil those breast lines and you went off and paid no attention to it." I said, "I supposed he had men that knew enough to coil down a breast line besides me." He said, "I'll fix you, you _____" and grabbed a sharp axe out of the rack and came at me and if there was ever murder in a man's eye, it was in his. I was scared stiff and thought it was all up with yours truly, but he tripped on the breast line and pitched forward. I don't know how I did it, but I grabbed him by the throat and shoved him back onto the stairs and I hit him right on the bridge of his nose.

As soon as I got him down, two of his rolling mills boys jumped on my back. An "old-timer" named Kelley came along just then, picked up the axe and said, "Hang on to his wind, Harry, he'll squeal if you let up, and if one of you rolling mill yaps put a hand in this, I'll cut him in two." I pounded him until I was tired and left him laying there on the stairs. The captain came aboard and there wasn't a man in sight. He looked at Langdon lying there on the stairs. Never asked a question and went up and "backed her out." Langdon finally came to and told me I had better get off the boat and right now, but Dick White told him to go up and get his gun and he would shoot it off for him.

I got off when we arrived in St. Louis and went to work the next day for Captain Slocumb's nephew on the Knapp Stout landing. The Knapp Stout boats all laid up Sundays and sometimes when we were going up river and happened to be forty or fifty miles from some town where some of the crew lived, we would run a few hours overtime so they could have a Sunday at home. One Sunday we laid at Canton, Missouri. Both engineers lived there, also the watchman. That day engineer Eagan's ten-year-old son had supper on the boat. We had a cook that summer from the lower river where he had been a packet cook. Every case like this when one of the crew brought a friend aboard at meal time, that meal went down in the cook's little black book. I don't know how Captain Slocumb heard of it, but one day we were lying at St. Louis all ready to go up the river and John H. Douglas, Secretary of the Knapp Stout Company, came down to the boat. Captain Slocumb went out on the bank and walked up to him and said, "Mr. Douglas, I don't care whether I go up in the doghouse and back that boat out or not, but that cook and I don't go out on the same boat." They didn't, but Captain Slocumb wasn't the one that got off.

Fourth of July I found myself in Keokuk, Iowa, and a few days after that I shipped on the steamer *DAN THAYER* owned by the P. S. Davidson Lumber Company, LaCrosse, Wisconsin. I. H. Short was captain; Chas. Short, second pilot; Chas. Burrell, chief engineer; Jas. Ferguson, second engineer; Dave Judson, mate. While on this boat I was in the hottest race I was ever in on any steamboat. The *THAYER* came out a new boat in the fall of 1884. That same fall, Turner and Hollingshead brought out the steamer *CLYDE*. This company also owned two other boats, the *ABNER GILE* and the *LILY TURNER*, and was towing lumber to Hannibal, Missouri. The *THAYER* was towing logs to Keokuk, Iowa.

In the spring of 1885, all the talk on the river was of the race that was to be run between the *DAN THAYER* and the *CLYDE* and the chances for and against each boat. Finally, the time came. The *THAYER* was on her way up the river and we met the *CLYDE* going down with a raft at the foot of Nine Mile Island, below Dubuque. A short time before, perhaps an hour, we had passed the *ABNER GILE*, also on her way upstream. Captain Short knew that the *CLYDE* would turn her raft over to the *GILE* as they had been doing so all that season.

We went on up the river and landed at Hurricane Island, eighteen miles above Dubuque, and pretended to cut windlass poles, really to wait for the *CLYDE*. We didn't have long to wait and Short let her go by and then pulled out after her. Before we caught up with her, the *CLYDE* landed and they claimed afterward that she "blew out a joint" on her steam line. We went on up the river and at Glen Haven, Wisconsin, rang down to a slow bell. Then, with our wheel barely rolling, we proceeded to get ready for what was to come. In a short time, the *CLYDE* came up alongside and her captain, Jerry Turner, went up and took the wheel, leaned out of the pilot house window and said, "Now come on Short, I am ready for you." When he ran the *THAYER* off the slow bell, it seemed to me that she jumped about one hundred feet before she hit the water again.

For about ten miles, it was nip and tuck, but the *CLYDE* was on the larboard side and on the crossing below Clayton, Iowa, she got a little behind and got into our stern swells and could not get alongside again. I looked at the steam gauge in the firebox and it read 265 pounds, then I went back to the engine room. Engineer Burrell stood there with his hand on the throttle valve and he said, "Harry, get out on the sharp end, she is liable to come back in here any time." His steam gauge showed 275 pounds. We were allowed 165 pounds!

At McGregor, Iowa, we were about three miles ahead and we had to land. Our "doctor," or boiler feed pump, wasn't putting any water into the boilers and about half of our wheel had been thrown off. When we got to LaCrosse, Captain Short hurried to the office of the LaCrosse paper with *his* account of the race and I'll bet that my partner and I pulled a skiff one hundred miles on our next trip taking a copy of the paper ashore to show to his friends. Our next trip up the river he brought the paper down and had me wrap a lump of coal up in it. Then he said he would "run in close at Port Byron, Illinois, and for me to throw it ashore, where, a *particular* friend would get it but I guess I only had one thickness of paper on one side of the coal. I threw so hard the coal went ashore and the paper dropped in the river. Short was a good pilot, but he spoiled it by always telling how good he was.

We landed in Clinton, Iowa, one day on our way up the river and he said we would be there about two hours. I went uptown to mail a letter and was gone about one-half hour, but when I did get back, the boat was making the crossing below Lyons and I didn't have a coat, vest, or a cent and had to "rail-road" to LaCrosse. Nice man. He was one of a family of five brothers, all pilots; Jerome E., Allen M., George C., Chas. M., and Ira H., better known as "Windy," all good pilots and all have made "their last landing." There were three of us left at Clinton and it took us two days to "brush the bumpers" and then had to nearly have a fight with Mr. Holmes, the secretary of the company, to get our money and then didn't get it all but if they were satisfied, we were. We balanced the books.

I was in LaCrosse one day and then shipped on the good steamer *DEXTER* owned by McDonald Brothers, LaCrosse, Wisconsin. John O'Connor was captain; George Nichols, second pilot; John Orait, chief engineer; Chas. Davidson, second engineer; and John Mills, mate. Our towing was logs to Quincy, Illinois and Hannibal, Missouri. It was getting late in the season, but I think I made three trips on the *DEXTER* and to this day I can't tell how she was kept afloat.

She was built at Osceola, Wisconsin, in 1867 and was dismantled at LaCrosse, Wisconsin, in 1888 and twenty-one years is a long life for a Mississippi raft boat with no more repairs than the *DEXTER* got. She came into LaCrosse late in 1888. Her kit was taken off and she was taken up into Black River to McDonald's boat yard and thirty-seven minutes later she was sitting on the bottom of Black River. The steam had gone down and the siphons had quit and "Old Faithful" was at rest. Peter O'Rourke, James Newcomb, Bony Lucas, Andy Lambert, and "Lome Short" are some of the pilots who did good work with the *DEXTER* and Jack Orait, James, and Henry Tully, Joseph, and Frank Dillon were some of her engineers.

Peace to her ashes.

1886 and 1887

Harry Dyer left no record of his river activities in 1886 and 1887, but from other records he indicated he was on the *LILY TURNER* in 1886 and the *HELENE SCHULENBURG* in 1887 and we resume his account in 1888.

1888—Aboard the *LOUISVILLE, NETTA DURANT* and *KIT CARSON*

After spending the winter on the lower river, I shipped on the steamer *LOUISVILLE,* one of the Knapp Stout fleet. This was the first time I had been on a Knapp Stout boat since 1885. There had been a great change since that time. John H. Douglas was now in charge of the boats and one of his first moves was to cut the crew's wages five dollars a month. Before his reign, the Knapp Stout boats always had a first-class crew; now it was anything they could get.

The *LOUISVILLE* was in charge of Captain H. C. Walker; Mr. Dobler, second pilot; Henry Horton, chief engineer; Ladd Gault, second engineer; Al Stone, mate; and Chas. Buchler in charge of the kitchen. We were towing lumber from Read's Landing to meet the *BART E. LINEHAN* generally about Burlington, Iowa. The *LINEHAN* took our raft on to St. Louis and we went back to Read's for another one. Our pilot, Mr. Dobler, was one of the best on the river, but Captain Walker and he didn't get along the best. I only stayed a month or so. The idea of working for five dollars less than anyone else made me sick, so I "hopped" her and the next day shipped on the *NETTA DURANT* with Captain Al Duncan, towing logs to the Clinton Lumber Company of Clinton, Iowa. I wanted all the experience I could get with different men as I was to go for my license. We soon found that Bailey was a "pet man"—one who always has a man in the crew who doesn't have to do anything. Some call him the handy man.

[Mr. Dyer shipped later in the season on the *KIT CARSON* and we pick up his narrative when he is on that craft.] The *KIT CARSON* was towing logs from Stillwater to Burlington. One trip, we were getting near the foot of Lake Pepin. It was about five o'clock P.M. Bailey came and called the crew to "tighten lines." I noticed he didn't call his pet, but he said to me, "Harry, you and your partner go up and sweep the boiler deck." Tom grabbed a broom and we started for the boiler deck, but we went in the office and got our money. Bailey wanted to know what was the matter, and Tom told him he was getting tired of doing another man's work. A short time after that I saw Bailey get the sweetest licking I ever saw one man give another and Gene Reeser gave it to him, and he didn't use anything but his hands and yet he never struck him with his fist. He simply slapped him to sleep.

I finished up the season of 1888 as I started it, on the steamer *LOUISVILLE*. I left her at Rock Island, Illinois, October 22 and headed for Louisville, Kentucky and the coal boats.

1889—A Season on the *LOUISVILLE*

I came up from the lower river in May 1889 and shipped on the *LOUISVILLE* again but this time H. C. Walker was master; Frank Wild, second pilot; Tom Chambers, chief engineer; David Shaw, second engineer; Owen Corcoran, mate; and George Newton in charge of the kitchen. Our trade was the same as last year, meeting the *LINEHAN*. I worked as night watchman all this season. All this season I only went to sleep once on watch and I picked a good night for the nap. We were lying at the head of Shohokan Chute with a raft. I was supposed to have ninety pounds of steam at five o'clock A.M., and then call the fireman. I went into the engine room about four o'clock and the steam was at seventy pounds, so I sat down on the foot box alongside one of the engines and soon was dead to the world. One of the boys woke up and saw me and woke me up. I looked at the steam gauge. I had sixty pounds. I ran out to the fire box and had about a hat full of fire under one boiler, called the fireman and went up and called the engineer. It happened that the second engineer and second pilot came on watch that morning. When it came time to call the pilot, we had ninety pounds of steam and Dave said, "Go up and call him, Harry." I did, and Dave backed her out with ninety pounds of steam. If I had called the chief, we would have laid right there until we had 150 pounds.

Frank Wild was a fairly good pilot, but very cranky. One night we were coming up river near Muscatine and he called me and told me to turn down the lights in the cabin as they blinded him. I turned them down and pulled down the curtains over the cabin doors. In a few minutes, he called again, same trouble that time. I put the lights out. Another call—"I said, what is it now?" He said go down and call the captain. I went down and called the "old man" and told him Frank wanted him. He got up, dressed and came out in the cabin, fell over a chair, ran into the table and said, "Harry, what have you got it so dark for?" I told him and he started for the pilot house and Frank told him that the d____n watchman had his lights so bright he was blinded. The old man took the wheel and told him to go down and fix the lights just as he wanted them and the trouble was over.

I laid the *LOUISVILLE* up that fall and when I left her I was hired to go as mate on her the next spring, but that winter the Knapp Stout boats were all sold to McDonald Brothers of LaCrosse, Captain Walker was put on the *MOUNTAIN BELLE* and I went with him. Captain Bob Cassidy was put on the *LOUISVILLE* and Captain Decker Dixon on the *BELLA MAC*. Cassidy and Dixon were old Knapp Stout men.

1890—Aboard the *MOUNTAIN BELLE* and *PAULINE*

In the winter of 1889-90, the Knapp Stout Company sold their boats, the *LOUISVILLE, HELEN MAR,* and *BART E. LINEHAN* to McDonald Brothers of LaCrosse, Wisconsin, and in April 1890, I shipped as mate and clerk on the *MOUNTAIN BELLE* with Captain Henry Walker; second pilot, Robert Erwin; chief engineer, Joe Stombs; second engineer, James Ferguson; and Mr. and Mrs. George Newton in charge of the kitchen. I should have taken a little more time to think it over before going on the *MOUNTAIN BELLE*, but in the fall of 1889 Captain Walker had hired me to go on the *LOUISVILLE* with him in 1890, but he didn't go on [her].

We got our first raft, a half of lumber for Hannibal, Missouri, and a half raft of logs for Quincy, Illinois. The lumber had laid all winter in Fountain City bay and the logs in Chimney Rock and it was the worst half raft I ever stepped onto. I don't believe there was a log in the raft that would scale two hundred feet. We landed alongside the raft about nine o'clock at night. When we left LaCrosse, I had orders to pay raftsman twenty dollars a month, so you can imagine what kind of a crew I had. Captain Walker had brought two "cornfield" sailors with him from his North Dakota farm, both good farmers but *very* poor raftsmen and I had six twenty-dollar-a-month men I had picked up in LaCrosse.

It was pitch dark when we landed at the raft and I was going to bed when the Captain said; "Harry, aren't you going to 'line her up,' and I said not until daylight and it will be bad enough then. If I got those fellows out there now I wouldn't have but one or two left in the morning, the rest of them would be under the raft." Pilot Erwin said, "that's right." Captain Walker said he didn't believe the company would stand for laying there all night. I saw what I was going to be up against, but he didn't say any more.

In the morning, we finally got the lines on and started down river. My Dakota boys were very homesick. At LaCrosse, we got orders to turn the raft over to the *BELLA MAC* and go to Stillwater. I soon found that Captain Walker knew very little about a log raft. He had always worked for the Knapp Stout Company and their work was nearly all lumber and our work was all logs.

We got along okay until about June 15. Pilot Erwin was a fine man and a good pilot, never had much to say, but when he did, he said it. One of our farmer boys had learned very fast. His name was Conrad Heider or "Coon," and he was formerly employed on the captain's North Dakota farm. He decided that the captain was the only man on the boat who could give him any orders, but one thing he learned was that when the second pilot was on watch, he was captain and when Bob Erwin got ready to tell a man a few things he told him in language that he could understand, and I guess Mr. Heider thought he meant it because when Erwin told him "a few things," the captain heard the whole conversation and never said a word.

We landed at Rock Island one night with two burned boilers and the next morning, who should walk aboard but Captain Dan McDonald, one of the owners. They sent for some boiler makers and then Walker said, "I suppose we had better lay the crew off," meaning my crew. Captain Dan said, "Oh no, I guess Harry can find work enough for them," but Walker told me to lay them off so I told them to get ashore and only come aboard at meal times. The boiler makers came and there was a lot of sidewalls to be torn out and then Walker said, "Harry, put your men to tearing out those side walls." I told him I didn't have any men, that he told me to lay them off. He looked at me about a minute and then said, "Put them to work again," but when he told me to lay them off he said I could keep "Coon" under pay and he would let him help the cooks. I had about enough of his work, but finally one of the [raftsmen] got permission for his wife to make a trip with us and I soon noticed they spent a lot of time in the pilot house when Walker was on watch and one day he said, "Harry, I guess I will let him do the clerk's work and you the mate's." I said, "It suits me. Send him up right now and we will balance the books and then you can get yourself a mate if you can find one."

I made another trip and one day I was called into the office of McDonald Brothers at LaCrosse and they asked if that was my signature on some bills and checks and I said "No." The head clerk said I need not be so emphatic about it. I knew it wasn't. That fall Captain Walker went back to his farm and stayed there. I guess he took "Coon" with him.

I put in the rest of the season on the steamer *PAULINE* with Captain Jerry Turner, Walter Hunter, mate and second pilot; Joseph Fuller, chief engineer; Chas. Fess, second engineer; and Mrs. Seeger in charge of the kitchen. Captain Jerry was an old-time steamboat man. He owned the *PAULINE* and he ran her to suit himself, and took orders from nobody. It was late in the fall when I shipped with him and he was standing watch all day. He wouldn't let Hunter run the raft. We laid up every night, but when we delivered the raft at Hannibal, Hunter took the boat back up the river and Captain Jerry took the train at Burlington and went home to Lansing, Iowa, and we picked him up when we got there. I laid the *PAULINE* up in Lansing Bay for the winter. One thing I learned from Captain Walker was to *never* make a "pet" of any of your men as he did of "Coon." If you did, you would never have a crew, but if you used them right and let them know that they all looked alike to you, there was never any trouble.

1891

Mr. Dyer left no account of his steamboating this year, but from other sources it was indicated that he was on the *PAULINE*.

1892—From the *ISAAC STAPLES* to the *CLYDE*

It was late when I shipped this spring and it was on the steamer *ISAAC STAPLES* with Charles B. Roman, master; Sam Lancaster, second pilot; George Van Bebber, chief engineer; William Allen, second engineer; Henry Polis, mate; and John Goff in charge of the kitchen. She was a Bronson and Folsom boat and was towing logs to Burlington, Iowa. Captain Roman was a good pilot, but he made a very bad mistake that spring. Late in the fall of 1891, he laid a raft up for the winter in the mouth of Black River at LaCrosse and that was to be our first trip. We "lined up" half of the raft and as it had been laid up with the bow upstream, he had to swing it. The LaCrosse highway bridge was but a short distance below the mouth of Black River and the water was high and swift and our raft did not swing fast enough and hit the bridge an awful rap. It didn't hurt the bridge any, but it was very hard on the raft.

It took us a week to gather it up and re-raft it. When we took the other half of the raft out of Black River, we swung it on a line. That was the only breakup Captain Roman had that season.

Early in June we had to lay up for a short time on account of high water at Burlington and part of the mill was under water, so I shipped on the steamer CYCLONE with Captain Bob Cassidy. She was a Durant and Wheeler boat, so I knew I would not be troubled with indigestion. She also was towing to Burlington, but the high water did not affect that mill. We made one trip and came back to Stillwater and laid at the levee all night. When we went up to breakfast the next morning, all that was on the table was bread and bacon. The slices of bacon were not more than an inch wide before they were cooked and looked like a lot of pork rinds. I said to the captain when we came down from breakfast, "You don't expect us to do much today do you, Bob." He said, "Why?" I said, "Men can't do much on that breakfast." He said, "It was pretty raw, let's both get off." I said, "I'm going to but you can't, you are hired by the season." The CYCLONE had two lady cooks and I'll bet neither of them got more than twenty-five dollars a month.

Next, I find myself on the steamer DAISY with Captain Ira Fuller and towing logs to Moline, Illinois. Ira Fuller was a good pilot and would have been a star but for one thing—liquor. After I had made one trip, the DAISY had to lay up for repairs and I shipped on the steamer BELLA MAC with Captain N. B. Lucas who was generally called "Bony." His name was Napoleon Bonaparte. Bob Ervine was second pilot; James Tully, chief engineer; and John McCann, mate. George Whalen, one of the best cooks on the river, had charge of the kitchen. I made a trip to Hannibal and one to St. Louis. When we got back to LaCrosse from the St. Louis trip, it was September 15 and we decided to ask for more money, the same as the rest of the boats were paying.

But when we asked Captain Dan McDonald about it, you would have thought we had asked for one of his eye teeth. Why he said, "The McDonald boats never pay more than a dollar a day until October 15," so we gave him a chance to hire some dollar-a-day men. The next morning I shipped on the steamer CLYDE, a Bronson and Folsom boat, for forty dollars a month. Captain Morrell Looney; second pilot, Frank Wetenhall; Milton Newcomb, chief engineer; Tom Buchanan, mate; Bob Moulton, better known as "Double-headed Bob" was in charge of the kitchen. Morrell Looney was a good pilot and a fine man to work for. Wetenhall was a good pilot, but very excitable and in a tight place would "go up in the air," but a few words from Morrell and he would come down again.

The CLYDE used to be called the "biggest little boat" on the upper Mississippi. Her towing was all to Dubuque, Iowa to the Standard Lumber Company. About October 15 the mate Buchanan quit and Looney put me in his place. Late in November I got off at LaCrosse as she was going to Stillwater to lay up for the winter. As I was going down the gangplank, Captain Looney told me I was hired for the next season, for 1893, which suited me perfectly. She was a good boat, belonged to a good company, and had a fine captain—what more could a man ask for? I worked seven seasons on the Bronson and Folsom boats, the CLYDE, the ISAAC STAPLES, and JUNIATA, and they were the best.

1893—A Banner Year on the CLYDE

This was the banner year of my service on the raft boats of the Upper Mississippi. Late in the fall of 1892, I was hired as mate of the steamer CLYDE for the season of 1893 and was ordered to report at Stillwater, Minnesota to get her ready, April 15. The CLYDE's crew for that season was Morrell Looney, master; Frank Wetenhall, second pilot; Harry Dyer, mate; Milton Newcomb, chief engineer; Sam Serene, second engineer; Rufus Newcomb, clerk; and George Wright in charge of the kitchen and let me say here that, with the exception of Wright, this crew laid up the boat that fall. Herman Thomas took Wright's place about July 1.

The CLYDE was one of the Bronson and Folsom fleet, the others being the *RAVENNA*, Captain Davidson; the *MENOMONIE*, Captain Dunn; and the *ISAAC STAPLES*, Captain Roman. The *CLYDE* was well named, "the biggest little boat" on the river. She was 125 feet long, nineteen-foot beam, four-foot hold. Two steel boilers allowed 198 pounds steam pressure. Engines, six-foot stroke and twelve-inch bore. Almost all of our towing was to Dubuque, Iowa, to the Standard Lumber Company.

In the entire season of 1893, the *CLYDE* had just one "break up" where we were forced to land. Coming around Bad Axe Bend one night our right-hand bow corner of the raft caught on the sand bar below the bend and we knocked out about two hundred logs. We landed at the foot of Battle Island and in about six hours had them back where they belonged and were going down the river again as if nothing had happened.

I had wonderful luck that season in keeping a crew. My log book for that season shows that I shipped fifty-three men. On our second trip in the spring I shipped a man at West Newton, April 29. His name was Billy Stanton. The next morning our clerk told me he didn't see why that man wanted to ship as he had given him twenty dollars and a gold watch to keep for him. On the 16th of October, Billy came to me at Dubuque and said, "Well, Harry, I am going to leave you and go to the Fair at Chicago." He took me back in the deck room, went to his bunk, turned down the blankets, stuck his hand down in the corner of his mattress and took out 175 dollars and said, "Good bye, Harry, you surely know how to mate a steamboat."

We laid the *CLYDE* up that fall at Dubuque, the 7th of November. Mr. David Bronson was there and he asked me if I wanted to go on the *CLYDE* the next season. I said, "I sure do." He said, "You are hired." That was all. He said, "the *CLYDE* has had the best season and made the most money of any season since we have owned her and I want the crew all back in 1894."

1894—On the *CLYDE* and *J. K. GRAVES*; Mr. Dyer's Mother Dies

In the winter of 1893-94 my old skipper, Captain Looney, bought the *THISTLE* from McDonald Brothers of LaCrosse, Wisconsin, and in the spring of 1894 put her in the packet trade between LaCrosse and St. Paul. As soon as I found that the *CLYDE* was to have a new captain, I wrote to Mr. Bronson and asked him who it was to be. His reply was that he hadn't fully decided, but it would make no difference to me as he would tell him he had hired a mate. I got orders to go to Dubuque to get the *CLYDE* ready, March 16, 1894, and left the next day. I heard that John Hoy was to be the *CLYDE*'s captain. He arrived in a few days and I told him if he had someone he would rather have it was OK with me. He said, "No, it is all right." The rest of the crew was the same as 1893, that is, Frank Wetenhall, second pilot; Milt Newcomb, chief engineer; Sam Serene, second engineer; Rufus Newcomb, clerk; and George Whalen, cook.

We pulled out March 22 and made a few trips to Dubuque from Lynxville and Waukon Bays with logs that had been laid up there. When I left home, my mother was quite sick and on March 27 we were forced to lay up at Lynxville as the river was running full of ice. The next morning I heard that my mother was much worse and I told Hoy I was going home. It was only sixteen miles and he said, "Sure, that is all right." I told one of my linesmen if the boat pulled out before I got back, to do my work. My mother died March 30, 1894. The *CLYDE* pulled out and made one trip to Dubuque and I was off eight days.

A few days after I got back I asked the clerk if Hoy had stopped my wages while I was gone and he said, "Why sure not, he didn't say anything about it but I will ask him." Hoy said, "sure and give it to Wetenhall." So there was sixteen dollars of my money to go into their booze fund. I stood it for about two months and then decided that it was no use to try to suit him, he was so ignorant he could not forget that "Bronson had hired me." I wrote to Mr. Bronson when I got home and told him of the deal I got from Hoy. He said, "Never mind, Harry, I will have another boat for you in a few days" and sent me a check on the Lumberman's Bank in Stillwater for sixteen dollars. In a very few days, I was on the steamer *J. K. GRAVES* and finished the season on her.

Captain Hoy was drowned when the steamer *RAVENNA*, another Bronson and Folsom boat, capsized at the foot of Maquoketa Slough near Dubuque, June 13, 1902. Five other men also drowned.

1895

Harry Dyer did not leave an account of his activity in this year but was on the *J. K. GRAVES* as mate.

When asked by George Merrick for a photo, Harry G. Dyer sent this one of him posing in his "engineering" regalia beside the furnaces and boilers he attended when he worked with the state of Wisconsin.
Photo courtesy of State Historical Society of Wisconsin.

George Winans at the time of his service in the Wisconsin Legislature of 1887. Captain Winans was already showing signs of early baldness. Like other men of the day he sported a heavy mustache.
Photo courtesy of State Historical Society of Wisconsin.

George Winans sported these white whiskers in his old age.
Photo courtesy of State Historical Society of Wisconsin.

Captain Fred Way, Jr., shown here at age ninety in *TELL CITY* pilothouse. Captain Way was the "dean" of western river steamboat historians and was a river pilot in his own right. He founded the Sons and Daughters of Pioneer Rivermen and was its first and only president until his passing in 1993. His data on towboats and packets was invaluable to producing this work.
Photo courtesy of William Penberthy, Sewickley, Pennsylvania.

George B. Merrick (1841-1931) was a Mississippi River steamboat clerk before the Civil War. During the war he was with the 30th Wisconsin Infantry. He was prominent in GAR (Grand Army of the Republic) circles and produced a weekly column for many years in the *Burlington Saturday Evening Post* about old steamboats and river men. He lived out the last years of his life in wretched health and blindness. He authored a well-regarded steamboat book, *Old Times on the Mississippi*.
Photo courtesy of State Historical Society of Wisconsin.

Captain Walter Blair, successful steamboat captain, pilot, and owner. He operated many raftboats and also had several packets on the river.
Photo courtesy of Murphy Library Special Collections, University-LaCrosse.

Stephan B. Hanks, cousin of Abraham Lincoln, was the "dean" of floating raft pilots and steamboat pilots on the river. He was master on the *ARTEMUS LAMB* for fifteen years and rode on the *OTTUMWA BELLE* on the last rafting trip in 1915.
Photo courtesy of Murphy Library Special Collections, University of Wisconsin-LaCrosse.

Rafting captain Thomas Forbush had served in the Civil War and when George Merrick asked him for a photo he sent this early one taken in uniform.
Photo courtesy of State Historical Society of Wisconsin.

Daniel Davison was pilot or master on the *ANNIE GIRDON*, both of the *J. G. CHAPMAN* steamboats, *JAMES FISK, JR., JULIA, LITTLE EAGLE* and *SILAS WRIGHT*.
Photo courtesy of State Historical Society of Wisconsin.

Captain John Lancaster was master of the *ECLIPSE* for several years and was on the *EVERETT,* which he owned, and the *MOUNTAIN BELLE.* Harry Dyer said, "Captain Lancaster was a first-class steamboat man."
Photo courtesy of Murphy Library Special Collections, University of Wisconsin-LaCrosse.

Captain Joseph "Tansy" Hawthorne. He served on the *NEPTUNE, ST. CROIX, GARDIE EASTMAN,* and many others. He was a cousin of Nathaniel Hawthorne and had lived in LaCrosse since 1856. He died in 1937 at the age of ninety-seven.
Photo courtesy of Murphy Library Special Collections, University of Wisconsin-LaCrosse.

Captain John McDonald, one of the McDonald Brothers of LaCrosse and a steamboat pilot and owner.
Photo courtesy of Murphy Library Special Collections, University of Wisconsin-LaCrosse.

Captain John M. Long was a Rock Island Rapids pilot and built the *JO. LONG*.
Photo courtesy of Murphy Library Special Collections, University of Wisconsin-LaCrosse.

Captain J. Wesley Rambo was a rafting pilot at LeClaire. The *WEST RAMBO* was probably named after him.
Photo courtesy of Murphy Library Special Collections, University of Wisconsin-LaCrosse.

Captain George Nichols was pilot on the *DEXTER, DAN THAYER, INVERNESS* and *KIT CARSON*.
Photo courtesy of Murphy Library Special Collections, University of Wisconsin-LaCrosse.

Captain Orrin Smith was master of the *PILOT* and was also a Rock Island Rapids pilot.
Photo courtesy of Murphy Library Special Collections, University of Wisconsin-LaCrosse.

Captain John Rook was in command of the *SILAS WRIGHT*.
Photo courtesy of Murphy Library Special Collections, University of Wisconsin-LaCrosse.

Captain Isaiah H. Wasson was owner and master of the *MOLINE* and master of the *STILLWATER*.
Photo courtesy of Murphy Library Special Collections, University of Wisconsin-LaCrosse.

One of the most successful rafting steamboat entrepreneurs was Captain Samuel R. Van Sant, a Civil War veteran, who was often a partner with Captain Walter Blair and P. Musser. Later, he was governor of Minnesota for two terms and national head of the GAR.
Photo courtesy of Murphy Library Special Collections, University of Wisconsin-LaCrosse and Winona County (Minnesota) Historical Society.

Captain R. "Charlie" Tromley was on the *FRONTENAC* in 1913 and also was pilot on the *SILVER CRESCENT*.
Photo courtesy of the Buffalo Bill Museum, LeClaire, Iowa.

Captain George Tromley was master of the *LYDIA VAN SANT* and also served on the *TEN BROECK*.
Photo courtesy of the Buffalo Bill Museum, LeClaire, Iowa.

Captain Asa B. Woodward was captain or master of the *HENRIETTA, LIZZIE GARDNER,* and the *SAM ALTEE*.
Photo courtesy of the State Historical Society of Wisconsin.

Captain Volney A. Bigelow owned many steamboats. He had the *JESSIE B.* built for his use, utilizing machinery of the *NATRONA,* and named her for his daughter. He also owned the *QUICKSTEP* and the *ALFRED TOLL* and was on the *BUCKEYE*.
Photo courtesy of the State Historical Society of Wisconsin.

Captain R. J. Wheeler was a partner with Ed Durant in Durant and Wheeler and was master of the *R. J. WHEELER* in 1890.
Photo courtesy of the State Historical Society of Wisconsin.

Captain W. W. Slocumb was known as "Old Will" because his nephew, also a pilot, was known as "Young Will." He was on the *CHAMPION, JULIA* and *KIT CARSON*.
Photo courtesy of the State Historical Society of Wisconsin.

Captain John Knapp (1825–1888) piloted the first steamboat on the Chippewa River circa 1848–49. He was a founder of Knapp, Stout and Company, a large lumber firm.
Photo courtesy of the State Historical Society of Wisconsin.

Captain Peter Kirns sent this 1896 photo to George Merrick, saying it was taken the year he quit the river. He was master on the *J. G. CHAPMAN* (2nd) and the *J. W. VAN SANT* (1st) and he had a rafter named after him in 1879.
Photo courtesy of the State Historical Society of Wisconsin.

Henry Whitemore (1821–1902) was a cub engineer in 1839 and left the river in 1892. He was repeatedly cited for his engine room excellence by Captain Walter Blair.
Photo courtesy of the State Historical Society of Wisconsin.

Captain John S. Walker of the *LUELLA* in the early 1890s was also on the *SILAS WRIGHT* for several years.
Photo courtesy of the State Historical Society of Wisconsin.

Thomas Hoy was master and pilot of the *CYCLONE* in the 1890s and was also on the *HENRIETTA*.
Photo courtesy of the State Historical Society of Wisconsin.

Captain William R. Young was a prominent lumber entrepreneur and owned many rafting steamboats.
Photo courtesy of the State Historical Society of Wisconsin.

Jerome "Jerry" M. Turner owned the *ABNER GILE* in 1880–88, and was master of the *CLYDE* for a time and also was on the *GOLDEN GATE*, *LILY TURNER*, *NELLIE* and *SILAS WRIGHT*.
Photo courtesy of the State Historical Society of Wisconsin.

Joseph "Big Joe" Perro was an old-time "floating" pilot and later served on rafters. Two of his vessels were the *MOONSTONE* and *PEARL*.
Photo courtesy of the State Historical Society of Wisconsin.

Captain Jerome E. Short, seen here with a model of the steamboat *HELEN*, was one of the last active captains.
Photo courtesy of the Putnam Museum of History and Natural Science, Davenport, Iowa.

Samuel Hanks, related to Stephan B. Hanks, served many years in the rafting trades.
Photo courtesy of the Putnam Museum of History and Natural Science, Davenport, Iowa.

P. M. Musser came to Muscatine from Pennsylvania and worked for his uncle. He took over the lumber business in Iowa City and later moved to Muscatine where he was prominent in many lumber and associated businesses.
Photo courtesy of the Edward A. Mueller collection.

Abner Gile early on was engaged in the logging and lumber business. A rafter was named after him.
Photo courtesy of the Edward A. Mueller collection.

Chancy Lamb, founder of Chancy Lamb and Sons of Clinton, Iowa, a profitable lumber works, had a stake in almost all businesses in Clinton, Iowa. His two sons, Artemus and Lafayette, were in business with him.
Photo courtesy of the Edward A. Mueller collection.

Henry L. Stout was a financier who bought into the Knapp lumber business. He was elected mayor of Dubuque for five years and arranged for lumber sales "down river."
Photo courtesy of the Edward A. Mueller collection.

Isaac Staples was a dominant factor in Stillwater, Minnesota, a prominent lumber town. He came to the area from Maine. He had a hand in most significant businesses in Stillwater.
Photo courtesy of the Edward A. Mueller collection.

F. Weyerhaeuser was said by many to be the catalyst that enabled rafting on the Mississippi to be as successful as it was. He was a leveling force and had the foresight to move to the West Coast and continue his lumbering dynasty there.
Photo courtesy of the Edward A. Mueller collection.

Captain Robert N. Cassidy, shown here in a sketch by Don Ingram, was on the *CYCLONE, FRONTENAC, JUNIATA, KIT CARSON, MENOMONIE, MINNESOTA, MOLLIE MUHLER* and others. He closed out his career as captain of the Mayo Brothers' *ORONOCO* in 1915.
Drawing courtesy of the Edward A. Mueller collection.

Captain Paul Kerz was born in Germany and came to America when he was seventeen years old. He started rafting with the *STERLING* and later was on the *J. W. MILLS*. He helped build the *DOUGLAS BOARDMAN* and also the *W. J. YOUNG, JR*. Captain Walter Blair stated, "if there ever was a man who really loved his work it was Captain Paul Kerz."
Photo courtesy of the Edward A. Mueller collection.

Captain Oliver P. McMahon, sketch by Don Ingram, was on the *SILVER CRESCENT* for a long time and helped build her.
Drawing courtesy of the Edward A. Mueller collection.

Captain William McCraney, sketch by Don Ingram, bought the *MOUNTAIN BELLE* (when she was *THE PURCHASE*) and ran her in the excursion business at St. Paul until the mid-1910s.
Drawing courtesy of the Edward A. Mueller collection.

Captain Joseph Buisson started working on the river when he was fifteen years old. He was master or pilot on the *CLYDE, GARDIE EASTMAN, L. W. BARDEN* and the *C. W. COWLES*. He later worked for the Streckfus Line and even was a United States Marshall.
Photo courtesy of the Edward A. Mueller collection.

Captain Cyprian Buisson, brother of Joseph, was widely known for his twelve seasons of service on the rafter *B. HERSHEY* from 1877 on. He then joined the Valley Navigation Company and spent another eight years on the *B. HERSHEY*. After a brief period of retirement he came back to the river and piloted large packets.
Photo courtesy of the Edward A. Mueller collection.

A sketch by Don Ingram of Captain Jerome E. Short in his eighties. He celebrated his eighty-ninth birthday in 1938 and was probably the oldest surviving pilot at that time.
Drawing courtesy of the Edward A. Mueller collection.

Benjamin Hershey came from Pennsylvania and was active in the lumber business at Muscatine until his death in 1893.
Photo courtesy of the Edward A. Mueller collection.

BEEF SLOUGH

The Beef Slough was a sluggish branch of the Chippewa River that provided an excellent storage pond for the logs floated downstream by numerous logging companies. Here loggers were employed to arrange the mixed-up logs into orderly rafts to be towed by steamboats to sawmills down the Mississippi.

The Chippewa Falls and Eau Claire sawmills felt threatened when the Beef Slough Manufacturing, Booming, Log Driving and Transportation Company was organized near here in 1867. Camp No. 1 built offices, a railroad depot, post office, church and dormitories to house 600 men during the rafting season.

The competition between the Eau Claire and Beef Slough interests developed into a brief dispute in 1868, sometimes called the "Beef Slough War." The most important result of the "war" was the arrival on the scene of Frederick Weyerhaeuser, whose Mississippi Logging Company brought skilled management and seemingly unlimited capital into the picture and changed the logging operations on the Chippewa from locally-operated activities into a major interstate industry.

Erected 1976

Roadside marker on Wisconsin Route 35 near Alma, Wisconsin commemorating Beef Slough and the rafting days.
Photo courtesy of Murphy Library Special Collections, University of Wisconsin-LaCrosse.

Below: Beef Slough rafting works, the "race" is at left, log pockets are on either side.
Photo courtesy of Murphy Library Special Collections, University of Wisconsin-LaCrosse.

Above: Scaling (measuring) logs at Beef Slough.
Photo courtesy of Murphy Library Special Collections, University of Wisconsin-LaCrosse.

Below: Sorting logs at Beef Slough.
Photo courtesy of Murphy Library Special Collections, University of Wisconsin-LaCrosse.

Horses and men retrieving logs stranded on a sand bar opposite Alma, Wisconsin.
Photo courtesy of Murphy Library Special Collections, University of Wisconsin-LaCrosse.

Two raftsmen stopping for a drink from the Mississippi River.
Photo courtesy of Murphy Library Special Collections, University of Wisconsin-LaCrosse.

The Fleming Brothers Lumber Works in McGregor, Iowa. The company was one of the processors of the many log rafts. There were good-sized areas for holding logs in the river there.
Photo courtesy of the Historical Society of McGregor, Iowa.

This photo is thought to be of the West Newton rafting works.
Photo courtesy of Murphy Library Special Collections, University of Wisconsin-LaCrosse.

A portion of the strung-out Beef Slough rafting works. The "race" is in the foreground. Photo courtesy of Murphy Library Special Collections, *University of Wisconsin-LaCrosse.*

A log raft makeup crew. The fifth man from the left and the fifth man from the right have hand augers for boring holes.
Photo courtesy of Murphy Library Special Collections, University of Wisconsin-LaCrosse and Winona County (Minnesota) Historical Society.

Photo taken at a river pilot's convention held in 1889 at LaCrosse.
Photo courtesy of Murphy Library Special Collections, University of Wisconsin-LaCrosse.

1896—With the Tromleys and Joe Buisson

This year I discovered what a vast difference there can be between two brothers. I hopped on the *J. W. VAN SANT* in 1896. George Tromley, Jr., master; Charles Tromley, second pilot; Henry Bingham, chief engineer; Ladd Gault, second engineer; Ben Metzer, mate; and Charles Buehler was in charge of the kitchen. George Tromley, Sr. was a *first class* pilot and a fine man but very quiet and did very little talking. His brother was just the opposite—lively, full of fun and a good mixer. I don't know what was wrong between the brothers, but they scarcely ever spoke. They would change watches time after time without saying a word. George Sr. was an old-time pilot from the floating raft days and would rather play poker than eat. French and Indian descent, no education and a perfect gentleman. He married Kate McCaffery of LeClaire, Iowa. He died at LeClaire, October 16, 1904, age seventy-six years. George Jr.'s health was never very good and he died at Davenport, Iowa in 1919, age sixty-three years. Charles committed suicide by drowning at Dubuque, Iowa.

Later in the season of 1896, I shipped on the steamer *C. W. COWLES*, Joseph Buisson, master; Ira Decamp, second pilot; Thomas Decamp, chief engineer; Milton Roundy, second engineer; Joe Larrivere, mate; and Mrs. Thomas Decamp was in charge of the kitchen. Here is another brother story. Joe Buisson had a brother, Cyprian, both of French and Indian descent. They were both good pilots, but to my mind Cyp Buisson was the best raft pilot on the Upper Mississippi. Neither had any education, but Joe married a school teacher and she taught him to read and he could "put on the dog" when he got started.

We were going down with a raft one trip and just above DeSoto, Tom Decamp asked me if I knew that the *COWLES* was going to lay up when we got to Muscatine. I asked Captain Joe if that was so and he said, "No, what put that in your head?" I told him I did not want to go to Muscatine and pay fare back and he said I wouldn't have to. We delivered at Muscatine Saturday, laid at the levee there Sunday, put on two hundred boxes of coal. Monday forenoon, we "dropped in" on a raft that had been laid up in Hershey Slough. After dinner the clerk called the crew up one at a time and paid them off and he left me until the last. I went up and he had my money all laid out and a receipt in full for me to sign. I said, "How about my fare back up the river, captain?" And he said, "This company doesn't pay any fare back." I said, "You are all the company there is. I won't sign that receipt in full so you will have to change it to so many days work." Well, he finally told the clerk to change it. There were eight of us to "railroad" back up the river. We stopped at Dubuque, Iowa, and had a talk with the U. S. marshal there and when we left he knew just how much railroad fare was due each man and we knew we would get it. The marshal sent it to us.

Captain Cyprian did not deny that he was part Indian. Their home was in Wabasha, Minnesota, and during the winter months they were given a part of their groceries by the grocers of that city. Captain Cyp used to go and get his but not so with Captain Joe and Captain Cyp had ten close friends where Captain Joe had one. Captain Joe was appointed Deputy Marshal when he retired from the river. He died at St. Paul, Minnesota, October 29, 1918. Captain Cyp was pilot on the steamer *MORNING STAR* in the packet trade between Davenport, Iowa, and St. Paul, two or three years and died at St. Paul, November 24, 1920. Another case of two brothers as different from each other as black is from white. There was another brother of the Buissons. His name was Henry and he was his brother Cyprian's double. They were plain everyday men, well thought of, lots of friends, but Joe wanted to be classed by himself and hadn't brains enough to carry it out.

1897—Salvaging the *BART E. LINEHAN*

In the spring of 1897, I was fool enough to ship on the *C. W. COWLES* again with Joe Buisson. That spring he had Frank LaPointe and he was signed as mate. He was an old-time pilot and was supposed to stand Captain Joe's watch going upstream and a good part of it going down, and I soon found that I was to do most of Frank's work on the raft, but Joe soon found that he had got his lines crossed and it wouldn't work, so I told Joe goodbye. A few days after that, I shipped on the *BART E. LINEHAN*, William Dobler, master; John Schmidt, second pilot; Bob Shannon, chief engineer; Fred Graham, second engineer; Louis Prommel, mate; and Si Barnes in charge of the kitchen. The boat was owned by McDonald Brothers of LaCrosse and her trade was towing logs from West Newton and Stillwater to Quincy, Illinois.

Captain Dobler was one of the best raft pilots. In

1887 he made eight round trips from the West Newton rafting works to Quincy, Illinois, in sixty-four days; a mark for all to shoot at. The *LINEHAN* was a good towboat, not as powerful as some, and not as fast as some, but a good all-around raft boat.

While steaming up the Mississippi River after delivering a raft of logs to the Gem City Lumber Company, Quincy, Illinois, about October 1, 1897, the *BART E. LINEHAN* sank after striking a snag above Buena Vista, Iowa. The water where the *LINEHAN* settled was about eight feet deep.

Captain Dobler was on watch at the wheel at the time the craft struck a snag, which proved to be a soft maple log about two feet in diameter firmly planted on the bottom of the river. The snag struck the boat just forward of the boilers, tearing a hole in the hull about fifteen feet long and three or four feet wide.

It took the boat about two minutes to settle on the bottom of the river.

The deck crew had its sleeping quarters on the lower or main deck, and immediately after the boat struck the snag, there was a race for the after stairs leading to the boiler deck.

Ed Lubey, one of the firemen, an old man and a cripple, was in the lead, and was followed by eight raftsmen, the second engineer, the fireman, and a helper, all of whom were trying to get up the stairway which was about thirty inches wide.

After the craft had settled down, the water was from two to three feet on the main deck and about three inches below the grate bars in the furnace.

McDonald Brothers at LaCrosse, owners of the boat, were immediately notified, and a diver was sent from St. Louis. Two large barges, each about the same length as the sunken boat, were procured from the Diamond Jo Company, Dubuque, Iowa.

On the arrival of the diver, the work of raising the *LINEHAN* began. The first phase of the work was for the diver to enter the hull and saw off the snag. This took about six hours. The snag was about seven feet long and was removed from the hull when the boat was pulled out on the dock at Dubuque.

While the diver was at work in the hull, the steamboat crew and an extra gang sent down from LaCrosse were engaged in putting large chains under the boat from one barge to the other. Seven of these chains were placed.

By means of large levers which were square timbers twelve feet long and a foot square, the chains were pulled up, gradually raising the sunken boat. Amidships, it was found impossible to get the chains to run "square across" under the boat because of the many small snags on the river bottom. This made it useless to go further with the chains as the boat would have broken in two.

After working three or four days it was decided to bulkhead the hold and pump the boat out. The diver went into the hull and built a double bulkhead of dry lumber around the hole. When this was finished, a strip of heavy canvas was run around the *LINEHAN*, the top edge of the canvas coming above the surface of the water. It was then tacked to the sides of the boat.

Steam was raised in the boilers on the *LINEHAN* and the *ETHEL HOWARD*, a small boat from LaCrosse, was brought alongside. All the siphons (pumps) were started, and two men with a wash tub were at each deck room door bailing out water. The *LINEHAN* came up until the crown of the main deck was three inches out of the water. Then, owing to a poor draft, the steam dropped, the siphons stopped working, and the *LINEHAN* settled back onto the river bed.

That night the *QUICKSTEP*, another McDonald boat, went to Fulton, Illinois, and brought back a sand pump having an eight-inch rotary pump and an eight-inch rubber hose for a suction line. The outfit arrived at the place of operations about 5:30 A.M. Steam was already up in the sand pump's boiler.

The suction hose was stuck down the *LINEHAN*'s forward hatchway, the pump started, and in one hour and a half the boat was afloat.

While she was coming up, we kept taking up the slack of the chains so that it was impossible for her to go down again. When the pumping out was finished, she was between the two barges and resting on the chains, and after steam was raised went to Dubuque under her own power and was pulled out on the ways and repaired. The time spent in raising and repairing the hull was thirteen and one-half days.

While tearing out the bulkhead that the diver built around the hole in the hull, one of the boat yard men made the remark that a good many men couldn't have built as good a one out of the water as the diver built underwater. The diver, Leron Jobin of St. Louis, surely was good and knew his business.

The *LINEHAN* was back in commission in time to make a trip from Prescott, Wisconsin, to Quincy, Illinois, and then back to LaCrosse where she was laid up for the winter on November 7, 1897.

The crew of the *LINEHAN* at the time of the sinking was as follows: captain, William Dobler; pilot, John Schmidt; chief engineer, Robert Shannon; second engineer, Fred Graham; clerk, Herman Lawson; steward, Si Barnes; cook, Fred Burrows; watchmen, William Lawson and Isaac Deschman; mate, Louis Frommel; firemen, Newton Nesbitt and Ed Lubey; linesmen, Harry Dyer and John Cronin; and raftsmen, Ed Frazier, Dennis Cronin, Arthur Hultz and Pete La Duke.

1898—With Captain William Wier on the *ISAAC STAPLES*

May 8th, 1898, I shipped as mate on the steamer *ISAAC STAPLES*. William Wier, master; Silas Alexander, second pilot; Edward Stokes, chief engineer; Elmer Stokes, second engineer; Harry Dyer, mate; and Ross Martin in charge of the kitchen. Captain Wier had the contract for towing all the logs of the John Paul Lumber Company and the C. L. Coleman Lumber Company from the West Newton rafting works to LaCrosse, Wisconsin where their mills were located. He had done this work for five seasons with the steamer *VERNIE MAC*, but in the fall of 1897 the *MAC* was sold to Memphis, Tennessee parties and he chartered the *STAPLES* to do his work.

He surely had the West Newton-LaCrosse trade down to a science. This meant to deliver three brails of logs at LaCrosse every twenty-four hours. That meant the raft had to be "lined up," towed fifty-one miles and "stripped" or unlined every day. At daybreak we were alongside the raft at West Newton, at 5:30 A.M. were lined up and going down river, past Winona about 10:30 A.M., Homer about noon, and about five o'clock P.M. we were landed and delivered at LaCrosse, and at supper time the raft was "stripped" and we were going back after another one. As soon as I "got on" to Captain Wier's way of getting underway, all I had to do was to get my crew to do the work his way. That was easy. I told them the sooner they got the lines on and "tightened up" they were done until we got to Winona. There we picked up a barge of wood, filled up the fire box and alongside the boilers. That took about an hour, then we landed the wood barge. Coming back that night, we picked it up, filled up the empty places and left it at Winona to be filled again. It was a fine trade.

Captain Wier was a fine man to work for and it was no trouble to keep a crew. One of my log books shows I didn't change a man for fifty days. The rafting works closed early in August and we had to lay up. Then I made a trip on the *LADY GRACE* and one trip was enough. I shipped at LaCrosse and she had a double-decker going to Burlington, Iowa. In a double-decker, a second tier of logs is put crosswise on top of the original raft. It makes a very stiff raft, also a very heavy one.

When I got on the *GRACE*, her captain, William Davis, was having trouble with his wife and was in the Rock Island jail and the boat was in charge of Captain Charles Roman and we had the *R. J. WHEELER* for a bow boat. When we got to Rock Island we found that Davis had sold the *LADY GRACE* to Stewart and Company, government contractors from Plaquemine, Louisiana, so we transferred her rafting kit to the *WHEELER*, put the *ZALUS DAVIS* on the bow, and were again underway for Burlington. But at Illinois Chute above New Boston, Illinois, Captain Roman stuck the raft on a sand bar. Now if there is any harder work than getting a double-decked raft off of a sand bar, I don't know what it is. We were ten days on that sand bar and when we finally got afloat and delivered the raft at Burlington, every man in the crew was so sore and lame he could hardly move. It was the worse breakup I was ever in and I had seen a lot of them.

When we got back to Stillwater, I got word from Captain Wier that the *STAPLES* was going to work again. She came out the 7th of September, and we finished up the season of 1898 towing logs to Zimmerman and Ives, Guttenburg, Iowa. The *STAPLES* was rebuilt in the winter of 1898–99 and came out a brand new boat in charge of Captain Walter Hunter, who was in charge of her from 1899 to the close of the 1907 season. The *STAPLES* was laid up for the winter of 1907 at Wabasha, Minnesota, and burned there December 6th that year with the *J. W. VAN SANT* and *CYCLONE*.

I think Captain Hunter has the longest record of any pilot on the Upper Mississippi. His first berth was a pilot on the Pan Line. He took the last raft down the river with the *OTTUMWA BELLE* in 1915. He was a long time pilot on the *CAPITOL* and for the last five seasons had been pilot on the *MARK TWAIN*, a government tow boat.

1899—A Season with Captain Wier on the *JUNIATA*

The year 1899 found me back with Captain Wier, but this time on the steamer *JUNIATA* but still in the West Newton-LaCrosse trade. Our crew this year was William Wier, master; Edward Huttenhow, second pilot; Ben Hanks, chief engineer; Arthur Fayerwether, second engineer; Harry Dyer, mate; and Ross Martin in charge of the kitchen. The *JUNIATA* was a much better boat for the LaCrosse trade than the *STAPLES*. She was much faster and that meant much time saved in getting back up the river. Everything went fine until June 3. At 12:30 P.M., engineer Hanks came on watch and as usual went out on the fantail to oil the journals and the cams. He found a cracked wheel shaft. He stopped the boat and notified the captain, who had also just come on watch and the next I heard was, "Harry, you will have to land her with the check line." We were just above Chimney Rock. It so happened that at this time the *J. M. RICHTMAN* came out of Richtman Slough with a barge of brush for a government contractor working near there. We hailed her and they landed the barge, took us in tow and took us into Winona. Captain Sam Van Sant, at that time governor of Minnesota, lived at Winona and he was at home and always ready to help a steamboat man and he told Captain Wier that the best place to take out the broken shaft was at the Laird and Norton dock at Winona. He also referred him to a machinist there who had done such jobs for him. Well, as soon as we got the wheel off, this man took his measurements and was all ready to start for Chicago to get the new shaft.

Of course, Captain Wier notified Bronson and Folsom of the accident and the man he had engaged to make the repairs. Then a telegram came from Bronson saying he would rather have D. M. Swain of Stillwater do the work and he would leave at once for Winona. Swain got there next morning. He went to the Winona man and wanted him to let him take his measurements but the Winona man said, "Nothing doing," so there was twenty-four hours wasted. When the shaft got to Winona and it came by express, you can believe it or not, it was so warm you couldn't bear your hand on it. Then it had to be machined in the Winona man's shop.

June 3, 4, 5, 6, 7, 8—we laid up at Winona putting in the new shaft. It could have been done in four days if the Winona man had done the work. Swain was a fool to think he would let him have his figures. Then, if anything was wrong, it would have been laid on the man from Winona. That was the only bad luck we had that season.

There was a short layup August 20 to September 8, then we pulled out and put in the rest of the season towing to Guttenburg, Iowa and Dubuque. We laid up for the winter at Stillwater, November 12.

In 1907, Bronson and Folsom sold the *JUNIATA* to Captain Milton Newcomb of Pepin, Wisconsin. He changed her name to *RED WING* and ran her in the packet trade a few years, St. Paul to Wabasha, Minnesota, then sold her to Ohio river parties. The last I heard of her, she was towing a show boat on the Ohio River.

1900—Harry Dyer Meets Captain George Winans

At the request of Captain Sam Van Sant, I shipped as mate on the steamer *MUSSER*, S. B. Withrow, captain; I. H. Short, second pilot; George Galloway, chief engineer; Bert Long, second engineer; Harry G. Dyer, mate; Gene Hanley, clerk and captain of the bow boat; and "Catfish Tom" had charge of the kitchen. Our trade was towing logs to Muscatine, Iowa, from Stillwater and West Newton. I had served two seasons with Captain Withrow, 1883 and 1884, on the steamer *MENOMONIE* and I soon found that he had changed greatly. All went well until we wrapped a 1,200-foot raft around the head of four mile island, just about Brownsville, Minnesota. Of course, Captain Steve was getting old and didn't have his old skill and nerve and had begun to lose confidence in himself and the second pilot didn't make things any better for him.

I stayed with him about three months and finally got tired of his eternal faultfinding and quit. Then he sent Gene Hanley, the clerk, to ask me to come back but I had gone. A few days afterwards I got a letter from Captain C. B. Roman asking me to go with him on a new boat he was building at Lyons, Iowa to be called the *NEPTUNE*. I went to Lyons to get her ready and then found Captain Roman would not take her out as Winans had work for another man so the *NEPTUNE* came out in charge of Captain Bob Mitchell; Joe Hawthorne, second pilot; John Zuckever, chief engineer; Otto Davenport, second engineer; Dyer, mate; and James Sweeny in charge of the kitchen. Our work was running lumber from Read's Landing and Stillwater down to meet the *JOHN H. DOUGLASS*. This was the first time I ever met Captain George Winans. He was a fine man to work for, a good pilot, and the first man to start a raft down the river with a steamboat behind it. That was in 1863 and the steamboat was the *UNION*. Bob Mitchell was also a good pilot but not the all-around steamboat man Captain Winans was, in fact, I think he was the *best* I ever worked for. He died at St. Paul in 1926. Captain Mitchell and Captain Hawthorne have also made their last trip. Captain Hawthorne was ninety-nine years old when he "landed on the other shore."

I was on the *NEPTUNE* until Captain Winans transferred me to the *JOHN H. DOUGLASS*, formerly the *DAN THAYER*, and I was on her the balance of the season. I laid her up in Rock Island, November 12, 1900, and was hired to come out on the new boat in the spring of 1901 as the *DOUGLASS* was to be given a new hull that winter.

1901—With Captain Winans and the *SATURN*

I got orders from Captain Winans to go to Rock Island to get the *NEPTUNE* ready. When I got there, I found the new boat nearly completed but still on the ways. The crew of the *NEPTUNE* had not reported yet. Captain Winans had got the contract to tow the Standard Lumber Company logs to Dubuque, Iowa this year, so he sent me up on the *NEPTUNE* until the new boat was ready. The new boat was named *SATURN*. When she was ready, the *NEPTUNE*'s crew took her out and took a lumber raft from New Boston Bay to St. Louis. The two boats met for the first time at Chimney Rock and we changed crews.

The *SATURN*'s crew that season was George Winans, master; Peter O'Rourke, pilot; Levi King, Sr., chief engineer; Levi King, Jr., second engineer; Harry Dyer, mate; Earl Winans, clerk and captain of the bow boat *PATHFINDER,* and Mrs. Ella Tesson in charge of the kitchen. She was a good cook, but oh boy, how she loved to gossip. Our trade was towing lumber from Read's Landing and Stillwater, Minnesota to Knapp Stout and Company, St. Louis, Missouri.

On my first trip on the *SATURN* at Oquaka, Illinois, just after supper, May 28, our wheel hit something that raised one side of the wheel up about fifteen inches, broke the cams, bent the cam rods and raised hell generally. There we were, it was beginning to get dark and we were going down the river with a big lumber raft and no boat.

Captain Winans told me to cut the *SATURN* off and let her hang on the anchor. Then he brought the *PATHFINDER* back to the stern of the raft and with her help and with two 1,200-foot check lines, we landed the raft at Eagle Island, four miles below Oquawaka. Then we took the *SATURN* in tow and took her to Burlington, Iowa, for repairs. On the 15th day of June, we left Stillwater with sixteen "forty-fours," that meant sixteen strings of lumber each forty-four cribs long. The raft was 1,430 foot long, 256 feet wide, 26 inches deep and covered an area of about eight acres and contained over 10,000,000 feet of lumber, the largest raft ever sent down the river.

The *SATURN* was a fine raft boat. Built at Rock Island in 1901, she was 145 feet long, 30 feet wide, and had a depth of hold of 4 feet and was of 175 tons. She had two steel boilers, was allowed 165 pounds of pressure, engines were of six-foot stroke, fifteen inch bore, a powerful towboat. Earl Winans was the captain's son. He had a pilot's license, St. Paul to St. Louis, and his home is Prescott, Wisconsin.

He and myself are the only ones left of the *SATURN*'s 1901 officers. Captain Winans died at St. Paul, January 22, 1926. Peter O'Rourke died at LaCrosse, Wisconsin, February 28, 1911, age sixty-five years; Levi King, Sr. died at LaCrosse, September 5, 1909, age sixty-six years. Levi King, Jr. died at LaCrosse, March 18, 1940, age seventy-one years. Captain Winans was eighty-seven years old when he died. I think this was the finest crew I ever worked with—Mrs. Tesson was a steamboat cook's widow, I am sorry I do not have the date of her death.

1902—Last Season on the River

I did not know when I shipped on the *JUNIATA* this spring that it was to be my last year on the river. I knew the timber in Wisconsin and Minnesota was getting short and already some of the sawmills had closed down and some of the boats had laid up or been sold. However, the last log raft went down the river in 1912, and the last lumber raft in 1915.

The fleet of boats that was there when I started had dwindled from seventy-five in 1881 to twelve in 1902. So this meant much less demand for men. This was my third season with Captain Wier and our crew for 1902 was William Wier, master; George Brasser, second pilot; Ora Oliver, chief engineer; Reed Tuttle, second engineer; Harry Dyer, mate; and Tom McAloon and his sister, Mabel, in charge of the kitchen, and believe me, the kitchen was well taken care of. We had very good luck all that season. We were in the West Newton-LaCrosse trade until August and then Bronson and Folsom, the owners of the boat, had enough work to keep her busy the balance of the season.

I laid the *JUNIATA* up at Stillwater, October 15, 1902, went over to St. Paul and the next morning shipped on the steamer *CYCLONE*, Captain Milt Newcomb, dropping logs from the St. Paul boom to Prescott, Wisconsin. I laid the *CYCLONE* up at Stillwater, November 7, 1902. The next morning I heard that Mabel McAloon, our second cook on the *JUNIATA*, had just died from pneumonia. She was a fine young lady and had a host of friends in Stillwater.

Conclusion

In looking over my records of twenty-two years service on the raft boats of the Upper Mississippi, I find that I served under thirty masters and thirty-two second pilots and I was on thirty-five boats beginning with the *RUBY* in 1881 and ending with the *JUNIATA* in 1902. Of the boats, the *R. J. WHEELER* was, to my mind, the model raft boat. She was low between decks to catch little wind. A big roomy fire box and deck room, good power, engines five-foot stroke, fourteen-inch bore, and three boilers to supply them with steam.

As to captains, my thoughts always go back to Captain William Wier. He was a good pilot; a fine man to work for and a "square shooter." He had no relatives or friends to furnish the pull to make him a pilot, but got there by his own efforts. If anything went wrong on the raft, he wasn't always yelling at the crew from the pilot house. If the mate was doing his work, he let him do it and did not interfere and always said, "the crew were supposed to take their orders from the mate and no man could work for two bosses." I think Captain George Winans was the best all-around steamboat man of the raft boat fleet and William Dobler and Cyprian Buisson two of the best pilots.

All of them have long since made their last landing and are tied up on the other shore.

In these sketches of my steamboating days, the years left out were seasons where, for various reasons, I only made a few trips. I met some very fine men and have never been sorry for the years I spent as a steamboat man and I want to thank Mr. Charles E. Brown (Curator for the State Historical Society of Wisconsin) and Mrs. Ruth Shuttleworth (assistant at the society) for their assistance.

Harry G. Dyer

Listing of Upper Mississippi River Rafting Steamboats and Their Owners

Harry G. Dyer

May 1942

Schulenburg and Boeckler
  CHARLOTTE BOECKLER
  HELENE SCHULENBURG
  MOLLIE WHITMORE
  ROBERT DODDS

Bronson and Folsom
  CLYDE
  ISAAC STAPLES
  MENOMONIE
  RAVENNA

Durant and Wheeler
  A. T. JENKS
  CYCLONE
  DAISY
  ED. DURANT, JR.
  NETTA DURANT
  PAULINE
  R. J. WHEELER
  ROBERT SEMPLE

Gillespie and Harper
  IDA FULTON
  MARK BRADLEY
  NINA

Van Sant and Musser
  J. W. VAN SANT
  JAMES FISK, JR.
  LeCLAIRE BELLE
  MUSSER
  SILVER WAVE

LeClaire Navigation Company
  B. HERSHEY
  EVANSVILLE
  GLENMONT
  J. W. MILLS
  LAST CHANCE
  NORTH STAR
  TEN BROECK
  VOLUNTEER

McDonald Brothers
  BELLA MAC
  BLUE LODGE
  CARRIE
  DEXTER
  INVERNESS
  JIM WATSON
  KIT CARSON
  LITTLE EAGLE
  LUMBERMAN
  MOLLIE MOHLER
  MOUNTAIN BELLE
  NATRONA
  SCOTIA
  THISTLE
  ZADA

Weyerhaeuser and Denkmann
  C. J. CAFFREY
  E. RUTLEDGE
  F. WEYERHAEUSER
  F. C. A. DENKMANN
  J. K. GRAVES
  STILLWATER

Keator Lumber Company
  J. S. KEATOR
  JAMES MALBON
  ROBERT ROSS

C. Lamb and Sons
  ARTEMUS LAMB
  CHANCY LAMB
  HARTFORD
  LADY GRACE
  LAFAYETTE LAMB
  VIVIAN
  WANDERER

W. J. Young and Company
  DOUGLAS BOARDMAN
  J. W. MILLS
  STERLING
  W. J. YOUNG, JR.

Knapp Stout and Company
  ANNIE GIRDON
  BART E. LINEHAN
  CHAMPION
  HELEN MAR
  JOHNNIE SCHMOKER
  LOUISVILLE
  MENOMONIE
  PHIL SCHECKEL

Valley Lumber Company
  B. HERSHEY
  C. W. COWLES

Drury and Kirns
 J. G. CHAPMAN
 PETE KIRNS

Burlington Lumber Company
 D. C. FOGEL
 MAGGIE REANEY
 WILD BOY

Dimmock Gould and Company
 MOLINE

Gardiner Batchelder and Wells
 GARDIE EASTMAN
 IOWA

Youmans Brothers and Hodgins
 CITY OF WINONA
 JULIA

George Winans
 JAMES MEANS
 JOHN H. DOUGLASS
 LONE STAR
 MARS
 NEPTUNE
 PATHFINDER
 SAM ATLEE
 SATELLITE
 SATURN
 SILAS WRIGHT
 WYMAN X

Paige Dixon and Company
 ECLIPSE
 PARK PAINTER
 SILVER CRESCENT

Daniel Shaw Lumber Company
 BUCKEYE
 L. W. BARDEN

Gem City Lumber Company
 PENN WRIGHT
 TABER

Building Rafts

How We Build a Log Raft

HARRY G. DYER

A large percentage of the pine and hemlock logs that were cut in northern Wisconsin and Minnesota had to be floated or driven down the tributary rivers to the Mississippi. Every log cut had to have two identifying marks to determine who it belonged to. One of these marks called the "bark mark" was cut through the bark into the sap with an axe. The end mark was cut on each end of the log four times equally spaced around the circumference of the log. This mark was put on with a stamping hammer.

Generally both marks were the same. The marks used would read Crowfoot, Rabbit track, notch, etc. The reason for the end mark was that no one could tell which side of the log would be on top when the log went into the water but two of the end marks would be in sight, while put on the top side of the log when it was in the woods, the bark mark might be on the bottom side when the log was in the water. The marks were all registered with the Surveyor General.

Now some place to hold these million of feet of logs must be found until they could be rafted for their journey down the Mississippi.

For ten years or more the Chippewa River logs were rafted in Beef Slough. This is a big slough that leaves the Chippewa River at Round Hill, nine miles above Alma, Wisconsin, twelve or fifteen miles from the head. A fin boom was stretched across the Chippewa at Round Hill and all the logs were turned into Beef Slough.

In the course of time the head of the slough began to fill with sand. Something had to be done. Two miles above Alma, but on the opposite side of the river is West Newton Slough. The foot of this slough is about ten miles below Alma but on the Minnesota side. There is where the rafting works were moved to. The fin boom was taken out of the Chippewa and placed across the Mississippi at the head of West Newton Slough.

Piling was driven at intervals of 150 feet on one or both sides of the Mississippi channel, and a boom, hung on the piling from one pile to another, kept the logs that now came out of the Chippewa into the Mississippi at Read's Landing in the channel until they got to the fin boom above Alma. There they were switched into West Newton Slough. All the boarding camps, the office, plug mill, blacksmith shop, etc., were moved to the new site.

In order to get West Newton Slough ready for the rafting business, the rafting works were at the foot of the slough. Piling was driven to hang the booms on and keep the logs in the race. The whole upper part of the slough is filled with logs from bank to bank. The race is a channel about a mile long. Here the logs are sorted. Pockets on either side of the race will hold logs enough to make one brail of logs. A brail is 600 feet long and forty-five feet wide. All logs having the same mark are put in the same pocket.

The first act in starting a brail is making the header; two or three logs are fastened and placed across the pocket and form the end of the brail. The logs are "tailed in" forming a tier across the brail. The outside logs in each tier lap about two feet and a two-inch hole eight inches deep is bored in each log and a boom chain and two round hard wood plugs make the joint. Two men on each side of the brail keep extending this boom and the brailers fill in the space between side booms with logs. One of the boomers is boring holes, the other, driving plugs. The brailers try to pick the longest logs for boom logs to saving boring holes, but when the brail is complete, you will find there are about forty boom logs on each side. Eighty holes have been bored, forty chains have been used, and eighty plugs driven on each side.

Now the six chains and twelve plugs used to make the header and the same for the rear boom would call for twelve more holes in each. So, a total of 208 holes had been bored and 108 chains used, and 210 plugs driven on each brail. Multiply this by six and we have 148 chains, 1,296 holes and plugs on a six-brail raft.

The augers used to bore the holes were made especially for the Mississippi River Logging Company. They had a very coarse feed screw and would cut very fast. The axe used to drive plugs weighed ten pounds and was wedge shaped. The head was about seven-by-three inches to the edge. Up to the time of the invention of the boom chain, all boom joints were made with new, one-inch manila rope. The holes were eight inches deep, the rope reached to the bottom of the holes and a hard wood plug 1¾ inches square was driven in each hole. Thus each joint took eighteen or twenty inches of rope.

Here is the reason for the ten-pound axe. You could cut the rope with the edge and drive the plugs with the head of the axe. In the first tier of logs across the head of a brail, there might be logs of twelve or fifteen different lengths and the logs in the second tier bulled the ones in the first. This was desirable because, the more the joints were broken, the stiffer the brail would be. When the brail was complete, two men came alongside in a skiff in which was carefully coiled a one-inch line, 1,200 feet long. These were the brail droppers.

Below the rafting works were a number of pilings and some tiers with a number on them. Holes had been bored in each pile or tree and wooden pins, three feet long, driven into the hole. On each pin was hung a shore line 1½ inches in diameter and 350 feet long.

Now the gate boom was opened and the brail floated slowly down the river. At one of these numbered piles or tiers the line is run and the brail gradually brought to a stop. Then the shore lines are made fast. Then the dropping line is coiled back in the skiff and the two men are on their way back for another brail.

Perhaps another brail of the same man's logs will be ready when they get back, perhaps not until the next day. It all depends on how the logs come into the race. As soon as another brail is ready, it is landed alongside the first one. Then one more and we have a half raft.

Now the "filling up" crew. The brail droppers pay no attention to the shape the stern of brails are in when they have them. The filling up crew square up the brails and build the check works, couple the brails in several places. Now each brail may have been scaled out as it left the "works," perhaps not. Well, a scaler, a handyman and ketch marker work together. The "ketch mark" is put on with an axe and shows that the log has been scaled.

A number is painted on each brail and the same number is cut on one boom log of each brail. Now we have three brails or a half raft all ready to go down river.

A raft boat lands at West Newton. Her clerk goes to the office and finds that her raft is "down on No. 19," but before the crew can get that half raft "lined up" to go down river a man comes along, hands the boat clerk a book, on one page of which he finds "received from the Mississippi Logging Company in good condition Brails No. 243, 244 and 245." The clerk signs the receipt with his name and the name of his boat.

The same day that the raft leaves West Newton, the scale sheet for that raft leaves West Newton by mail to the company that owns the logs. Arriving at its destination, the logs are scaled as they go into the mill and if there is any shortage, the owner of the boat that towed the raft must pay for them. Well, we will suppose that the boat had bad luck, a storm, a sandbar, a bridge or breakup, resulting in a loss of forty or fifty logs. The captain of the boat has to pay for them. Now suppose you were living along the river, and occasionally you saw a log or two floating along, you went out in your boat, caught it, and towed it to shore and tied it up. Then in the course of three months you had forty or fifty logs you had got in this way.

Who would you consider owned these logs? You? NO. The captain of the boat? NO. The Mississippi River Logging Company? YES. The captain of the boat had to pay the sawmill company for the lost logs and then the logging company owned them again. They never had owned theirs.

A blacksmith at West Newton invented the boom chain. Just as he finished the first one, a Mr. Rutledge came along and asked him what he was doing. On being told, he said, "Oh that would never work, they would drown them faster than you could make them." Inside of two weeks the chain was patented. Did the blacksmith have it patented? No, it was Mr. Rutledge.

What It Costs to Run a Raft Boat a Month

Harry G. Dyer

This would vary somewhat for different reasons. One, it depended on who owned the boat; two, the size of the boat; three, the trade she was in; and four, the skill of the pilots and mate. Wages for the captain were $200 to $250 and the captain always "stood a watch at the wheel." Second pilot, $100 to $175, mate, $45 to $75, clerk, $35 to $45, cook or steward, $60 to $90, firemen, $35 to $45, watchman, $30, raftsmen, $30 to $35, linesman, $35 to $40.

On the Bronson and Folsom, C. Lamb & Sons, Weyerhaeuser, Van Sant, Schulenburg and W. J. Young boats, the scale would amount to $1,075 a month. The pilot who could get a raft down the river the quickest, deliver at the mill or lumberyard, and get back again generally got the best money. Fuel was hard to average. All the raft boats that belonged to the big sawmill companies burned "ratlines" almost entirely. These were edgings off one inch lumber four feet long and tied up in bunches about the size of a bundle of lath. An old fireman on the *LADY GRACE*, a C. Lamb and Sons boat, once said, "poking ratlines in the *LADY GRACE*'s furnace was like poking hay in hell" but they were cheap fuel at $1.00 to $1.25 a cord and the mill company had lots of them.

A coal burner would burn from twenty to forty tons in twenty-four hours. Any of the W. J. Young boats would burn 250 or 300 cords of ratlines on a six day trip, so the fuel bill would be from $20 to $40 a day.

The kitchen expenses was figured at so much per man per day. On the *JUNIATA*, a Bronson and Folsom boat, our food cost 57¢ a day per man *and we were fed.* There were some boats on which it was less than half that. I have heard old captains say that a good cook would save half his wages and I believe it is true.

So, for a month we will say—wages $1,075, fuel from $600 to $800, kitchen expense, $200 to $350, mate's stores, oil, etc., $15; total about $2,100. So, with good management and good luck a boat would clear from $5,000 to $7,000 in a season. The lines in a raft kit have to be carefully looked after, new ones added and kept in good shape, so there are often additional expenses.

Raft Pilots

Harry G. Dyer

The raft pilots of the Upper Mississippi were a fine lot of men. Captain Al Day, now inspector of hulls in the St. Louis District and a very good pilot himself, once said to me, "Since the rafting business closed, I have been on every navigable river in the United States and nowhere did I find any pilots that equalled ours. The tow boat pilots on the Ohio and the Lower Mississippi are experts but they have a better channel on the Ohio and on the Lower Mississippi, they have lots of room."

Many times on the Upper Mississippi the raft fills the channel width and often laps over a little. The raft is so long that in some places the bow of the raft is in one current, the middle in another, and the stern in yet another. If the raft is properly handled, it will go around these short bends with their tricky cross currents without trouble, but there is no room to spare.

I have worked for many of these pilots and when it comes to handling a raft, my star pilot would be Captain Cyprian Buisson, followed closely by Captain William Dobler, Jerome Short, William Whistler, John Hoy, George Winans, Ira Fuller, Otis McGinley and some others. Two of these men would have been in the same class with Captain Buisson but for the interference of Captain John Barleycorn.

If we are to classify the pilots, we must put Peter O'Rourke, George Trombley, Jr., John Lancaster, Walter Blair, George Reed, Morrell Looney, James Newcomb, Walter Hunter, Stephen Withrow, Andrew Loken, William Kratka, John O'Connor, Al Duncan, Charles B. Roman and N. B. Lucas in class A or class I. We must also remember that many of these pilots came up from the days of the floating raft. The raft looks very different from the stern of the raft than from the pilot house of the boat. Also, the company that owned the boat had much to do with a pilot's work.

Age was also either a help or a handicap. A pilot between thirty and forty was considered in the prime of life or at the age where he did his best work. Another thing was health, and I have known two or three pilots where this was the main reason for their good or bad work. Some people had the idea that the first requirement for a good pilot was that he be a prize fighter, but this was a great mistake, though I will admit that some of them would have been a bad customer for a prize fighter to tackle.

When I picked Captain Buisson as the star of the raft pilots, I did so because I never saw him in any trouble. He seemed to handle his raft easily and carefully, had a good crew, a good mate and knew how to use them.

The steamboat *B. HERSHEY* came out in the spring of 1877 and Cyprian Buisson was her captain then and was her captain until 1902.

Some of the lumber companies wanted their rafts delivered in good shape, even if it took a little longer to make a trip. William Denkmann of the Weyerhaeuser and Denkmann Company used to say to his pilots, "Go quick up and quick back and bring down all you start mit." Robert Dodds, Ezra Chancy and George Brasser of the Schulenburg and Boeckler Company were all good pilots, but they took their time because the company wanted their rafts delivered at St. Louis, Missouri, in the same conditions that they left Stillwater, Minnesota.

Some pilots bragged about the quick trips they made, others about the trip they made without "breaking a boom." Many of these pilots were well past middle age and had lost some of their nerve and a few of them were not in the best of health. Captain Steve Withrow, one of the best pilots that ever slipped into a pilot house, had some stomach trouble and at times I could not see how he took his watch.

Captain Bill Slocomb of the Knapp Stout Company was a good pilot and one who knew his rights and wasn't afraid to say so. Hank Walker of the same company would rather meet the devil than one of the company.

Cornell Knapp at one time was captain of the *ARTEMUS LAMB* of Chancy Lamb and Sons and Mr. Lamb was making a trip on the boat. They were in a close place and Mr. Lamb began giving orders to the crew and Captain Knapp told him to shut his mouth or he would put him on the bank. Mr. Lamb said, "I own this boat." "Yes," Cornell said, but "I am captain of her." After he got home, Lamb was telling the story in his office to some of his friends and he chuckled and said, "by gad I believe he would have put me ashore."

Some pilots, in fact, most of them, were ace high with their employers and the main reason was that most employers were ace high with the pilots. In fact, the pilots were proud to be working for such men. But I don't believe I knew any that were proud they were working for Durant and Wheeler or the P. S. Davidson Lumber Company. The *DAN THAYER* of this line had P.S.D.L.Co. painted on their bulkheads. The hoboes used to say that it stood for "Pack Slabs Damn Lively Come On."

Steamboat Cooks

Obviously, good and plentiful well-cooked food was essential for good morale and the general well-being of steamboat rafting crews. Cooks on the steamboats were therefore very important. Mr. Dyer's observations on this subject follow.

The raftsmen classed the cooks as "forward table" and "after table" cooks and they generally fought shy of a boat that carried a forward table cook.

On most of the raft boats, the food was good, well cooked, and plentiful. Most companies and captains realized that the cook had a lot to do with keeping a crew. I was on the *NETTA DURANT* when Christine and her sister shipped on her. It was her first boat and she was a long ways from being a steamboat cook. A couple of years later, Christine was on the *DOUGLAS BOARDMAN*. She was a big, powerful boat, hard on a raft, there was lots of work and new men every trip, but that year the vessel made two or three trips without changing a man and the "hoboes" couldn't understand it. One would say to another, "Are you going to stay on her all summer?" and the answer would be, "I am going to stay as long as Christine does." So Christine must have had a lot to do with holding a crew.

Meals served on the rafting boats generally were as follows. For breakfast, the meal was fried potatoes, ham and eggs, pancakes, bread and butter, rolls, cookies, ginger bread or snaps, and coffee. At dinner, the meal was a roast, mashed potatoes, two or three kinds of vegetables, pie and cake, ice cream and so forth for dessert. The pancakes were omitted in hot weather. At supper, once in a while it would be only "cold meat tonight, boys," but it was generally steak of some kind. George Whalen of LaCrosse once served boiled rice and sauce for dessert at noon and had quite a lot left, but it didn't go overboard. The next morning, he put the leftovers in a large frying pan, added a big slice of ham or two slices, diced, then a can of tomatoes; the diced ham, rice and tomatoes were then browned, seasoned quite highly with a touch of red pepper and then it was "jambolya" (jambolye) and fine for a hungry river man. He was believed to be the originator of this "steamboat" dish. Lunch was always set and coffee was on the stove in the kitchen at night and in fact there was hot coffee all day and night.

Durant and Wheeler and McDonald Brothers of LaCrosse were firms that had the reputation among the men of being the meanest firms on the river. They were cheap concerns when it came to both wages and food.

Billy Durant of Stillwater was the only cook I ever knew that really hated to see a man eat and to give a man enough to eat. He was on the *ED DURANT, JR.* in 1884. One trip we had some butter that was perfectly able to walk. No one made a kick but the next trip, coming out of Stillwater, one of the boys asked if that was the same old butter and was informed by Mr. Durant that it was and that we would eat it before we got any more. Well, that night, "the boys" used about five pounds of that butter to grease the door knobs in the cabin and about ten pounds more was used to decorate various kitchen utensils, drawer pulls and anything else that they thought would look better with a coat of butter. The next day the clerk went ashore at Lake City to get some butter. Durant knew it wouldn't do to put that rotten butter on the forward table or the officer's table and he thought he would work it off on the "boys" in the mess room or after table.

The Durant and Wheeler Company was always looking for something cheap. On the *CYCLONE* in 1892, they had three women in the kitchen for about $65 a month for the three and a long ways from service because they didn't know how. Women,

STEAMBOAT COOKS

somehow, did not "catch on" as readily to the steamboat style of cooking. A good cook generally got from $80 to $90 a month and hired his own helper.

A few of the cooks, Fred Tuttle, Harvey Black, George Newton, and others had their wives with them and then the service was good. Mrs. Ella Tesson, of LeClaire, Iowa, a widow lady, served her apprenticeship with her husband before he died and she was a good cook, but oh boy, she did love to gossip.

Chancy Lamb, head of the C. Lamb and Sons, used to say, "Cook—cut everything in two in the middle and send half of it each way," meaning that the forward and the aft table should each have their share. The flunkey on the *JUNIATA* used to stick his head in the mess room at meal times and say, tea, coffee, iced tea, lemonade, or milk and you could take your choice.

Perhaps I should tell you that the after table was set in the mess room and the forward table in the cabin. We had fish at least once a week—catfish, bass, and pike. Fishermen brought fish to the boats. Ducks were served during the hunting season. Berries were brought in crates, especially around LaCrosse and Trempealeau. The kitchen and pantry were in between the mess room and the cabin. On a packet they had a steward or head cook, meat cook, pastry cook, and a baker, but as to cleanliness, the raft boat cook was 100 percent ahead of the packet cook.

Many of the cooks had their own peculiarities. Robert Moulton—"Double-Headed Bob,"—as he was termed, had a large head, wore a No. 8 hat. We called his wife "Molly Two Head." They lived in LaCrosse. He was a good cook and loved to see a man eat. George Whalen—"Short Arm." One arm was shorter than the other. He had gotten wounded in the arm and development was stunted. Charlie Buehler was said to always have either a butcher knife or a dipper of coffee in his hand. Fred Burrow worked his way up from flunkey to cook and he was a good one.

Smiler McAloon knew what the boys needed when they had been out late. James Sweeney was called the best meat cook on the Upper River. Ross Martin was noted for his fine rolls. Fred Harms had been on more rivers than any other cook. He had a very fine collection of steamboat pictures. George Howard was drowned on the *EVERETT* when she capsized in a storm at Burlington.

In 1942, Mr. Dyer noted that there were only five steamboat cooks that he knew that were still living. "The others have made their last landing and are 'tied up' on the other shore. When I make the final crossing, I am going to find George Whalen and a plate of JAMBOLAY WITH RED PEPPER."

A list of the old time steamboat cooks would include: Silas Barnes, LaCrosse; Harvey Black, Read's Landing; Charles Buehler, Read's Landing; Fred Burrow, LaCrosse; Catfish Tom, Davenport; Christine (a Dane), Lyons; Billy Durant, Stillwater; Tom Finley, Brownsville; John Goff, Stillwater; Fred Harms, Read's Landing; Billy Holmes, LaCrosse; George Howard, Burlington; Jimmy Luker, a hobo cook; Ross Martin, Wabasha; Smiler McAloon, Stillwater; Tom McAloon, Stillwater; Robert Moulton, LaCrosse; George Newton, Lynxville; Jim O'Brien, LaCrosse; Mrs. Rhodes, LeClaire; Steubenville Jim (original home at Steubenville, Ohio); James Sweeney, LeClaire; Mrs. Ella Tesson, LeClaire; Herman Thomas, LaCrosse; Fred Tuttle, Wabasha; George Whalen, LaCrosse; Andy Woods, Stillwater; and George Wright, LaCrosse.

Steamboat Hoboes on the Upper Mississippi River

(The following information is taken from Mr. Dyer's notes on the subject and recast by the author into a narrative style.)

Double-headed Bob, Brockie Shang, Scotty the Singer and Flopper Murphy—actual people. These might lead one to wonder, "what's in a name?" Unusual names aside, these people were steamboat hoboes, roustabouts and tramps who served primarily on Upper Mississippi River craft in the log rafting decades just before and after the turn of the century.

Men such as The Owl, The Camel, The Fox, Black Andy, Chicago Fatty and Three Brail Billy were the tramps of the day but instead of hopping freights, they worked as deck hands on the steam-powered rafting boats. A few were firemen and pilots; most, however, were deckhands who worked for a season or a few weeks as the "spirits" moved them. When they drew their pay it was usually quickly squandered in river town saloons. When the money was gone and the hangover only a dull headache, they sought another boat and another job. In the winter, they often drifted south to the lower Mississippi or the Ohio. When springtime came, like the robins, northward they would trek and the cycle started over again.

"Double-headed Bob" was Robert Moulton. He was an excellent steamboat cook and a very heavy drinker. He had a very large head, hence his nickname. He wore a size eight hat and loved to see a man eat. His wife was called "Molly Two-head." Brockie Shang was a tall man named Davis. A fireman on raft boats, he also had a prison record. His favorite saying was, "the cemetery, that's where people get next to each other." The word, "Shang" originally was the name of P. T. Barnum's Chinese giant and many hoboes used it.

The real names of the river tramps are mostly unknown, but by nickname they were celebrated up and down the river and were undoubtedly the subject of many a long winter's yarn. Scotty the Singer, for example, as one might expect, had a fine voice, baritone, no less, and sang sentimental songs. In his leisure time, he made silk match hangers and sold them. Flopper Murphy worked for Harry Dyer on the *JUNIATA* and *NEPTUNE*. He had a crippled arm and hand, hence the name, "Flopper."

The Owl, The Camel, and The Fox were all tramp deckhands. Once they were rowing across the Mississippi River at Clinton, Iowa in a skiff when it overturned, throwing all in the water. When help arrived, The Owl said, "Save The Camel and The Fox. The Owl can save himself."

Black Andy was a deckhand; originating in New Hampshire, he was a small wiry man and as dark as an Indian. Chicago Fatty, as one might assume, came from the Windy City and formerly was a Great Lakes sailor. Three Brail Billy served as a deckhand on the rafter *VERNIE MAC* for three years. Since the vessel only towed three brails of logs at a time, it was just a matter of time before someone gave him his nickname.

Others of these hobo tramps were personages such as Keokuk Shang, some 6'7" high in his stocking feet; The Squirrel who reportedly lived with a negro lady at Cairo during the winter months; Redwing Dutch who jumped off the Red Wing, Minnesota bridge every time he got drunk. Reportedly, this not too difficult feat was accomplished some twenty times. A Swede, his real name was Fred Seestrom.

LaCrosse French's forte was being good at card tricks and he loved to entertain all who could spare the time, both on steamboats and in saloons. Another hobo was Buffalo John, a German whose home was in Buffalo, Wisconsin. Chief Higbey was President of the "Silent Nine," a LaCrosse, Wisconsin beer drinkers club. Regretfully, we don't know much about Mush Head Ryan, a river boat bum, nor are Kid Dailey and Black Dailey, two Lower River roustabouts who worked on Upper Mississippi River Boats in the summer and drifted south during the winter, any better known.

Tattered Jack Welch earned his name the hard way as he was a fireman on the D. A. McDONALD when she blew up, killing eighteen of the thirty-three aboard. He was blown into the air and came down on the deck of a nearby ferry boat. Recovering from this accident, he lived for years afterwards. Not so lucky was Pittsburg Crutch who died at a hobo drinking party on the big island in the Mississippi at Clinton, Iowa. His hobo friends were thoughtful enough to bury him there.

Some of these tramps were named after the work they did. So, Smokestack Billy, in reality John Reddick, painted steamboat smokestacks. Joe "Nosey" Willard who lived at Fulton, Illinois had no nose at all hence his name, while Mushrat (Muskrat) John McCarty had his nose cut off in an accident. He was a good pilot but had a booze problem.

As one might surmise, a tramp named Jo Cleary was named after "Jo, Jo the Dog-faced Boy." He was neither very homely nor very handsome. Spike Ike who headquartered out of Bellevue, Iowa, was named after the spike or fid used to loosen rope knots on steamboats. Red Murphy and Red McCarty, alas, are only known to us as "two good old soaks."

The darling of Read's Landing, Minnesota, a tough river town, was undoubtedly Overcoat Johnny. He once appeared on the Fourth of July wearing a straw hat and overcoat. Speaking of apparel, we have Dirty Shorty. There were three of these "Dirty Shorty's," No. 1, 2, 3—all well—known river hoboes who shared the dubious reputation of putting on a clean shirt in the fall and wearing it through the winter. Without change or cleansing action, that is.

"Noisy" Bill Smith, an old broken-down river pilot from the floating days hardly ever spoke. Then there was the LaCrosse Kid, a thief and "tough gink" according to Dyer. Whitey Tate hailed from Pittsburgh and was a roustabout with a very white complexion and very light hair.

Today one could go a long time before finding anyone who knows what a kiwah is (or was). Hobo Kiwah Billy did, for in his spare time he cut out "kiwahs" from blocks of pine. Kiwahs in river parlance were artistic wooden fans. Kiwah Bill would trade one of his creations, which sometime took two or three days to carve, to a saloon keeper for a pint of whiskey. Bill passed on at Keokuk after consuming a pint of alcohol.

"Shang" was a popular nickname, for Dyer speaks of both Shang Nolan, an old fireman, and Shang McCann, a tall man. There was also Minneapolis Shang, who was Joe Rudiver, pilot and captain of the raft boat NETTA DURANT. Lost to history are the exploits of Flopeared Shang, unfortunately.

One Costell was Big-Handed Mike, due to the fact one of his hands was nearly twice as large as the other. Monk (Monkey) Morgan was so named because of his face and Dubuque, Iowa was his home. Snow Gallagher managed to be fireman and bum at the same time. We suspect that Jimmy The Section Boss, a roustabout, might have had a railroad background and we know that Billy Irish was an Irishman named Billy Simmons.

The names go on; Forepaugh Billy, Chicago Simpson who married at LaCrosse, Keithsburg Clark from the Illinois city of that name, Foxy Norton, a hobo deckhand named Harry Norton. Whistling Charley, Hobo Kelley (and Sawed-Off Kelley), Handsome Charlie, Big Nick Hargett, Cooper Jack, Gentle Willy, Blondie Joe, Black Haley, Grits Miller, St. Louis Slim, Whiskey Farrell, Buffalo Dutch, Big Eyed George, Clever Willie Young and Seneca.

Seneca, a hobo steamboat man, died at Read's Landing and Old Jerry Lanigan gave Bulger, a "floating" hobo, some whiskey and told him to bury Seneca. Bulger managed to get the corpse laid out according to orders, but then got drunk and laid himself out beside the corpse!

One hobo even made good. Dude Wilson, who is described as a big, powerful brute, later engaged in commercial fishing on Lake Pepin and made money.

There is something pathetic about these lonely drunks, however picturesque they seem in hindsight. The old river towns of Clinton, Iowa; Cassville, Wisconsin; Fulton, Illinois; LaCrosse, Wisconsin; Lansing, Iowa; Rock Island, Illinois; Read's Landing, Minnesota; Winona, Minnesota; Keokuk and Guttenburg, Iowa; Cairo, Illinois; Quincy, Illinois; Fort Madison, Iowa; and Red Wing, Minnesota, where evidently Redwing Dutch jumped one too many times, are the last resting places of many of these rascals.

Scotty the Singer, who died at Kewanee, Illinois, even had a rival in Mickey the Singer, who vied with him in singing on the steamboats and in saloons. A match was once arranged between the two river songbirds, but the silence of time does not tell us who won.

Bell and Whistle Signals of Mississippi River Rafting Steamboats

Harry G. Dyer

October 1941

Bells

For *sternwheel* steamboats, the stopping and starting bell was on the starboard side of the engine room, the right side facing the bow. The backing bell was on the left or larboard side.

We will suppose that the boat is under way and it becomes necessary to stop and back. The pilot rings the stopping bell, the engineer then closes the throttle valve and stops the engines. The backing bell is rung and he reverses the engines. This is done by merely pulling a lever. At the next ring of the backing bell he opens the throttle valve wide open. The boat is then backing strong. If the backing bell rings again, he closes the throttle valve part way and she is backing slow. If the bell rings again or the fourth time, she is again backing strong.

At the ring of the stopping bell, the engines are stopped. Then, if the stopping bell rings again, the engines are reversed and she comes ahead full speed. Then, if the backing bell rings while she is coming ahead, she is slowed down to half speed. Another ring of the backing bell and she is again put at full head. The starting and stopping of the engines is governed by the stopping bell, the shipping up and rate of speed by the backing bell.

On *sidewheel* boats, the bells and signals are the same, but there are two bells for each engine, as the engines are separate. On a sidewheeler, one engine may be coming ahead and the other backing at the same time if necessary, as in turning the boat around or getting out from a landing. The sidewheel boat was easier to handle as the rudder was behind the wheels. The sidewheel boat had one rudder, the sternwheel boat always two and sometimes three or four according to the size of the boat.

Whistles

The whistle was used in landing, and when two boats were meeting. In meeting the descending, i.e., the boat going downstream has the choice of the river, but the ascending boat whistles first. Why, I do not know. In meeting, one blast of the steam whistle means keep to the right and two blasts means keep to the left. So two boats are meeting, the ascending boat blows one whistle and, if agreeable to the pilot of the descending boat, he answered with one whistle; but in case he does not agree, he must blow five short whistles, then after a short interval, blow two whistles which the pilot of the ascending boat must answer with two whistles, then both boats bear a little to the right.

The blowing of five short whistles is also a "call to quarters" in case of fire or a serious accident when each man on the boat has his place and duty. The landing whistle of a company owning two or more boats is the same. For instance, the landing whistles of the Diamond Jo line boats were two long and two short whistles; the Bronson and Folsom Company, three long and one short; the C. Lamb and Son Company, two long, a short, and a long, etc. Five long whistles meant the boat was in trouble or in distress.

Other Bells and Whistles

The big bell on the hurricane roof of the boat was used to let the leadsmen know when to sound water. One tap of the bell meant sound on the right, two taps, sound on the left, one tap, stop sounding. When the boat was at a landing, three taps of the bell meant the boat was nearly ready to leave.

A small whistle was located on top of the boilers. It was called the ready whistle. At the three taps of the bell at a landing, if the engineer was ready to leave, he would answer the three blasts of the ready whistle. Also, in a close place or an emergency, one blast of the ready whistle meant, "give her the gun" or all the engine power.

Steamboat inspection law says that all engine bells must have wire bell pulls and the two engine bells may be rung on either side of the pilot house. For instance, the pull from the stopping bell comes into the pilot house on the starboard side, goes through a small pulley in the roof of the pilot house, goes across the pilot house through another pulley and ends in a ring six or eight inches in diameter. The backing bell pull is arranged just the opposite.

If the pilot is on the right side of the pilot house he rings the stopping bell by taking hold of the bell pull. If he is on the left side, he takes hold of the ring in the end of the pull. The whistle was always blown using the pilot's foot, as sometimes he could not let go of the pilot wheel with either hand. A treadle on the floor of the pilot house took care of this.

There were some beautifully-toned roof bells on the Mississippi boats, the one of the steamer *OCEAN WAVE*, which burned at Frontenac in Lake Pepin on June 11, 1868, was known from St. Paul to St. Louis. When she burned, the bell went down into the water. Sometime afterward, Captain George Knapp fished it out and found it to be cracked; he had it brazed but the tone was never the same. It is now on a church in some small town in Minnesota.

Rafting Steamboat Histories

These brief histories of rafting steamboats have been assembled from many sources. A list was compiled of all possible vessels engaged in this trade and then data was assembled under each name. Dyer's and Winans' writings were useful. Captain Walter Blair's work was helpful and Frank Fugina had significant material. Captain Fred Way's two directories (towboats and packets) were extremely helpful. George Merrick's columns that he wrote and published in the *Burlington* (Iowa) *Saturday Evening Post* were of great interest; most of the material that he edited and published weekly had been initially furnished by steamboat participants.

The Lytle-Holdcamper (LH) Vessel List published by the Steamship Historical Society of America and the various Lists of Merchant Vessels published annually by the government had necessary data on all steamboats. Each vessel was checked through the various sources and data was noted and written into the histories. This data provided a control for the vessels.

Each vessel built and enrolled by the U. S. government has a separate and unique registry number ascribed to it, which enables one to trace the vessel through time. Names can be changed, but the registry number stays with the vessel until she is no longer in existence.

There are so many notations such as "rebuilt," machinery placed in another vessel, cabins removed, hulls changed, etc., that the registry number had to be used for control purposes. Combined with this basic data are the anecdotal accounts found in Merrick, Way, Dyer, and others. Therefore, these histories are based on facts found in records and first-hand accounts. Of course, this material is evaluated, and sifted out and contradictions are resolved if possible.

It should also be noted that these inland water vessels were required to be enrolled or documented.

The official government documentation included the *name* of the vessel, *when* and *where built*, *statutory dimensions*, *tonnage* and the name of the owner and other information. A change in ownership, dimensions, etc., required a new enrollment.

The *official number* was applied to vessels in documentation after 1866 so vessels documented before that date did not have numbers. The statutory *length* of a vessel is less than the actual length due to the way the measurement was taken. The *breadth (width)* or beam was the widest part on the outside of the vessel but did not include wide guards such as those used on sidewheel vessels. The *depth of hold* was measured from the underside of the tonnage deck plank amidships to the ceiling of the hold, average thickness.

The length was measured on the top of the tonnage deck from the forepart of the outer planking on the side of the stem to the afterpart of the rudder post. This is often referred to as the length "between perpendiculars." The *overall* length of the vessel was used for the public by owners who, often, did not mind a bit.

Tonnage is a cubic measurement and is not related to weight. After 1882, certain space in the vessel was deducted from the total or *gross* tonnage to arrive at *net* tonnage, and so both gross and net tonnage appeared in the documents and also in the official listings of vessels. These histories give both when available and it should be noted that "gross" and "net" are often the same.

Where known, numbers, dimensions, etc., of boilers are given. Boilers often changed during the lifetime of a vessel. All steamboat engines had pistons and cylinders and these data are given where known.

In order to keep track of the vessels as they changed names, a numbering system is used. Thus *(A)* means the initial name, *(B)* is the second name, etc. Where possible the history of the steamboat under each name is presented even though some part of the vessel's career may not have been as a Mississippi rafter.

This material cannot be guaranteed to be completely accurate but certainly has significant information on these vessels, most of which has not been set forth before in this fashion.

A

A. REILING   #105677

Sternwheel or sidewheel rafter, wood hull, built 1816 in Bellevue, Iowa. 76 tons, 100' x 21' x 4.4'. Built by I. A. Reiling of Bellevue, who sold her to Ingram, Kennedy and Day, Dubuque, Iowa, October 25, 1881. George Martin was pilot in 1882. A. J. "Jack" Davis of Trempealeau, Wisconsin, was master in 1880 and 1883 when she was owned by A. J. Davis and the Standard Lumber Company of Dubuque. Dismantled at LaCrosse, 1886. Machinery went to the *INVERNESS*.

A. T. JENKS   #105974

Sternwheel rafter, wood hull, built Cincinnati, Ohio, 1880 by C. T. Dumont. 230 tons, 153 tons, 113' x 22' x 3'. Engines were 10" cylinders by 6' piston stroke. Had two boilers, 34" diameter, 20' long. Built for Durant, Wheeler and Company, Stillwater. Named for Captain Austin T. Jenks, a junior member of the firm. First enrolled at Cincinnati, May 22, 1880. James Newcomb of Pepin, Wisconsin, was captain and pilot in 1883, and Frank Clemmons was mate. In 1883 she burned at South Stillwater while in winter quarters and was rebuilt in 1884 (149 tons, 115' x 27.3' x 4.5') and renamed *(B) ED DURANT, JR*. After 1890, she was renamed *(C) JOSEPHINE LOVIZA*.

ABNER GILE   #105124

Sternwheel rafter, wood hull, built 1872, LeClaire, Iowa. 124 tons, 110' x 21' x 3'. Engines 14" cylinders, 4' piston stroke. She had three boilers. In 1880-1882, she was owned by Captains Jerry Turner and Al Hollingshead; Horace Hollingshead (brother of Al) was master. 1883-1888, owned by Jerome E. Short, also master, 1890. Sold to Canton Sawmill Company, Canton, Missouri. Ran several years for them, Captain John Wooders, Captain Brown Jenks, 1893. Sold in 1895. Ran logs from St. Paul boom to Prescott, Wisconsin, Captain I. H. "Windy" Short. Dyer says she burned at South Stillwater in the winter of 1898 in U.S. marshal's hands. Blair says she gave out like the "one hoss shay," remaining good parts used in other boats. Listed as being in Burlington, Iowa, 1901 (last year).

ACTIVE   #105544

Wooden sidewheel rafter initially, later, a sternwheel. 105 tons. Built 1867, Brownsville, Pittsburgh. Lost January 29, 1877, Brashear, Louisiana, unknown loss of life.

ALFRED TOLL   #105889

Sternwheel, wood hull, built 1880 LaCrosse, 97 tons, 126.2' x 24' x 3.5'. Owned by Captain P. S. Davidson (LaCrosse) in 1883. In 1890, owned by Captains G. L. Short and V. A. Bigelow, Captain Albert M. Short, master. Sunk and wrecked near Dubuque, 1890, while being used as a bowboat by rafter *THISTLE*. Abe Looney of LaCrosse and Lyman Short were master and pilot for a time. George Dansbury was chief engineer for some time.

ALICE D.   #106477

Screw tug. Built 1887 in Stillwater, Minnesota, documented at St. Paul until 1920 or later. 27 tons, 12 tons, 60' x 12' x 5.7'—four crew. Owned by William Sauntry, lumberman of Stillwater. Used at Stillwater as a make-up boat.

ALICE WILD   #1622

Sidewheel rafter. Built circa 1860. 11 tons, 10 h.p. Home port Galena, 1877.

ALVINA—(Number Not Known)

Sidewheel rafter, wood hull, built LaCrosse, 1865, 47 tons. Owned for some time by Captain Russell Smith of LaCrosse. In a fight between a wood merchant (Starlocki) at Genoa, Wisconsin, and *ALVINA*'s second engineer, both were wounded, and the latter died (he was Captain Smith's son-in-law). *ALVINA* was later changed to a sternwheeler. Mrs. Laura Lowe of Reads Landing was master for a time. Hauled from Reads Landing in 1873. Not in LH.

ALVIRA   #1234

Sidewheel towboat, wood hull, built 1865 Reads Landing or Onalaskca, Wisconsin. First port, St. Paul, inspected Galena, 1872. She was of 46 tons, 110' x 25', had six staterooms, a small kitchen. Another source says she was built 1862-63 by Captain Thomas Benton. Owned by Captain H. B. Whitney and son, river contractors in 1880. Captain Whitney master. Firm also owned *A. J. WHITNEY*. *ALVIRA* was dismantled in 1881.

Annie Girdon   #1918

Sidewheel rafter, wood hull, built 1866, Burlington, Iowa, 41 tons, 83' x 14.2' x 2.5'. Owned new by James L. Harris and a partner, sold in 1870 to Knapp, Stout & Company, who used her in their rafting business on the Chippewa and Red Cedar Rivers until 1882 when she ran from Reads Landing to St. Louis. Dan Davison, Captain; Jerome Short, pilot; Hiram Wilcox, engineer; L. N. Edwards, clerk; Harvey Black, cook. Stephen Withrow was captain, 1879–82. Out of service and dismantled by 1884. Named for daughter of George W. Girdon, U.S. government inspector of hulls at Galena. This vessel was a twin-engine boat but instead of each engine turning its own sidewheel, a short shaft connected the engines. On the shaft a one-to-four gear wheel was affixed. It, in turn, was geared into a larger cog wheel on the shaft. One reason for this arrangement was to save weight. Shallow draft vessels were essential in the tributary rivers such as the Chippewa.

Annie H.   #120445

Sternwheel, wood hull. Originally (A) F. C. A. DENKMANN, then (B) WABASH, (C) ANNIE H., (D) HALLIE. Captain C. H. Matthews of Pt. Pleasant, West Virginia, bought her in July, 1916 and gave her this name for a short period, later changing it back to WABASH. The engines were of 14.5" cylinders, 6' piston stroke. 120' x 32'.

Artemus Gates   #107258

Sternwheel rafter, wood hull, built 1896 at Clinton, Iowa for Chancy Lamb and Sons. Dwight Lamb oversaw her construction. Often used as bowboat for the CHANCY LAMB. 90 tons, 70 tons, 85' x 18' x 3'. Engines were 10" cylinders, 4' piston stroke. Used around Clinton to tow logs. Later owned by Clinton Sand and Gravel Company, Captain John Lind of Clinton. Listed as having a crew of four, 50 h.p. in 1920. Burned on September 4, 1927. Captain Lafayette Lamb used her as a pleasure boat towing the barge PASTIME. Artemus Gates became president of New York Trust Company, was Secretary of Naval Aviation during WW II.

Artemus Lamb   #105366

Sternwheel rafter, wood hull, built in 1873 at Clinton, Iowa for Chancy Lamb and Sons. 176 gross tons, 176 net tons, 140' x 30.6' x 4.0'. Powerful rafter named for son of Chancy Lamb. Stephen B. Hanks was her master for fifteen years followed by William McCaffrey, master in 1890 (formerly her mate). Around 1881 may have been a substitute packet between Davenport and Clinton, Iowa. Around 1893–94, sold to Joy Lumber Company of St. Louis, used to tow barges of lumber from Stillwater and Winona to LaCrosse. Thomas Duncan was her captain in 1893. In June 1894, she had a record tow of logs from Stillwater, 1,200' x 265'.

She was sold to the Chicago and Eastern Illinois Railroad as a railroad transfer boat to handle barges at Joppa, Illinois. In 1899 she was sold and rebuilt at Paducah, Kentucky, and renamed CONDOR (given a new registry number). She burned in early March, 1917.

B

B. F. Weaver   #2940

Sidewheel (or sternwheel) rafter, built in 1872 at Galena, Illinois. 75 tons, 75 tons, 80' x 21.8' x 4'. Home port LaCrosse, 1877 to 1886; St. Paul, 1887; Paducah, 1888. Perhaps dismantled at LaCrosse, late 1880s.

B. Hershey   #3050

Sternwheel rafter, built 1877, Rock Island, Illinois, for Hershey Lumber Company of Muscatine, Iowa. 170 tons, 170 tons, 125.3' x 27.5' x 3.9'. Named for Benjamin Hershey, head of Hershey Lumber Company. Engines were 17" cylinder, 4.5' piston stroke; had three boilers, 283 h.p. Captain Cyprian Buisson was on her twenty years, used EVERETT as bow boat. From 1901 to 1913, had passenger license and did some excursion work; eighteen crew. Antoine LaRoque was a pilot for Buisson; Steve Withrow, captain 1901–02; William Dobson, 1905. Burned at Stillwater, November 1906. Rebuilt, sold to Valley Navigation Company. Sank in 1913 while doing levee work at East St. Louis. Raised by insurance company and sold to Captain Joseph Chotin. Other personnel were Ira DeCamp, pilot; John Smith, pilot for a long time; Bert Archer, mate in 1902; John Wright, chief engineer for five or six years.

Bart E. Linehan   #3132

Sternwheel rafter, wood hull, built in 1880 at Burlington, Iowa for Hansen and Linehan of Dubuque who were in the boat-store business. Named for Linehan. Builders were brothers F. J. and A. A. Fogel. Engines were built by the firm of McElroy and Armitage of Keokuk. 178 tons, 178 tons, 127' x 23.5' x 3.9'. Sold to Knapp, Stout & Company in 1883. Captain William Slocumb was master and Jack Bradley pilot under Knapp, Stout ownership. She was sold in 1889 or 1890 to McDonald Brothers of LaCrosse. Captain William Dobler made eight round trips with her in sixty-four days from West Newton to Quincy, Illinois in 189__.

In October 1897, while coming up river, she struck a snag near Buena Vista and sank in eight feet of water, William Dobler, master. She was raised in eighteen days. Her crew was twenty-one. In 1902 she was sold to the lower Mississippi and placed in the Paducah-Golconda packet trade, Captains Bauer and Karns. Later on the Ryman Line of Nashville used her for towing on the

Cumberland River (railroad ties). Burned at Nashville in the same fire that destroyed the Ryman elevator there, circa 1904.

BELLA MAC   #3119

Sternwheel rafter, wood hull, built in 1880 at LaCrosse for McDonald Brothers. 83 tons, 83 tons, 111′ x 22′ 3.8′. Engines were 14″ diameter cylinders, 5′ piston stroke. Named for Captain Dan McDonald's daughter, Bella. Nicknamed "Bella Danger" due to her many misfortunes. In spring 1882 exploded her boilers a short distance above Brownsville, Minnesota, killing nine men and scalding a number of others. Captain W. W. Gordon, master; James Tully, chief engineer; Charles Monahan, second engineer. The latter was on watch but asleep, awakened, started the doctor pump and created the dangerous combination of hot boilers and cold water; he lost his license. Rebuilt 1882-83 and later burned at LaCrosse, 1895. Rebuilt and enlarged to 126′ x 26′ x 3.8′. Sunk at West Newton, 1896, and raised. Harry Dyer was on her in 1884 and was in two of the worst raft breakups he was ever in, one at Bullet Chute just below Genoa, Wisconsin, and on the same trip in Crooked Slough above Lynxville, Wisconsin, breaking her shaft. Captain E. D. Dixon, 1890; Captain N. B. Lucas, 1893.

Finally lost in 1898, when upbound with owners as passengers aboard, she began to roll and sank above the Merchants Bridge, St. Louis opposite Salt Point light. Crew was Captain Tom Withrow, master; W. R. Slocumb, pilot; John Slocum(b) mate; Charlie Bradbus, chief engineer; "Dago" Clem, second engineer.

BEN FRANKLIN   #136270

Originally *(A) E. RUTLEDGE*, rafter, *(B) JOHN M. RICH, (C) ORONOCO*. In 1921 the Mayo Brothers sold their ORONOCO to the Ben Franklin Coal Company of West Virginia, and they changed the name to *(D) BEN FRANKLIN*. She towed coal between Moundsville and Parkersburg. From July 1922 until January 1926, she was owned by the Independent River Sand Company. In July 1925, she was cut down "pool style" at the Morgan-David Dock Company, Glenwood, Pennsylvania. The Ben Franklin Coal Company (A. O. Kirschner of Cincinnati and John Donald of Ripley, Ohio) bought her in January 1926. Captain John Donald sold out in June 1927 and the *BEN FRANKLIN* did job towing. She burned at Cincinnati, December 2, 1935 due to a fire from a signal lantern.

BERNICE   #3861

Sternwheel rafter, wood hull, built in Clinton, Iowa, 1899. 51 tons, 75′ x 18′ x 4′. Was bowboat for the *CHANCY LAMB*. In 1913, owned by Douglas Jones of Golconda, Illinois and engaged in general towing. Then at Paducah, and towed ties. Later bought by Williams Brothers of Evansville, Indiana, towed around Ohio River Dams 47, 51, and 52 when they were being built. Burned on December 16, 1932, in fire which also destroyed the *DICK WILLIAMS, RIVAL* and packet *SOUTHLAND*.

BESSIE KATZ   #161681

Built 1892 at Wabasha as *(A) VERNIE MAC*, sternwheel. 124.3′ x 22′ x 3.8′. Meyer Katz of St. Louis owned her and renamed her circa 1920. Towed garbage and was sold to Jefferson Distributing Company in 1925 and was renamed *(C) JEFFERSON*.

BLUE LODGE   #2533

Sternwheel towboat, wood hull, built Pittsburgh, 1866. 103 tons, 103 tons, 155′ x 25′ x 4.4′. Engines 17″ diameter cylinders, 5′ piston stroke, three boilers. In coal trade, owned new by James Matthews. Was largest towboat to go up on Allegheny River to oil fields, but only made one trip. Towed for W. H. Brown Coal Company of Pittsburgh. Sold at U. S. marshal sale on June 6, 1874 and bought by J. W. Williams. Used in Grand Lake Coal Company fleet.

Bought by McDonald Brothers in 1875, brought to LaCrosse to serve as a raft boat. In 1878 during low water season, chartered by Diamond Jo Line to tow grain in barges. While cleaning boilers, night of June 11, 1882 (or 1888), at St. Louis, she broke loose and sank, a total loss; N. B. Lucas, master. The hull was raised, slung between two barges and towed to LaCrosse. She was dismantled and engines placed in the new *THISTLE* owned by McDonald Brothers.

BOREALIS REX   #3407

Sternwheel rafter/packet. Built at Stillwater, 1888. 163 tons, 125.5′ x 22′ x 4.5′. Had cross compound engines, 12″ and 24″ cylinders, 6′ piston stroke. She had two boilers, 40″ by 16′. Was in rafting trade until 1891, then ran on Illinois River until she was sold downriver and ran out of Natchez. Later on, was working out of Lake Charles, Louisiana. Sold in 1938 for $110.

BROTHER JONATHAN   #2761

Sternwheel rafter, wood hull, built 1871, LeClaire, Iowa. 110 tons, 110.6′ x 21′ x 4′. Engines 12″ diameter cylinders, 4′ piston stroke. Captain Brown Jenks, master; Stephen Hanks, pilot three seasons, 1874 to 1876. Towed logs from St. Paul. Early in 1877, Captain A. T. Jenks associated with Durant & Wheeler and placed the *BROTHER JONATHAN* with them. Henry Peavey, captain, and pilot in 1870s. C. C. Carpenter, master in 1883. Registered Galena 1887 and 1891, St. Paul, 1884-86. In February 1890, owned by Lachmund, George W. Ashton and George S. Sardam, Fulton, Illinois, George Reed, master.

BUCKEYE #2727

Sidewheel-geared boat, built 1868, Reads Landing for Captain E. C. Bill. 69 tons, 69 tons, 102' x 16.4' x 3'. Captain Bill, master; son Fred A., clerk; one of best built of the early raft boats. Built in spring 1868 by Pearl Roundy. Drew 16" light. Engines built by Coe and Wilkes of Painesville, Ohio. Engines attached to bed-plates which were very light, with very short pitmans. Boiler built by Funk and Lauer, LaCrosse. It was 16' long x 42" diameter, had ten 6" flues. Had separate "oscillating" engine for capstan located under stairs leading to boiler deck.

Captain E. C. Bill would take contracts for running logs or lumber or else charter his *BUCKEYE*. In 1869 she was chartered to George Winans to run lumber from Pound, Halbert & Company's mill at Chippewa Falls. One trip was made with fifteen strings, sixteen long. About 2.1 million feet of lumber was towed with 33,000 pickets, 412 shingles and 75,000 laths as deck load.

In 1870 *BUCKEYE* towed material for Chicago Northwestern Railroad at Winona. Other pilots or officers on the *BUCKEYE* were George Winans, Stephen Hanks, W. R. Slocumb, Volney A. Bigelow, Eli Minder and Jack Young. Engineers were John Phillips, Hiram Fuller, Frank Clark, Alfred Fuller and James Shaw. Dismantled 1890, worn out.

BUN HERSEY #3248

Sidewheel rafter, wood hull, built 1883, Stillwater by Captain Register. 35 tons, 35 tons, 91.5' x 20.4' x 3.6'. Named for son of one of the owners. Built for and owned by Charles Hersey of Hersey, Staples and Company of Stillwater. Make-up boat around Stillwater for many years. Owned by the Matt Clark Transportation Company of Stillwater, 1883, John Quinlan, captain. Rebuilt 1894, Stillwater, six crew. Captain Dan Rice, master, November 1891. Used in rafting 1890 to 1903. May have towed coal around Paducah in latter days. Off list 1907.

BURDETTE #3150

Screw tug, built 1881, Baytown (Stillwater), Minnesota. 30 tons, 30 tons, eq. 76' x 14.5' 5.2'. Off list after 1892. Dismantled at a South Stillwater yard. Used as a make-up boat around Stillwater.

C

C. J. CAFFREY #4658

Originally sidewheel packet, *(A) J. H. BALDWIN*, built in 1860 in Louisville, first home port Nashville, 173 tons. Captured as a Confederate steamer, spring 1862, on the Cumberland River. Sold for $12,000 to Wiley Simms and A. Hamilton, vessel agents at Nashville. Bought by U.S.Q.M.D. (along with packets *MATTIE CABLER, EMMA, H. O. BIRD*) for federal transports. Sold to private interests, redocumented as *(B) C. J. CAFFREY*, October 4, 1865, then sold to the U. S. engineers who used her as a snagboat, August 13, 1867. As a snagboat, she was used to "scrape off" sand from high places between St. Paul and LaCrosse, one of first on the upper Mississippi.

Around 1875, she was sold to Weyerhaeuser and Denkmann and built (or rebuilt) at Rock Island as a sternwheel rafter, retaining the *C. J. CAFFREY* name. 197 tons, 197 tons, 131' x 26' 4.5'. Captain Oliver P. McMahon, Clinton, Iowa, master for many years. George Carpenter was master in 1890 and thereabouts. A powerful vessel and heavy on fuel. Dismantled in 1892 at Rock Island and the machinery used in the *F. WEYERHAEUSER*.

C. W. COWLES #125929

Sternwheel rafter, wood hull, built 1881, Madison, Indiana for Fleming Brothers who had a lumber mill at McGregor, Iowa. 180 tons, 180 tons, 128.5' x 26.6' x 4.0'. Named for son-in-law of Captain Fleming, who was later employed by the Diamond Jo Line. In 1881 David Hanks of Albany was captain and pilot; Albert Withrow was captain and pilot in 1886; and Richard Dixon in 1887. Sold around 1890 to Valley Navigation Company (Buisson Brothers) Joseph Buisson, master of *C. W. COWLES*; Antoine LaRoque, pilot. They ran logs to the Hershey mill at Muscatine, Iowa. Frank LaPointe of Wabasha was mate and pilot in 1896; Joseph Larrivere, mate; Ira DeCamp was pilot also.

Captain George Winans bought her in 1900, and when he quit rafting, sold her to the Deere family of Moline who used her to tow their houseboat, *MARKATANA*. Rebuilt in 1909 at the Kahlke yard at Rock Island, given a new and wider hull and renamed *KALITAN* (given new registry number).

CARRIE #125838

Sidewheel bowboat, wood hull, built 1880, LaCrosse. 29 tons, 70' x 24' x 3.4'. In 1888 listed at 34 tons and 72' x 24' x 3.5'. Last on 1892 list. Owned by McDonald Brothers in 1883. Said to have burned at LaCrosse.

CHAMPION #5844

Sidewheel-geared rafter, built in 1867 at Reads Landing by Benjamin Seavey & Polley for the Chippewa River trade. 21 tons, about 85' long. In 1868 sold to Knapp, Stout & Company for $6,000. Remodeled at Durand, Wisconsin and rigged as a rafter. She towed lumber from Reads Landing to St. Louis. W. W. Slocumb, and his nephew, W. R. Slocumb, were captain and pilot for many years. Hiram and Alvin Fuller were engineers. Abandoned in 1879.

CHANCY LAMB #126836

Sternwheel rafter, wood hull, built 1872, Clinton, Iowa for Chancy

Lamb and Sons. 194 tons, 194 tons, 136′ x 28.8′ x 4.5′. Named for Chancy Lamb, founder of the Clinton lumber firm. J. E. Short, captain, 1872, 1873, and in 1880. He was a *star* pilot. Engines were of 12″ diameter cylinder, 6′ piston stroke. (Blair says 8′ stroke.) She had three boilers. In 1902 I. E. "Harry" Short, J. E. Short's nephew, was master, and his father was second pilot. Rebuilt in 1892, Dubuque. George E. Rockwood was chief engineer on her for some time.

In 1905 Lamb sold her to the Ryman Line at Nashville, who used her as a packet in their Nashville-Burnside trade; sold by them to John B. Ransom & Company, Nashville. Operated as a towboat on Cumberland River, seventeen crew, 200 h.p. Struck a pier of the Cumberland River bridge at Clarksville, Tennessee, sank in twenty-five feet of water February 18, 1911 drowning a fireman and a female cook.

Charlotte Boeckler   #125934

Sternwheel rafter, wood hull, built in 1881 in New Albany, Indiana. 143 tons, 143 tons, 140′ x 29.4′ x 4.1′. Engines were of 15″ diameter cylinders, 7′ piston stroke. She had two steel boilers, 28′ long, 44″ diameter. Owned by Schulenburg & Boeckler Company of St. Louis. Captain Robert Dodds, master most of her rafting career. "Smile" Gleason was second pilot; William Milligan was chief engineer and James Gleason was mate. In 1897 sold to Captain John McCaffrey, later sold to Cairo, Illinois parties. Rebuilt in 1908, name changed to *J. N. FRIEND* (given new registry number) and later sold to Barrett Line and renamed *MAMIE BARRETT*, engaged in general towing on lower Mississippi River. Seventeen crew, 50 h.p. as towing vessel.

City Of Winona   #126010

Sternwheel rafter, packet, wood hull, built in 1882, Dubuque, Iowa. 147 tons, 147 tons, 126.2′ x 25.5′ x 3.8′. Engines had 13″ diameter cylinders, 5′ piston stroke. Owned by Youmans Brothers and Hodgins of Winona. Henry Seyfert, mate, 1882 and 1883. In 1883 master was William McCraney, O. James Newcomb in 1893 and first captain was James Follmer. Rebuilt with new and faster hull at Kahlke's shipyard at Rock Island in 1894, changed to 212 tons, 178 tons; 137′ x 29.1′ x 4.6′. Her engine cylinders were rebored to 14.5″ diameter. In 1895 crew was O. J. Newcomb, captain; Bob Irvine, second pilot; Hiram Fuller and E. J. Newcomb, engineers; Herman Johnson, mate; Guy Newcomb and E. E. Fuller (son of Hiram), watchmen.

Used in rafting trade until 1896 when she was sold to Captain John Streckfus who, with his *VERNE SWAIN*, plied her in the Davenport-Clinton trade. As a packet, she carried a crew of thirteen and was of 305 h.p. As background in 1896, Captain Newt Long of LeClaire put his *JO LONG* up against the *VERNE SWAIN*. Streckfus then bought the *CITY OF WINONA* (at Winona). Captain Long then chartered the laid-up *DOUGLAS BOARDMAN* at Clinton, Iowa and ran her against the *CITY OF WINONA*. So there were four boats instead of one!

In the fall of 1896 after a very competitive summer, hot-headed Captain Long got into a fight and stabbed Captain James Osborne, the Streckfus agent at Rock Island. He was fined, and it took the *JO LONG* to pay the chartering cost of the *DOUGLAS BOARDMAN*. In 1897 the Davenport-Clinton interurban electric line put all vessels out of business. Captain Long retired and Streckfus had the *CITY OF WINONA* rebuilt at Paducah in 1905 as the excursion vessel, *(B) W. W.*

Clerimond   #86556

Sternwheel towboat, wood hull, *(A) GAZELLE*, built 1901, Wabasha, Minnesota. 124′ x 23.2′ x 3.9′. Brought to Wheeling, West Virginia in June 1904, by a Mr. Mendel, his daughter was named Clerimond, hence, the renaming and possible rebuilding to *(B) CLERIMOND* in February 1905 after she "turned turtle" and sank in the ice. Sold in June 1909, to Captain Steve Green of New Albany, Indiana. Towed in that area and also Salt River, also worked for the Kosmosdale Portland Cement Company. In 1922 she was rebuilt at Madison, Indiana and her name was changed to *KOSMOSDALE* (given new registry number).

Climax   #127007

Sternwheel towboat, built 1893, Burlington, Iowa. 58 tons, 49 tons, 82′ x 18.5′ x 4′. In August 1900, chartered by George Winans and used as a bowboat in conjunction with the *NEPTUNE*. Was sold to Captain Robert Mitchell and engineer John McDeever in 1901 and used by them to tow barges of wood from upper river points to Clinton. On the upper Mississippi until 1903, then ran out of Memphis. Crew of ten. Dismantled at Carter's Point, Mississippi, July 28, 1907.

Clyde   #125806

Sidewheel, later sternwheel rafter, built at Dubuque, Iowa, 1870 by the Iowa Iron Works. Iron hull. As a sidewheeler, she was 96′ x 19′ x 4.5′. Her two engines developed 75 h.p. She originally had either Clyde or Scotch type boilers, but these did not work out and were changed to conventional Western River boilers. Owned by Ingraham and Kennedy, Eau Claire lumbermen. Hugh Douglas became part owner and master in 1872. "Biggest little boat on the upper river" and one of the fastest. Named after the River Clyde in Scotland. First iron-hulled steamboat on the Mississippi. In 1870 sunk below Oquawaka, October 20 while loading lumber for Dubuque. Badly careened, the water level was up to the roof.

The *CLYDE* was rebuilt into a sternwheeler, being lengthened to 125' in the process. The year may have been as early as 1875; another source says 1888. Her tonnage was then 121 tons, 121 tons. The work was done at Dubuque. Rebuilt for Captain J. M. Turner and Captain A. E. Hollingshead. Received new engines, 12" diameter cylinders, 6.5' piston stroke and a new cabin. They ran logs for the Empire Lumber Company of Eau Claire and the Standard Lumber Company. In 1883 E. D. Dixon was captain.

She had a "race" in 1885 with the *DAN THAYER* which beat her but carried one hundred pounds of steam more than allowed! Bronson and Fuller may have owned her in 1885 and thereafter. Morrell M. Looney, master 1889–93; John Hoy, 1894 to 1897; Isaac Newcomb, 1898 to 1910 when she was laid up and out of commission for two seasons. She resumed business in 1913, sold then to Captain John E. Massengale of St. Louis and put in the Illinois River trade. The *CLYDE* was owned briefly by Captain Frank Fugina of Winona who chartered her to the Corps of Engineers. During rafting days, George Williams, Charles Fisher, Sam Serene and Milt Newcomb were some of her engineers. Harry Dyer, Frank Newcomb and Tom Buchanan were some of her mates.

The *CLYDE*'s usual bowboat was the *MARY B*. This vessel started life as the *ETHEL HOWARD* which had been built as a Lake City, Minnesota ferry. The Arrow Transportation Company of Paducah bought her around 1900 and used her to tow ties out of the Tennessee River to Joppa, Illinois. Sank at Paducah on November 9, 1933, in wind swells. Raised and rebuilt. She failed a stability test and her cabin was removed and she was changed to a "single decker." Sold in 1933 to Tennessee Valley Sand and Gravel Company. She made her last trip for them in October 1941. Her iron hull was afloat for many years thereafter.

Columbia #127436

Constructed from former rafter, *PAULINE*. Built or rebuilt 1900 in Stillwater. 82 tons, 82 tons, 117.3' x 24.0' x 4.6'. Owned by Captain William Henning and Frank J. Fugina. Sold January 1906 to Florida interests (Henry Flagler). Used in lower Keys building the Overseas Railroad to Key West. Burned at Milton, Florida, March 13, 1911. Still in 1914 LMV.

Commander #202938

Sternwheel towboat, wood hull. Built *(A)* as rafter *NORTH STAR*, Dubuque, 1906, 140' x 32' x 4.2'. As *(B) EUGENIA TULLY*, bought at U.S. marshal's sale by Captain James Ostrander. He took her to the Missouri River and worked her under charter to the UGI Contracting Co. As *(C) COMMANDER* in 1928, sank at Booneville, Missouri on April 3, 1929 and lost. Twelve aboard; no lives were lost. Captain Will Menke bought the wreck and some of the equipment was recovered.

Conquest #77345

Sternwheel towboat, wood hull, built *(A)* as *J. M. RICHTMAN* in 1899 at Sterling Island, Illinois, 120' x 23.5' x 3.9. Engines 12" diameter cylinders, 6' stroke, two boilers. Renamed *(B) CONQUEST* in 1904 after being bought by Captain Harvey Neville of Chester, Illinois. Used in towing wheat barges and excursion parties.

Sold in 1905 to showboat operators William R. Markle and M. O. Swallow of St. Marys, West Virginia. Enrolled at Wheeling, August 12, 1905. In the spring of 1909, while towing showboat *SUNNY SOUTH* on the Monongahela River, she got caught in high water and could not get under the low bridge at Monongahela City, Pennsylvania for ten days.

CONQUEST was sold (along with the *SUNNY SOUTH*) to W. C. Quimby, Zanesville, Ohio on April 21, 1909. Later, on September 20, 1909, lost at Bayou Sara, Louisiana in a big storm that also wrecked the *HARVESTER* and packet *HANDY* and caused a great loss of coal to the Combine.

Cyclone #126755

Sternwheel packet/rafter, wood hull, built 1891, Stillwater, Minnesota for Durant and Wheeler. 138 tons, 138 tons, 121' x 22.6' x 4.0. Crew of nine. Robert N. Cassidy was captain and pilot in 1892; Thomas Hoy, master and pilot for a time. Captain Albert Wempher took the *CYCLONE* from Keokuk to Quincy November 7, 1898 and was stricken with paralysis three days later, which ended his life shortly thereafter. Ran Wabasha to St. Paul as a packet from 1900 to 1907, Captain Milt Newcomb. Burned in winter, December 2, 1907, on ways in Wabasha along with the *J. W. VAN SANT* and *ISAAC STAPLES*. The hulls were dry and made a hot fire.

D

D. A. McDonald #6528

Sternwheel rafter, wood hull, built 1872, LeClaire, 168 tons, 120' x 24' x 4'. Engines were 14" diameter cylinders, 4' piston stroke. Engines were from packet *GUIDON* built in 1861. Built by and for J. W. and S. R. Van Sant. Named for Captain D. A. McDonald of LaCrosse, who chartered her for the rafting trade. Exploded her boilers on June 10, 1872 when but fifty-eight days old opposite McGregor, Iowa, while upbound to LaCrosse. Some sixteen to eighteen of the crew of twenty-seven were killed, including Captain "French" Martin. Survivors were picked up by the *JENNIE BROWN*; ten or twelve of crew were buried on an island between McGregor and Prairie du Chien.

RAFTING STEAMBOAT HISTORIES

The accident was due to foaming of water in the boilers. The license of the second engineer was revoked. Accident happened just below wooden pontoon bridge owned by John Lawler. [The Chicago, Milwaukee, St. Paul and Pacific Railroad ran trains across and paid tolls.] On July 31, the *JAMES MALBON* exploded near the same spot; she also had foaming boilers.

The hull of the *D. A. McDONALD* was raised. The upper "works" from the *HARTFORD*, an Evansville packet (which had sunk), were bought by the Van Sants and skidded over onto the *D. A. McDONALD*'s hull. The *D. A. McDONALD* sunk later in May 1876 at the Keokuk drawbridge and lost her upper works to a loose barge of stone. She was raised by the Van Sants under extreme difficulty and ran for some time without a cabin or pilot house. Owing to her two mishaps, she was always termed "ill-fated." In 1878 she was rebuilt and renamed *(B) SILVER WAVE*. Her engines later went to the towboat *VERNIE MAC*. The vessel was commanded by Captains Samuel Hitchcock, James Hugunin, George Rutherford, Harry Short, "Lome" Short and Stephen B. Withrow.

Captain Samuel R. Van Sant says of her, "while at first she was unfortunate, owing to no fault of construction but by reason of gross carelessness in some cases and mistaken judgment in others, she had a long career of money-making and she laid the foundation of the success of the Van Sant Navigation Company that, at one time, owned her and operated thirty to thirty-five steamboats. Like a bad child in the family, I was yet very fond of her."

D. C. FOGEL   #157072

Sternwheel towboat, hull built 1882 at Covington, Kentucky, (opposite Cincinnati), 89 tons, 89 tons, 121.9' x 21.6' x 4.4'. The engines were built by McElroy and Armitage of Keokuk and shipped to Covington where they were installed. Only in rafting trade a couple of seasons. In 1883 owned by Fogel Brothers (F. J. and A. A.) of Burlington, Iowa, Fred Fogel, master. Sold to New Orleans parties by the Fogels in 1884. She was engaged in towing staves and lumber from Red River and Quichita River points to New Orleans. Registered in New Orleans, 1888 to 1891 in Brashear, Louisiana in 1892 and after. Dismantled there in 1896 or else sunk in the Achafalaya River at Alma Grove, Louisiana.

DAISY   #157199

Sternwheel rafter, wood hull, built Stillwater, 1887 for Durant and Wheeler, 106 tons, 106 tons, 122' x 22' x 3.8'. Used in rafting business until 1898 or so, sold to lower river parties. Charles White, Ira Fuller and Thomas Hoy were masters and pilots. Charles Murray of Pepin was chief engineer in 1893 and 1894. Felix Bruner and Henry White were mates. On October 26, 1893, she was snagged and sank near Pontoosac, Illinois. The break was bulkheaded, the boat raised and taken to Stillwater where she was hauled out and repaired. Documented in New Orleans from 1897 to 1900.

DANDELION

Sternwheel lighthouse tender. Originally *(A) F. WEYERHAUSER*; obtained by the U.S. Lighthouse Service, Department of Commerce, around 1913. They sold her in October 1927 to steamboat broker John K. Klein. Lost in collision with towboat *HERBERT HOOVER* in February 1929.

DAN HINE   #6236

Sternwheel packet/towboat and rafter, built 1860 Pittsburgh, Pennsylvania. 100 tons, 100 tons, 135.5' x 24.6' 3.3'. Belonged to the Northern Line Packet Company (P. S. Davidson) of LaCrosse, 1883, G. L. Short, master. She was of especially light draft configuration. Was in rafting trade 1885 to 1890 for the Jellison Towing Company of Wabasha. Captains and pilots were Albert M. Short, Lyman Short, Abe Looney and Frank Looney, and George Lansbury was chief engineer for some time. Dismantled at Wabasha or LaCrosse about 1896. Lytle List says A91.

DAN THAYER   #157126

Sternwheel rafter, wood hull, built 1884, LaCrosse. 139 tons, 145.5' x 26' x 4.3'. Owned by the Davidson Lumber Company; captains and pilots were Albert M. Short, I. H. Short and Lyman Short, George Nichols (1890), Charles Burrill was chief engineer (1885), George Dansbury later on. An ornamental, "pretty" rafter. Dismantled at LaCrosse in 1896 and machinery went to the rafter *JOHN H. DOUGLASS* for Captain George Winans, who later named her *SATURN* (2) after his first *SATURN* had burned.

DAVID BRONSON   #76076

Sternwheel rafter, built as *(A) I. E. STAPLES* at Stillwater (1879). 95 tons, 95 tons, 130' x 21' x 4.3'. Had machinery of *WYMAN X*. Sold by Isaac Staples in 1883 to the Matt Clark Transportation Company of Stillwater. Matt Clark was a son-in-law of Isaac Staples and renamed her *(B) DAVID BRONSON*. Captain was James Newcomb. In 1889, 153 tons, 153 tons. In 1896 the Clark Company failed and the *DAVID BRONSON* was sold to the Durant and Wheeler Company. She was later renamed *(C) HENRIETTA*.

DEXTER   #6571

Sternwheel rafter (may have been sidewheel originally). Wood hull, built 1867, Osceola, Wisconsin, 188 tons, 188 tons, 130' x 25.7' x 3.5'. McDonald Brothers added her to their fleet in 1874. In 1880 Henry Buisson was captain; Joe Gardapie, pilot; and Frank Wetenhall, mate. In late 1880 she was caught by the

Mississippi River icing up and had to stay at McGregor until spring. In 1884 George Nichols, Jr. was pilot. In 1885 John O'Connor was captain and John Mills was mate. James Newcomb was captain in 1888. Captain Peter O'Rourke was on her many years for the McDonalds. Some of her engineers were George Dansbury, Charles Higbee, John Craft, Joseph Stombs, and James and Henry Tully (brothers).

On her last trip in 1888 or 1889, she came into LaCrosse and laid up at McDonald's boat yard. Some thirty-seven minutes afterward, she was sitting on the bottom of the Black River. Her pumps and siphons had stopped and the vessel was abandoned.

DISPATCH #6951

Steam propeller, built at Stillwater by Durant, Wheeler and Company, 61 tons, 96.5' x 15.4' x 5.0'; The List of Merchant Vessels says built at Hudson, Wisconsin, 1877. Used as a brail boat at Stillwater rafting works. On July 14, 1878, she was bumped and sunk by the packet *RED WING*, a few miles south of Savanna, Illinois. She was raised and later was engaged in rafting from St. Paul in 1881. Later taken to White Bear Lake and used as an excursion and pleasure vessel, eventually dismantled.

DOUGLAS BOARDMAN #157034

Sternwheel rafter, built Dubuque in 1881. 182 tons, 182 tons, 120' x 32' x 4', engines 14" diameter, 6' piston stroke. Built on Diamond Jo ways at Eagle Point. Two identical vessels, the *F.C.A. DENKMANN* and *DOUGLAS BOARDMAN* were built at the same time, the *F.C.A. DENKMANN* for Weyerhaeuser and Denkmann and the *DOUGLAS BOARDMAN* for W. J. Young and Co. of Clinton. Lots were drawn to see who got which boat and Denkman got his choice. He got the better twin as the bottom planking on the *F.C.A. DENKMANN* was 3" compared to 2½" for the *DOUGLAS BOARDMAN*. Boardman was the largest eastern stockholder of the W. J. Young Company.

Paul Kerz was the first captain and Conrad Kraus was chief engineer; both were transferred to the *W. J. YOUNG* in 1882. James Rellis was captain, 1882 to 1884. He became insane in 1885 and retired. Isaac Newcomb was captain 1891 to 1893. In 1896 she was placed in the packet trade between Davenport and Clinton. In 1897 she was dismantled at Clinton.

Her machinery and part of her upper works went into the building of the packet *COLUMBIA* which was built at Lyons, Iowa by M. J. Godfrey and son for C. H. Young of Clinton. The *COLUMBIA* was 166.5' x 33.6' x 5'; 122 tons, 123 h.p. Walter Blair bought her from W. J. Young Company in 1904 after she had been laid up for a year. Blair sold her in April 1912 to Captain H. F. Mehl of Chillicothe, Ohio. Blair used her in excursion work and as a substitute in the Davenport-Burlington trade. *COLUMBIA* sank on the Illinois River with a loss of eighty or ninety lives on July 5, 1918.

E

E. DOUGLAS #136542

Sternwheel rafter, built 1896, Wabasha, Minnesota. Originally, 107 tons, 107 tons, 112.3' x 24.3' x 4.6', 45 (est.) h.p.. Owned by the Mississippi River Logging and Boom Company rafting works. Adam Kerz was captain and Charles Murray was chief engineer for several years. Charles B. Roman was master in 1900. Caught in an ice jam in 1904 at the West Newton works. Sold "south" in 1907 and registered in Mobile. 93 tons, 93 tons, 112' x 24.0' x 4.0'. Operated by Black Warrior Lumber Company of Demopolis, Alabama. Captain E. V. Pickley and pilot Charles Nichols took her downriver. As tow vessel, had crew of twenty-five. Dismantled in April 1916.

E. RUTLEDGE #136502

Sternwheel rafter, built 1892, Rock Island for Weyerhaeuser and Denkmann. Named for Ed Rutledge, prominent honcho in that firm. 212 tons, 132.7' x 30.5' x 4.7', engines were 15" diameter cylinders, 5' piston stroke. She had three boilers and developed 375 h.p. Used as a pleasure boat as well as a towboat. Had twelve fine staterooms. From 1896 to 1902 William Whistler was master. Her bowboat for many years was the *H. C. BROCKMAN*. In 1907 the *E. RUTLEDGE* brought a large raft to Rock Island, 1,430 feet long and 285 feet wide. Sold to Captain Frank Fugina who in turn sold her to the Woods Produce Company of Red Wing who changed her name to *(B) JOHN H. RICH* in 1910 and used her as a pleasure boat. Rich was president of the company.

In 1912 she was sold to the Mayo Brothers of Rochester, Minnesota and they changed her name to *(C) ORONOCO*. They used her as a private pleasure craft. Captain Robert N. Cassidy was in charge for the Richs and Mayos. Jack Richtman was pilot. Captain William Whistler died in an Illinois sanitarium in 1913, hopelessly insane. The Mayos sold her and she operated on the lower Mississippi as *(D) BEN FRANKLIN*. She burned in 1935 on the Ohio River. Had seventeen crew in 1905, twenty-one in 1908.

ECLIPSE #135593

Sternwheel rafter, built in 1882, LeClaire for Lindsay and Phelps and the Cable Lumber Company of Davenport. 148 tons, 148 tons, 124' x 24.6' x 4.1'. Engines 13" diameter cylinders, 5' piston stroke, three boilers, 30" diameter by 16'. Captain John Lancaster, master for much of her rafting career. John McKenzie was her first captain. Captain John Lancaster bought an interest in her

RAFTING STEAMBOAT HISTORIES

in 1904-1905, entered packet trade between Davenport and Clinton, had nineteen crew, 241 h.p. Due to a parallel electric interurban line, the venture was not a success. She later ran between Prairie du Chien and Dubuque. She sank in 1913 while idle in Cat Tail Slough south of Albany, Illinois. Captain Ralph Emerson bought her to tow his showboat, *GOLDENROD* (1914-1917). *ECLIPSE* also did contract towing in the winter. In December 1917, while towing an Atlantic Refining Company gasoline barge from Pittsburgh to Sistersville, West Virginia, on the night of the 8th, she struck the dike at the foot of Neville Island (White's Riffle Dike). As she sank, a stove overturned and the *ECLIPSE* burned; the crew escaped in yawls.

Harry Dyer said, "Captain Lancaster was a *first class* steamboat man." He died at his LeClaire home, May 9, 1914.

ED DURANT, JR.   #105974

Sternwheel rafter. Built *(A)* as the *A. T. JENKS* which burned at Stillwater in 1883. Rebuilt 1883 as *(B) ED DURANT, JR.*, named for lumber entreprenuer at Stillwater. Owned and rebuilt by Durant and Wheeler. 230 tons, 153 tons, 113' x 22' x 3.7'. Albert Withrow master in 1884; Frank Clemmons, mate; George Griffin, chief engineer for most of her service. Burned at South Stillwater, February 19, 1887 with loss amounting to $7,500. Machinery placed in new, rebuilt *ED DURANT, JR.* In 1890, listed as 149 tons, 149 tons, 115' x 27' x 5.3'. At Memphis, 1894, renamed *(C) JOSEPHINE LOVIZA*, 1897.

ELLEN   #203944

Sternwheel rafter. Built 1907 at LaCrosse, 96 tons, 96 tons, 145.5' (126.6' by another source) x 26' x 4.4'. Her engines were 14" diameter cylinders, 6' piston stroke, 150 h.p. Original owner was the Sawyer Austin Lumber Company. The boat was named for wife of W. W. Cargill of the Cargill firm. Captain Charles White, Sr. was her usual master. Documented as steam yacht originally. Used in rafting, excursions, and private parties for firm members. Once, while tied up at Trempealeau, Wisconsin, Austin Cargill was bitten by a rattlesnake. Captain White cauterized the wound with a heated sluice bar. Captain White was a guest aboard the *OTTUMWA BELLE* in 1915 when she towed the last raft.

The *ELLEN* was bought by the Corps of Engineers at Rock Island around 1930. They put a steel hull under her, 150' x 30' x 5.2'. Captain John Suiter, master in the 1930s. During Franklin Roosevelt's presidency, her cabin was air conditioned and an elevator was installed, but President Roosevelt cancelled the visit for some reason. Captain Joseph Hawthorne of LeClaire was a guest aboard *ELLEN* several times in 1935 and 1936. He died January 24, 1937 at age ninety-seven. He was a cousin of Nathaniel Hawthorne and had been in LaCrosse since 1856. *ELLEN* was sold at public auction to Ralph James in 1943, then to Standard Oil of Ohio, who, in 1944 sold her to Industrial Marine Service of Memphis, who converted her to a twin prop (diesel).

EMERSON   #91248

Sternwheel towboat. Built as *(A) MOLINE* in Cincinnati in 1880. 140' x 26.2' x 4'. Purchased December 1907 by Captain Ralph Emerson and Edwin A. Price who renamed her *(B) EMERSON*, February 7, 1908. She towed their *GRAND FLOATING PALACE* showboat. The *EMERSON* turned over at 6:00 A.M. October 3, 1908 at Osceola, Arkansas while towing the *NEW GRAND* showboat to New Orleans. A musician on board died.

EMMA   #8364

Sidewheel bowboat, built 1867 Lynxville, Wisconsin. 101 tons. Burned December 9, 1872 at Shawneetown, Illinois, no lives lost.

ETHEL HOWARD   #136134

Sternwheel towboat. Built 1890, Lake City, Minnesota, 90 tons, 90 tons, 95.4' x 22.9' x 4.2' or 91' x 23' x 4.2'. Engines 10" diameter cylinders, 4' piston stroke. One steel boiler, one stack. Built for Captain J. S. Howard and named for his daughter. Originally a ferry, running between Lake City, Stockholm, Maiden Rock and Red Wing. Sold to McDonald Brothers, 1896 and used as a bowboat. She was a single deck towboat, renamed *(B) MARY B.* in 1898, after rebuilding at Lake City, Minnesota.

EUGENIA TULLY   #202938

Originally rafter *(A) NORTH STAR*. Built in 1906, Dubuque, 138 tons, 138 tons, 140' x 32' x 4.2'. Renamed *(B) EUGENIA TULLY* when sold circa 1917 to Patton-Tully Transportation Company, Memphis. Then sold in 1927 and went to Moundsville, West Virginia to tow coal. Sold at U. S. marshal's sale in August 1928. Bought by Captain James B. Ostrander who repaired and renamed her *(C) COMMANDER*.

EVANSVILLE   #8626

Sternwheel packet/rafter. Built in Evansville, Indiana, 1869. 158 tons, 158 tons, 109.2' x 26' x 3.9'. Equipment from *ADA LYON* used in construction. Ran in the "Green River trade" (Bowling Green, Kentucky to Evansville, Indiana) for the Green and Barren River Navigation Company. Sold in 1882 or 1883 to the Rapids Transit Company of LeClaire, S. R. Van Sant. She was then sold to the Matt Clark Transportation Company of Stillwater, Captain Edward Root, master. Captain Ira Fuller, master and pilot under Clark; Sol Fuller, chief engineer. The company failed and she was sold to John Robson of the

Lansing Lumber Company for an overdue fuel bill. Sunk at Stillwater, October 12, 1885, but raised within a few days.

Captain Walter Blair and the Van Sants bought her in 1888 or in 1889 and used her as a rafter. On June 1, 1889, she collapsed a flue below Winona, scalding seven of the crew. Two died, the second engineer and a mate. John O'Connor was master at the time. Towed to Winona afterwards and the boiler was repaired. Blair had Captain Thomas Withrow as master. Dismantled in 1891 and her machinery went to the *VOLUNTEER*, built by J. Van Sant, and his son.

EVERETT   #135880

Sternwheel rafter. Built 1886 South Stillwater for Captain Charles H. Meads by Josiah Batchelder. 85 tons, 85 tons, 110' x 16' x 3.5'. She had the machinery of the *WM. WHITE* which had been dismantled the same year by Meads. She had one boiler, 31" diameter, 14' long, with ten 5" flues. Engines were 10" diameter cylinders, 3½' piston stroke. Captain Meads owned her one season and then sold her to Vincent and Thomas Peel, brothers in Burlington. Captain Meads took the Peel's *MAGGIE REANEY* in exchange. In April 1889, she was caught in a tornado near Oquawka, Illinois and capsized, drowning Captain Vincent Peel; his daughter, Mary Bell; his granddaughter, Velva Bell; a nurse girl; and George Howard, the cook.

She was raised and sold to the Empire Coal Company of Fulton, Illinois, and then to Captain John Lancaster who used her as a bowboat for the *ECLIPSE*. Captain Darwin Dorrance of LeClaire was master and pilot. Van Sant bought her for a bowboat for the *B. HERSHEY*. Then the *B. HERSHEY* and *EVERETT* were sold to Captain A. L. Day, and he sold *EVERETT* to the Burlington Lumber Company. Dismantled at Burlington, 1913.

F

F. C. A. DENKMANN   #120445

Sternwheel rafter. Built at the Eagle Point boat yard in 1881, Dubuque. 182 tons, 182 tons, 120' x 32' x 4'. Engines 14" diameter cylinders, 6' piston stroke. Named for Frederick Carl August Denkmann and owned by Weyerhaeuser and Denkmann of Rock Island. Captain William Whistler in charge from 1881 to 1892. Captain Otis McGinley then in charge until 1897 when he resigned to go to the Yukon River. He brought a raft 1,625' long x 275' wide from West Newton to Rock Island. This was one of the largest rafts.

The *F.C.A. DENKMANN* was a twin to the *DOUGLAS BOARDMAN* except that she had 3" bottom plank contrasted to the *DOUGLAS BOARDMAN*'s 2½" plank. Denkmann drew lots with W. J. Young as to who got which boat and "won." *F. C. A. DENKMANN* was sold to Mrs. Mary Shelby in October 1899 and used to tow corn in barges from the Wabash River to Henderson, Kentucky; was renamed *(B) WABASH*.

F. WEYERHAEUSER   #120930

Sternwheel wooden rafter built at Rock Island in 1893 for the Weyerhaeuser and Denkmann Lumber Company of Rock Island, Illinois. She was 140' long, 31' wide, and had a depth of hold of 4.5'. This vessel (or at least her machinery) started in the packet *J. H. BALDWIN* built at Louisville, Kentucky in 1861. She was captured by Confederates on the Cumberland River in 1862 and sold at Nashville. Later on the *U.S.Q.M.D.* bought her and used her as an army transport. After the war, under the name of *C. J. CAFFREY*, she was sold to the U.S. Army Corps of Engineers who used her as a snag boat. She was a sidewheeler initially, but changed into a sternwheeler somewhere along the line. Around 1870 Weyerhaeuser and Denkmann bought the *C. J. CAFFREY* and used her in the rafting trade. As *C. J. CAFFREY*, she had a new hull and her dimensions were 131' x 26' x 4.5'.

When the powerful timber barons, Weyerhaeuser and Denkmann built the *F. WEYERHAEUSER* in 1893, they used the *C. J. CAFFREY*'s machinery, but after a year it proved too small and she had two new engines placed in her of 15" cylinder bore and 7' piston stroke, some of the largest engines ever used in a rafter. She had three boilers also. As built, or rebuilt, from the *C. J. CAFFREY*, the "Big Fred," as she was known to raftsmen, was of 216 tons and her dimensions were 140 x 31 x 4.5'. She was also used by the Weyerhaeusers as a pleasure craft for several years.

About 1913 she was sold to the U.S. Lighthouse Service and renamed *DANDELION*. They used her as a lighthouse tender on the Upper Mississippi until 1927 when she was sold to the steamboat broker, John K. Klein. A new steel tender, *WAKE ROBIN*, replaced the *DANDELION* in service. The old rafter was finally lost in a collision with the towboat *HERBERT HOOVER* at Cairo, Illinois in 1929.

FLYING EAGLE   #100431

Sternwheel. Built as rafter *(A) IRENE D*. 142 tons, 142 tons, 133.5' x 20.6' x 4.8'. Rebuilt and name changed to *(B) FLYING EAGLE* in 1898 when she was bought by Captain Thomas Adams of Quincy and converted into an excursion boat. Wrecked June 3, 1903 on the Hannibal bridge. A Sunday School group was aboard and at least four lost their lives including the cook, "Peggy" Harvey; Frank Slaten was pilot; Edward Meads was engineer.

FRANK   #120361

Originally a sidewheeler, built in 1879 at LaCrosse. 27 tons, 64' x 19'

The *ABNER GILE* was a LeClaire, Iowa-built vessel of 1872. She was owned by Captains Jerry Turner and Al Hollingshead in the early 1880s, then owned for a half dozen years by Jerome E. Short. Burned or dismantled around the turn of the century.
Photo courtesy of Murphy Library Special Collections, University of Wisconsin-LaCrosse.

Early sidewheel rafter ANNIE GIRDON, shown here with a record (for that time) lumber raft in June 1868. Owned from 1870 on by Knapp, Stout and Company. Named for George W. Girdon's daughter. Girdon was a government inspector of hulls at Galena, Illinois.
Photo courtesy of Murphy Library Special Collections, University of Wisconsin-LaCrosse and Winona County (Minnesota) Historical Society.

The *ANNIE GIRDON*'s propulsion system consisted of an engine for each sidewheel, but instead of turning each wheel with the individual engine, the wheels were connected by a shaft and gearing. This photo shows her when she was in service on the Chippewa River. *Photo courtesy of Murphy Library Special Collections, University of Wisconsin-LaCrosse.*

The *ARTEMUS GATES* was an 1896 sternwheel rafter built at Clinton, Iowa for Chancy Lamb and Sons. She was often used as the bowboat for their *CHANCY LAMB*. Her namesake became a prominent New York banker and was Secretary of Naval Aviation in WWII. *Photo courtesy of Murphy Library Special Collections, University of Wisconsin-LaCrosse.*

A Chancy Lamb and Sons rafter and packet at times, this photo of the *ARTEMUS LAMB* shows her with a full passenger complement. Named for a son of Chancy Lamb. *Photo courtesy of Murphy Library Special Collections, University of Wisconsin-LaCrosse and Winona County (Minnesota) Historical Society.*

The BART E. LINEHAN was built at Burlington, Iowa in 1880. In October 1897 she struck a snag and sank and was later raised by William Dobler. (See account by Harry G. Dyer elsewhere.) Owned at times by Knapp, Stout and Company and McDonald Brothers. *Photo courtesy of Murphy Library Special Collections, University of Wisconsin-LaCrosse and Winona County (Minnesota) Historical Society.*

Raising the BART E. LINEHAN. Captain William Dobler is probably the man in the center (with the hat) on one of the barges used to raise the LINEHAN. Photo courtesy of Joe Dobler Collection.

McDonald Brothers of LaCrosse built this steamboat which was named for Captain Dan McDonald's daughter, Bella. The BELLA MAC had many misfortunes, exploding her boilers and killing nine, burning in 1895 and sinking a year later. Finally lost in 1898 at St. Louis by sinking. Her nickname was "BELLA DANGER." Photo courtesy of Murphy Library Special Collections, University of Wisconsin-LaCrosse.

BEN FRANKLIN was the fourth name of this one-time rafter, shown here rigged as a coal towboat on the Ohio River after 1921. Other names were (A) *E. RUTLEDGE,* (B) *JOHN M. RICH* and (C) *ORONOCO.* Photo courtesy of Murphy Library Special Collections, University of Wisconsin-LaCrosse.

Benjamin Hershey, head of the Hershey Lumber Company of Muscatine, Iowa, was the namesake for the 1877 *B. HERSHEY*. The celebrated Cyprian Buisson was her master for twenty years. She also did excursion work, 1901–1913. *Photo courtesy of Murphy Library Special Collections, University of Wisconsin-LaCrosse and Winona County (Minnesota) Historical Society.*

A plainer, less elaborate *B. HERSHEY* lying at a Mississippi River bank. Note the access planks going from boat to bank. *Photo courtesy of the Joe Dobler Collection.*

BOREALIS REX was a packet for most of her career as shown here, but saw some rafting service. Built at Stillwater in 1888, she was one of a few rafting vessels to have cross-compound engines.
Photo courtesy of Murphy Library Special Collections, University of Wisconsin-LaCrosse.

An early George Winans craft, the sidewheel-geared steamboat BUCKEYE of 1868 is shown here before bowboats were employed and raftsmen had to man large sweeps to help steer rafts. In 1869 Captain Winans made a trip with the BUCKEYE pushing a raft fifteen strings wide, sixteen long; about 2.1 million feet of lumber was towed. Photo courtesy of Murphy Library Special Collections, University of Wisconsin-LaCrosse.

The C. J. CAFFREY was rebuilt from sidewheeler to a sternwheeler around 1875. Owned by Weyerhaeuser and Denkman of Rock Island. Dismantled and machinery used in the F. WEYERHAEUSER.
Photo courtesy of Murphy Library Special Collections, University of Wisconsin-LaCrosse.

The sidewheel-geared rafter CHAMPION of 1867, built at Reads Landing. Owned after 1868 by Knapp, Stout and Company. Towed lumber rafts from Reads Landing to St. Louis.
Photo courtesy of Murphy Library Special Collections, University of Wisconsin-LaCrosse.

The *CHARLOTTE BOECKLER* was built in 1891 at New Albany, Indiana and was owned by the St. Louis firm Schulenburg and Boeckler. Captain Robert Dodds was her usual master during her rafting days. *Photo courtesy of Murphy Library Special Collections, University of Wisconsin-LaCrosse.*

The first fourteen years of the CITY OF WINONA's life were spent in the rafting business. In 1896 she was sold to Captain John Streckfus and was paired with his VERNE SWAIN in the Davenport-Clinton trade. She was built at Dubuque in 1882. Streckfus rebuilt her in 1905 at Paducah as the excursion vessel W. W. Photo courtesy of Murphy Library Special Collections, University of Wisconsin-LaCrosse and Tulane University.

As *CLERIMOND* this former rafter was a towboat and worked on the Ohio River from 1904 until 1922 when she was rebuilt, given a new registry number and had her name changed to *KOSMOSDALE*. Photo courtesy of Murphy Library Special Collections, University of Wisconsin-LaCrosse and Cincinnati/Hamilton County Public Library.

Durant and Wheeler used the 1887 *DAISY* until 1898 in their rafting business. She served a few years thereafter on the lower river. Shown here on an excursion. *Photo courtesy of Murphy Library Special Collections, University of Wisconsin-LaCrosse.*

The U.S. Lighthouse Service used the DANDELION as a lighthouse tender on the river. She was originally the rafter *F. WEYERHAEUSER*. She was obtained around 1913 and lost by a collision with the towboat *HERBERT HOOVER* in February 1929.
Photo courtesy of Murphy Library Special Collections, University of Wisconsin-LaCrosse and Tulane University.

The well-cared for lighthouse tender DANDELION as seen in the Keokuk, Iowa drydock in 1922. Photo courtesy of Murphy Library Special Collections, *University of Wisconsin-LaCrosse.*

The *DAN HINE* was built in 1860 at Pittsburgh. She was a packet for a time and then was in the rafting trade for the Jellison Towing Company of Wabasha. Dismantled about 1896. *Photo courtesy of Murphy Library Special Collections, University of Wisconsin-LaCrosse.*

The Davidson Lumber Company had the *DAN THAYER* built in 1884 at LaCrosse for rafting service. She was rather ornamental for a rafter. After a dozen years she was dismantled and her machinery placed in the rafter *JOHN H. DOUGLASS*.
Photo courtesy of Murphy Library Special Collections, University of Wisconsin-LaCrosse.

The DAVID BRONSON started life as (A) I.E. STAPLES. The Matt Clark Transportation Company of Stillwater bought her in 1883 and used her in rafting until 1896 when she was sold to Durant and Wheeler. She was later renamed (C) HENRIETTA. Photo courtesy of Murphy Library Special Collections, University of Wisconsin-LaCrosse and Winona County (Minnesota) Historical Society.

The *DEXTER* was constructed at Osceola, Wisconsin in 1867 and went to the McDonald Brothers fleet in 1874. In 1880 she was caught by ice at McGregor and had to stay there until spring. She was abandoned in 1888 or 1889 at LaCrosse when her leaky hull gave out and she sank. *Photo courtesy of Murphy Library Special Collections, University of Wisconsin-LaCrosse.*

In 1881 two identical craft were built at Dubuque, the *F.C.A. DENKMANN* and the *DOUGLAS BOARDMAN*. W. J. Young and Company of Clinton owned the *BOARDMAN* and named her after their largest eastern stockholder. In 1897 she was dismantled at Clinton and her machinery and part of her upper works went into the *COLUMBIA*.
Photo courtesy of Murphy Library Special Collections, University of Wisconsin-LaCrosse.

Ed Rutledge, a prominent official of Weyerhaeuser and Denkmann, was the namesake for this 1892 sternwheeler, *E. RUTLEDGE*. Fitted out with twelve fine staterooms, she was often used as a pleasure craft. The *H. C. BROCKMAN* was her bowboat for many years. In 1907 she brought a large lumber raft to Rock Island, 1,430 feet long and 285 feet wide. *Photo courtesy of Murphy Library Special Collections, University of Wisconsin-LaCrosse and Winona County (Minnesota) Historical Society.*

The ECLIPSE was built in 1882 at LeClaire. Captain John Lancaster was her master for much of her career. She was later a packet and also towed the showboat GOLDEN ROD. She burned in December 1917. Her bowboat was often the EVERETT, an 1886 craft built at South Stillwater. Dismantled at Burlington in 1913. Photo courtesy of Murphy Library Special Collections, University of Wisconsin-LaCrosse and Winona County (Minnesota) Historical Society.

The *ED DURANT, JR.* was a Durant and Wheeler rafter, built in 1883 from the (A) *T. JENKS* after a fire to the latter. Named for the Stillwater lumber tycoon. Burned in 1897 at South Stillwater and rebuilt and renamed (C) *JOSEPHINE LOVIZA* in 1897. Photo courtesy of Murphy Library Special Collections, University of Wisconsin-LaCrosse.

The *EVANSVILLE*, built in Evansville, Indiana in 1869, initially ran on the Green River as a packet. In the early 1880s she was acquired by Samuel Van Sant of LeClaire and later by the Matt Clark Transportation Company. Afterwards she went back to Van Sant and Captain Walter Blair. Dismantled in 1891. *Photo courtesy of Murphy Library Special Collections, University of Wisconsin-LaCrosse.*

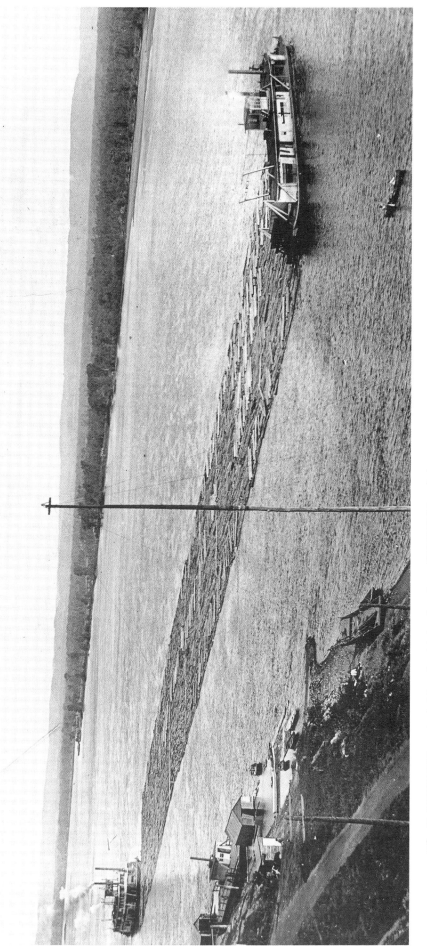

The *B. HERSHEY* pushed this raft with her bowboat *EVERETT* assisting.
Photo courtesy of Murphy Library Special Collections, University of Wisconsin-LaCrosse and Winona County (Minnesota) Historical Society.

Frederick Carl August Denkmann named the Dubuque-built 1881 *F. C. A. DENKMANN* after himself, fortunately using only the initials of his first three names. She was a twin to the *DOUGLAS BOARDMAN*, but supposedly had 3″ bottom plank as contrasted to the *BOARDMAN*'s 2½ inch. Sold in 1899 and renamed (B) *WABASH*. Photo courtesy of Murphy Library Special Collections, University of Wisconsin-LaCrosse.

This riverbank view shows two former rafters, the *FLYING EAGLE* (second from left) and the *SILVER CRESCENT* (third from left). *FLYING EAGLE* was originally (A) *IRENE D.*, but in 1898 her name was changed and she was converted for excursion work. She was wrecked June 3, 1903 at the Hannibal, Missouri bridge with the loss of at least four lives. The *SILVER CRESCENT* started life in 1881 as a rafter. In 1892 Captain Walter Blair remodeled her as a packet. She was dismantled at Winona in 1909.
Photo courtesy of Murphy Library Special Collections, University of Wisconsin-LaCrosse.

The sidewheel bowboat *FRANK* shown here is about to help guide a lumber raft through a Mississippi River bridge. Owned by George Winans at one time. Converted to a sternwheeler about 1900.
Photo courtesy of Murphy Library Special Collections, University of Wisconsin-LaCrosse.

The Laird, Norton Lumber Company of Winona had the hull of their *FRONTENAC* built at Wabasha in 1896. The completed hull was then taken to Winona and the engines and boilers of the *JUNIATA* were transferred to her and then her cabin was constructed. She was a rafter for eleven years and around 1906 was remodeled for the excursion business out of St. Paul.
Photo courtesy of Murphy Library Special Collections, University of Wisconsin-LaCrosse and Winona County (Minnesota) Historical Society.

The *F. WEYERHAEUSER* was built in 1893 for Weyerhaeuser and Denkmann. Her initial machinery came from the *C. J. CAFFREY*, but was too small, so she was refitted with new engines. She was also a pleasure craft for the Weyerhaeusers for many years. *Photo courtesy of Murphy Library Special Collections, University of Wisconsin-LaCrosse and Winona County (Minnesota) Historical Society.*

Jacksonville, Florida artist Mike Stevens' rendering of the *F. WEYERHAEUSER*, perhaps the most substantial rafter on the river. *Photo courtesy of the Edward A. Mueller collection.*

The *GARDIE EASTMAN* was built at South Stillwater in 1882. She was rebuilt at Rock Island and retained her name, but was given a new registry number. *Photo courtesy of Murphy Library Special Collections, University of Wisconsin-LaCrosse.*

The *GARDIE EASTMAN*. Captains at times on her were Joseph Hawthorne and Joseph Buisson. Sold to do river improvement work. *Photo courtesy of the Joe Dobler Collection.*

The GLENMONT and her bowboat, PARK BLUFF, are returning upriver after delivering a raft. The GLENMONT was built in Dubuque in 1885. After years of service she was condemned in 1905 and many of her components went into the NORTH STAR. The PARK BLUFF was built at Rock Island in 1884 and was named for a summer resort at Muscatine, Iowa. She was in the excursion business starting about 1896. Rebuilt at Wabasha in 1906 and renamed HARRIET. Photo courtesy of Murphy Library Special Collections, University of Wisconsin-LaCrosse.

GOLDEN GATE, at a riverbank, is in the process of hitching to a raft. She was built in Dubuque in 1878 and was later owned by the Van Sants. She was also in the excursion business and ran on the Illinois, Ohio and Kentucky rivers and was dismantled in 1903. Photo courtesy of *Murphy Library Special Collections, University of Wisconsin-LaCrosse.*

GYPSEY was the humblest of bowboats and had started life as (A) LUMBER BOY. Lost at St. Paul in 1907. Photo courtesy of Murphy Library Special Collections, University of Wisconsin-LaCrosse.

HALLIE was the ex-rafter (A) *F. C. A. DENKMANN* and by 1933 was towing barges on the Ohio River. Photo courtesy of Murphy Library Special Collections, University of Wisconsin-LaCrosse.

Formerly the rafter (A) NEPTUNE, HARDWOOD served as a bowboat and was probably also used in excursion work. Photo courtesy of Murphy Library Special Collections, University of Wisconsin-LaCrosse.

The *HENRIETTA* was owned by Durant and Wheeler in 1890 and had been built at Stillwater in 1879 as (A) *I. E. STAPLES*. Toward the end of the century she was in occasional excursion work. She was on the Cumberland River in 1902 and was converted to a towboat in 1909 and dismantled in 1914. Photo courtesy of *Murphy Library Special Collections, University of Wisconsin-LaCrosse.*

INTERSTATE was not a rafter, but parts of the famed *OTTUMWA BELLE* (the steamboat that made the last "official" rafting trip in 1915) were used in building her in 1920 at Rock Island. Used as a towing vessel and also in the construction trade. Sank at Alton, Illinois in December 1929. *Photo courtesy of Murphy Library Special Collections, University of Wisconsin-LaCrosse.*

Captain Dan McDonald named this 1888 vessel INVERNESS after his birthplace in Scotland. Five men were lost on her in May 1888 when she collapsed a flue. After 1902 she towed ties on the Tennessee and Kentucky rivers for a few years.
Photo courtesy of Murphy Library Special Collections, University of Wisconsin-LaCrosse.

The *IRENE D.*, built at Kahlke yard in Rock Island in 1888, was named after the daughter of Captain D. A. Dorrance of LeClaire. Used as a bowboat for the *LIZZIE GARDNER*. Also used as a towboat in 1893 and rebuilt to become (B) *FLYING EAGLE*, an excursion vessel. *Photo courtesy of Murphy Library Special Collections, University of Wisconsin-LaCrosse.*

ISAAC STAPLES was named after a lumber baron in Stillwater who had her built there in 1878. She was sold in 1881 and again in 1884. In 1886 Bronson and Folsom bought her and ran her several years. Some of her better-known captains were: John Hoy, Vincent Peel, Charles B. Roman and William M. Weir. She burned in December 1907 on the ways at Wabasha.
Photo courtesy of Murphy Library Special Collections, University of Wisconsin-LaCrosse.

The *J. C. ATLEE* was built in 1886 at Rock Island by S. and J. C. Atlee and named for the latter. She was later traded to the Parmalee brothers for the *OTTUMWA BELLE*. Went to the lower river in 1895 and was a towboat there. Burned around 1922. Photo courtesy of *Murphy Library Special Collections, University of Wisconsin-LaCrosse*.

The *J. K. GRAVES* was a steel hull rafter built in Dubuque in 1885 for the Matt Clark Transportation Company. Sold to Weyerhaeuser and Denkmann in 1886. Sunk in 1894 on the Upper Rapids, raised and continued to serve.
Photo courtesy of Murphy Library Special Collections, University of Wisconsin-LaCrosse.

The *J. S. KEATOR* started life as (A) *ROBERT ROSS* and was purchased in 1880 by the Keator Lumber Company of Moline. The vessel was sold to Captain L. E. Patton of Memphis in 1900.
Photo courtesy of Murphy Library Special Collections, University of Wisconsin-LaCrosse.

The J. W. MILLS spent the first year of her life towing coal. She was acquired by Clinton's William R. Young Company in 1873. Captain Walter Blair and Samuel Van Sant purchased her in 1883 and in 1894 they traded her to the Parmalee brothers for the CITY OF QUINCY. She was dismantled shortly thereafter and the machinery was used in constructing the OTTUMWA BELLE.
Photo courtesy of Murphy Library Special Collections, University of Wisconsin-LaCrosse and Winona County (Minnesota) Historical Society.

This *J. W. VAN SANT* was the second of her name and was built in LeClaire for the Van Sant and Musser Company. Harry Dyer thought that "she, with the *LYDIA VAN SANT* as a bowboat, made an outfit hard to beat." She burned at Wabasha in December 1907. Photo courtesy of Murphy Library Special Collections, *University of Wisconsin-LaCrosse*.

J. W. VAN SANT (2nd) is shown here helping to raise the *BART E. LINEHAN*.
Photo courtesy of Murphy Library Special Collections, *University of Wisconsin-LaCrosse and Winona County (Minnesota) Historical Society.*

The *JAMES FISK, JR.*, built in Ironton, Ohio in 1870 was in the Cairo-Paducah trade as a towboat. The Van Sants owned her from 1880 to 1886 and used her in rafting. She was dismantled in 1886.
Photo courtesy of Murphy Library Special Collections, University of Wisconsin-LaCrosse.

The *JESSIE B.* was built in Dubuque in 1891 for Captain Volney A. Bigelow and named after his daughter. She was sold to the Staples Towing Company of Stillwater. She was also an excursion vessel when not rafting. Dismantled in 1907. *Photo courtesy of Murphy Library Special Collections, University of Wisconsin-LaCrosse.*

The JO LONG was one of the fastest rafting steamboats on the river in her time. She was placed in the packet trade in 1895 (Rock Island to Clinton) and sold in 1898 to Vicksburg, Mississippi interests. Her name was changed to (B) PROVIDENCE. Photo courtesy of Murphy Library Special Collections, University of Wisconsin-LaCrosse.

A close-up of the JOHN H. RICH. The famed Mayo Brothers obtained her as part of an investment settlement and converted her to a pleasure vessel, ORONOCO. The JOHN M. RICH had started life as (A) E. RUTLEDGE in 1892 at Rock Island. Photo courtesy of Murphy Library Special Collections, University of Wisconsin-LaCrosse and Omstead County Historical Society.

A side view of the JOHN H. RICH while underway.
Photo courtesy of Murphy Library Special Collections, University of Wisconsin-LaCrosse.

Owned by two **R**ichtman brothers and their father, the *J. M. RICHTMAN* was built at Sterling Island, Illinois in 1899. She was renamed (**B**) *CONQUEST* in June 1904. *Photo courtesy of Murphy Library Special Collections, University of Wisconsin-LaCrosse.*

The unpretentious *JULIA* was built at Winona in 1871. Originally owned by Laird, Norton and Company and sold to George Winans in 1884. Lost by ice at Rock Island, March 24, 1893.
Photo courtesy of Murphy Library Special Collections, University of Wisconsin-LaCrosse.

The JUNIATA was a Laird, Norton craft built in 1889 at Winona. Later owned by Bronson and Folsom. She was sold in 1904 and became the packet RED WING (St. Paul —Wabasha).
Photo courtesy of Murphy Library Special Collections, University of Wisconsin-LaCrosse.

Bronson and Folsom owned and rafted the JUNIATA for 12 years (1895–1907). Harry Dyer was her mate in 1898, 1899 and 1902. Photo courtesy of Murphy Library Special Collections, University of Wisconsin-LaCrosse.

KIT CARSON was one of the most powerful river rafters and was built at South Stillwater in 1880. She was named for the daughter of one of the owners (Carson and Rand), not the famed frontier scout. She was owned by many of the well-known rafting companies. She was dismantled in 1916 at Memphis. Photo courtesy of Murphy Library Special Collections, University of Wisconsin-LaCrosse.

The *KIT CARSON* shown here with Captain William Dobler in the pilot house circa 1900–1904. *Photo courtesy of the Joe Dobler Collection.*

The LACROSSE had been built in 1889 as (A) RAVENNA and was sold in 1908 for use as a packet between LaCrosse and Wabasha. Photo courtesy of Murphy Library Special Collections, University of Wisconsin-LaCrosse.

The *LADY GRACE* was an 1881, Clinton-built rafter owned by Chancy Lamb and Sons. She was named for Chancy's granddaughter. She was sold in 1896 to Captain William Davis of Rock Island and sold a year later to government contractors. In 1915 her hull was cut in two and used as hulls for two quarter boats. *Photo courtesy of Murphy Library Special Collections, University of Wisconsin-LaCrosse and Winona County (Minnesota) Historical Society.*

The bowboat *LAFAYETTE LAMB*, shown here with a large raft, was built in 1874 in Clinton. The Lambs sold her in 1891 and in 1899 she was sold to Bronson and Folsom. They used her for one season with the *ISAAC STAPLES* and then dismantled her. *Photo courtesy of Murphy Library Special Collections, University of Wisconsin-LaCrosse.*

The *LAFAYETTE LAMB* was named for one of Chancy Lamb's sons, Lafayette, who died in a train wreck in 1901 and left an estate of seven million dollars. *Photo courtesy of Murphy Library Special Collections, University of Wisconsin-LaCrosse.*

The *LAST CHANCE* was Captain Walter Blair's first command. Samuel Van Sant and Blair acquired her in 1881. She had been built in 1870 at Burlington, Iowa. In 1884 she went to South Dakota and was lost in 1899.
Photo courtesy of Murphy Library Special Collections, University of Wisconsin-LaCrosse and Winona County (Minnesota) Historical Society.

An 1866 Dubuque-built rafter, the *LECLAIRE* is shown here at the end of her days. She was involved in an 1879 collision with the *VICTORY* near Muscatine and sank, a total loss. She was towed to Rock Island and dismantled.
Photo courtesy of Murphy Library Special Collections, University of Wisconsin-LaCrosse.

The LITTLE EAGLE came to the upper Mississippi in 1870, having been built in Madison, Indiana in 1868. Purchased by McDonald Brothers in 1875. Struck a drawbridge at Hannibal in 1882 and was a total loss. Three men drowned. *Photo courtesy of Murphy Library Special Collections, University of Wisconsin-LaCrosse.*

The *LIZZIE GARDNER* was a Cincinnati-built rafter (1871). She rafted on the Ohio and Kanawha rivers for a time and then came to the Mississippi. She burned in 1908 or 1909 due to a careless fire while laid up.
Photo courtesy of Murphy Library Special Collections, University of Wisconsin-LaCrosse.

One of the smallest rafters was the sixty-eight foot LONE STAR, built in 1868 at Lyons, Iowa. She ran on the Allegheny River initially and was brought to the Mississippi as a rafter by Durant and Wheeler. Later owned by Knapp, Stout and Company and McDonald Brothers. Dismantled at LaCrosse in 1891. *Photo courtesy of Murphy Library Special Collections, University of Wisconsin-LaCrosse.*

The *LOTUS* was a rafter for ten years and was usually a bowboat (seen here going through a swing-span railroad bridge). Built at Rock Island in 1893. In 1904 she was on the Green River in Kentucky.
Photo courtesy of Murphy Library Special Collections, University of Wisconsin-LaCrosse.

The *LOUISVILLE* was an 1864 Pennsylvania vessel brought to the Mississippi by Durant and Wheeler. She was later sold to the McDonald Brothers. *Photo courtesy of Murphy Library Special Collections, University of Wisconsin-LaCrosse.*

The 1866 Oshkosh-built LUMBERMAN was an early sternwheel rafter, which probably came to the Mississippi in the early 1870s. Used by Cairo, Illinois owners to tow lumber by barge to that port.
Photo courtesy of Murphy Library Special Collections, University of Wisconsin-LaCrosse.

An early rafting sidewheeler, the *L. W. BARDEN* was an 1864 vessel built in Berlin, Wisconsin. Captains Joseph and Cyprian Buisson were mates on her. She was dismantled in 1881 at Dubuque.
Photo courtesy of Murphy Library Special Collections, University of Wisconsin-LaCrosse.

The *L. W. CRANE* was an 1865 sidewheel rafter. Shown here in a famous line-up of steamboats at Reads Landing. Dismantled in 1881. *Photo courtesy of Murphy Library Special Collections, University of Wisconsin-LaCrosse.*

The *LYDIA VAN SANT* (in foreground) and the *J. W. VAN SANT* (2nd) with a pleasure vessel in their company. *LYDIA VAN SANT* was the usual bowboat with the *J. W. VAN SANT* and was built in 1898 at LeClaire as (A) *NETTA DURANT*. She was later chartered to the Taber Lumber Company for ten years. *Photo courtesy of Murphy Library Special Collections, University of Wisconsin-LaCrosse.*

The *LYDIA VAN SANT* as a bowboat with a raft going through a double-track railroad swing bridge. She had been rebuilt from the (A) *NETTA DURANT*. Photo courtesy of Murphy Library Special Collections, University of Wisconsin-LaCrosse.

The *LYDIA VAN SANT* shown bow-on.
Photo courtesy of Murphy Library Special Collections, University of Wisconsin-LaCrosse.

The *MARS*, shown here after a sinking, probably in August 1912 at Winona, was owned by Captain George Winans for a time. Winans liked to name his rafters after planets. She was built in 1902 at Lyons, Iowa and towed logs from St. Paul to lower river points for many years. *Photo courtesy of Murphy Library Special Collections, University of Wisconsin-LaCrosse.*

A lad poses in front of the *MARY B.* Built as (A) *ETHEL HOWARD* at Lake City, Minnesota in 1890. She burned on the Wolf River, Tennessee in August 1915. *Photo courtesy of Murphy Library Special Collections, University of Wisconsin-LaCrosse.*

The *MARY B.* shown rafting a combined log and lumber raft.
Photo courtesy of Murphy Library Special Collections, *University of Wisconsin-LaCrosse.*

The 1896 *MASCOT*, shown here at a river bank, supposedly sunk. This rafter was sold to C. H. Deere of Moline in 1899 who converted her to a pleasure craft. Burned at Kahlke Yard, Rock Island in April 1900.
Photo courtesy of Murphy Library Special Collections, University of Wisconsin-LaCrosse.

The diminutive *MAUD*, built at Wabasha in 1890. Sold to Tennessee River interests circa 1896. *Photo courtesy of Murphy Library Special Collections, University of Wisconsin-LaCrosse.*

The *MENOMONIE* had a fifteen-year career. An 1880 Madison, Indiana product, she was owned initially by the Knapp, Stout Company and later by the Matt Clark Transportation Company of Stillwater. Sold to Bronson and Folsom circa 1883. In that year she took a 192' wide by 576' long lumber raft from Reads Landing to Alton, Illinois in six days, four hours, non-stop. Some of her well-known pilots and masters were Stephen B. Withrow, Robert N. Cassidy, "Deck" Dixon, and D. Dorrance. *Photo courtesy of Murphy Library Special Collections, University of Wisconsin-LaCrosse.*

Captain E. E. Heerman named this vessel *MINNIETTA* after his daughter, a combination of her two names. Completed in LaCrosse in 1871. Rafted from Beef Slough to St. Louis and at times a daily trip from Reads Landing to Eau Claire, Wisconsin. Later taken to North Dakota and destroyed. *Photo courtesy of Murphy Library Special Collections, University of Wisconsin-LaCrosse.*

Built in 1880 at Cincinnati, this rafter, *MOLINE*, was in charge of Captain Isaac Wasson when she came out. About 1900 she was an excursion steamboat on the Missouri River. In 1908 she was renamed (B) *EMERSON* and towed the showboat *GRAND FLOATING PALACE*. *Photo courtesy of Murphy Library Special Collections, University of Wisconsin-LaCrosse.*

As her name might imply, the *MOUNTAIN BELLE* was originally a packet on West Virginia's Kanawha River. Four years after her 1869 Pittsburgh construction she was brought to the Mississippi and converted to a rafter. She was renamed (B) *THE PURCHASE* around 1902. She was dismantled at Wabasha in 1911. *Photo courtesy of Murphy Library Special Collections, University of Wisconsin-LaCrosse.*

The *MUSSER* was built at LeClaire in 1886 for the Van Sant and Musser Towing Company. Captain Walter Blair bought her in 1907 and put a new hull under her and ran her as the packet *KEOKUK* for fifteen years. *Photo courtesy of Murphy Library Special Collections, University of Wisconsin-LaCrosse and Winona County (Minnesota) Historical Society.*

The *MUSSER* with a large excursion group is seen here at LaCrosse, Wisconsin; note the wharf boat at left. *Photo courtesy of Murphy Library Special Collections, University of Wisconsin-LaCrosse.*

A Fourth of July excursion. The photo of the MUSSER was originally sold by the LeClaire Drug Company, a publisher of steamboat post cards for many decades. *Photo courtesy of Murphy Library Special Collections, University of Wisconsin-LaCrosse and LaCrosse County Historical Society.*

NATRONA had a varied career from her construction in Pittsburgh in 1863 until the early 1870s when she was purchased by the McDonalds for rafting. She sank in 1891 near East Dubuque.
Photo courtesy of Murphy Library Special Collections, University of Wisconsin-LaCrosse.

Another one of Captain George Winans' "planet" steamboats was his *NEPTUNE* of 1900. After a few years in rafting she towed out of the Green River and in 1910 was renamed *HARDWOOD*.
Photo courtesy of Murphy Library Special Collections, University of Wisconsin-LaCrosse and Tulane University.

An 1881 Durant and Wheeler craft was the NETTA DURANT. By 1883 she was owned by the Clinton Lumber Company. She was rebuilt in 1898 and became the LYDIA VAN SANT (owned by Van Sant and Musser). Photo courtesy of Murphy Library Special Collections, University of Wisconsin-LaCrosse and Winona County (Minnesota) Historical Society.

NINA was an 1881 rafter built near Stillwater. In 1890 one of her owners was Mrs. Ida S. Lachmund, one of the few women in the rafting trade. Burned at Clinton in June 1894.
Photo courtesy of Murphy Library Special Collections, University of Wisconsin-LaCrosse.

One of the last rafters was the 1906 Dubuque-built *NORTH STAR*, which had parts of the *GLENMONT* used in her construction. Photo courtesy of *Murphy Library Special Collections, University of Wisconsin-LaCrosse.*

The NORTH STAR was renamed (B) EUGENIA TULLY, and later, (C) COMMANDER.
Photo courtesy of Murphy Library Special Collections, University of Wisconsin-LaCrosse.

Artist Mike Stevens' rendering of the NORTH STAR. She was built in 1906 at Dubuque and was one of the last rafters. Captain William Dobler was her initial master.
Drawing courtesy of the Edward A. Mueller Collection.

The COMMANDER was formerly the rafter (A) NORTH STAR. As the COMMANDER she was lost in 1929, sinking at Booneville, Missouri. Photo courtesy of Murphy Library Special Collections, University of Wisconsin-LaCrosse and Cincinnati/Hamilton Public Library.

PARK BLUFF was an 1884 Rock Island steamboat. She was the bowboat to the *GLENMONT*. She was in the excursion business in 1896 and rebuilt in 1906 at Wabasha and renamed *HARRIET*.
Photo courtesy of Murphy Library Special Collections, University of Wisconsin-LaCrosse.

The 1878 PAULINE was a Durant and Wheeler steamboat. They sold her in 1880 to Captains D. C. Law and Al Hollingshead. In 1888 she was in the packet trade between Burlington and Keithsburg for two years and was later placed back in the rafting business. She was a packet again in 1894. In 1898 she was rebuilt and became COLUMBIA and later was owned by Henry Flagler who used her in building the Overseas Railroad to Key West. *Photo courtesy of Murphy Library Special Collections, University of Wisconsin-LaCrosse.*

The rafter PAULINE (circa 1885) by artist Mike Stevens. She was owned at this time by Captains J. M. Turner and Al Hollingshead who painted the two "eyes" on her forward bulkheads.
Drawing courtesy of the Edward A. Mueller Collection.

PHIL SCHAECKEL was built at Waubeck, Wisconsin for Knapp, Stout and Company. Used as a bowboat for the *B. HERSHEY*. Shown here going through a swing bridge. Photo courtesy of Murphy Library Special Collections, *University of Wisconsin-LaCrosse*.

The PHIL SCHECKEL was rebuilt in 1896–97 from the former PHIL SCHAECKEL. Named for a prominent Knapp, Stout employee. A few years after her rebuilding at Wabasha she was sold to Captain Samuel R. Van Sant in 1901–2. In 1905 she was sold to Henry Flagler and worked over a decade on the Overseas Railroad to Key West. She was modified extensively for this work.
Photo courtesy of Murphy Library Special Collections, University of Wisconsin-LaCrosse.

A side view of the *PHIL SCHECKEL* showing her at a bank: note the skylights for her lower deck. *Photo courtesy of the Joe Dobler Collection.*

The *PHIL SCHECKEL* as seen on the Mississippi in 1880.
Photo courtesy of the Edward A. Mueller Collection.

The *PHIL SCHECKEL* in Florida in 1914 helping to build the Overseas Railroad to Key West for Henry Flagler. A large quarters for personnel has been erected on the top deck and the pilot house has been shifted forward. *Photo courtesy of the Edward A. Mueller Collection.*

Built at Prescott, Wisconsin in 1870, this steamboat, *PRESCOTT*, was one of the initial bowboats. For her first few years she worked as a short-line packet. She was finally owned by Weyerhaeuser and Denkmann and used as a bowboat.
Photo courtesy of Murphy Library Special Collections, University of Wisconsin-LaCrosse.

Built in 1893 at Dubuque, this vessel, QUICKSTEP (at right), was owned by Captain Volney A. Bigelow of LaCrosse. (The *BELLA MAC* is at the left.) *QUICKSTEP* was usually a bowboat for the *BART E. LINEHAN*. By 1901 she was towing logs on rivers in Arkansas and she burned in June 1906. *Photo courtesy of Murphy Library Special Collections, University of Wisconsin-LaCrosse.*

The *R. J. WHEELER* was built for Durant and Wheeler in 1880. Ten years later she was sold to Captain William Davis who used her in towing. Harry Dyer said, "she was built low between decks so as not to catch the wind, was large and roomy in the deckroom and fire box, had good power with three boilers and was light on fuel." *Photo courtesy of Murphy Library Special Collections, University of Wisconsin-LaCrosse.*

The rafter *R. J. WHEELER* with her stacks partially dismantled. She had raised letters on her sides near the stern. *Photo courtesy of Murphy Library Special Collections, University of Wisconsin-LaCrosse.*

The *RED WING* started life as (A) *JUNIATA* in 1889. She was renamed (B) *RED WING* circa 1906–7. She then was in the Wabasha-St. Paul packet trade. She towed an excursion barge, *MANITOU*, for many years and finally burned in December 1926. *Photo courtesy of Murphy Library Special Collections, University of Wisconsin-LaCrosse.*

The 1880 Dubuque-built rafter/packet REINDEER was a rafter for her first eight or nine years. In the fall of 1897 she was a tri-weekly packet, Dubuque to Clinton. She was rebuilt in 1901 at Quincy and was then the ILLINOIS of the Illinois Fish Commission. *Photo courtesy of Murphy Library Special Collections, University of Wisconsin-LaCrosse.*

The *ROBERT DODDS* was an 1882, Stillwater-built rafter and was owned by Schulenberg and Boeckler for ten years. She then towed for the firm under different owners for another four or five seasons.
Photo courtesy of Murphy Library Special Collections, University of Wisconsin-LaCrosse.

The *ROBERT DODDS* was owned and managed by Mrs. Ida Moore Lachmund of Clinton for six years. In 1909 she towed showboats. She ended her days as a coal towboat and was dismantled circa 1919.
Photo courtesy of Murphy Library Special Collections, University of Wisconsin-LaCrosse.

The *RUBY* was Harry G. Dyer's first steamboat. This photo of the DeSoto, Wisconsin-built craft of 1882 shows her as fitted for the packet trade. *Photo courtesy of the Minnesota Historical Society.*

This photo displays the *RUTH* just behind another vessel at right. She was built at Wabasha in 1892 and owned by Captain Samuel Van Sant for several years. *Photo courtesy of Murphy Library Special Collections, University of Wisconsin-LaCrosse.*

A side view of the RUTH.
Photo courtesy of Murphy Library Special Collections, University of Wisconsin-LaCrosse.

This group of steamboats is on the ways at Kahlke's Yard in winter lay-up. Left to right—TEN BROECK, ECLIPSE, NETTA DURANT (obscured), SAM ATLEE and an unknown vessel.
Photo courtesy of Murphy Library Special Collections, *University of Wisconsin-LaCrosse.*

The *ST. CROIX* ran on her namesake river as a packet for two years. Captain George Winans ran her thirteen seasons in the rafting trade. Bought by Samuel Van Sant and Walter Blair in 1887. Dismantled in 1894 after sinking near Dubuque and her machinery was placed in the *QUICKSTEP*. Photo courtesy of Murphy Library Special Collections, University of Wisconsin-LaCrosse.

A George Winans rafter, *SATELLITE*, built in 1890 at Rock Island. Used primarily as a bowboat. Sold "south" and capsized in a storm on the Mississippi in February 1917, no lives lost.
Photo courtesy of Murphy Library Special Collections, University of Wisconsin-LaCrosse.

PATHFINDER (foreground) and *OTTUMWA BELLE* on one of their last rafting trips. Photo courtesy of Murphy Library Special Collections, University of Wisconsin-LaCrosse and Winona County (Minnesota) Historical Society.

The *OTTUMWA BELLE* had the distinction of being the last rafter. In August 1915 she took the last lumber raft from Hudson, Wisconsin to the Atlee Mills at Fort Madison, Iowa. This last raft was 128 feet wide and 1,150 feet long. *PATHFINDER* was the bowboat on this historic trip. Photo courtesy of Murphy Library Special Collections, University of Wisconsin-LaCrosse.

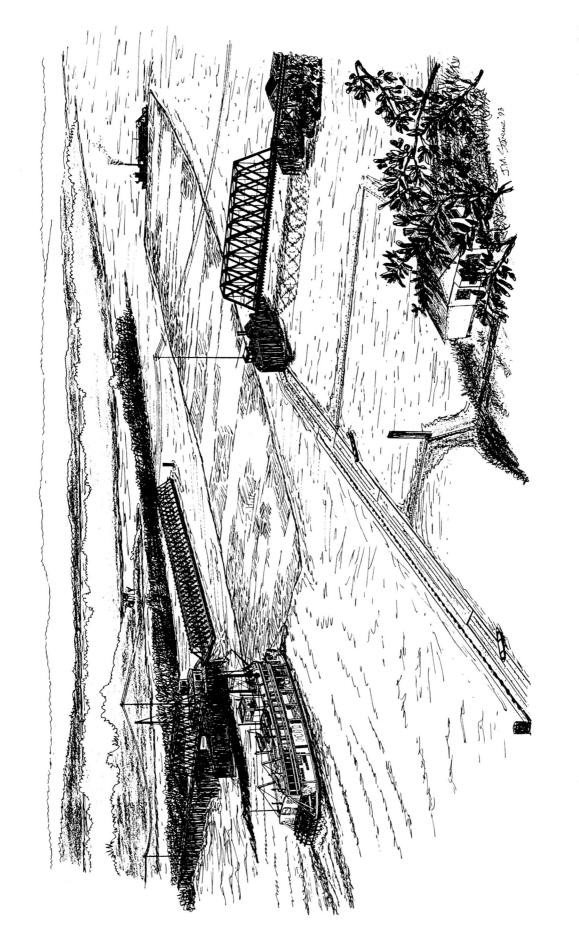

Artist Mike Stevens depiction of the rafter *OTTUMWA BELLE* and her raft passing through the CMSP&P railroad's pontoon bridge in 1915—"the last raft." View is from an overlook at Marquette, Iowa, Wisconsin is in the background. *Drawing courtesy of Edward A. Mueller Collection.*

RAFTING STEAMBOAT HISTORIES

x 2.9'. She was converted to a sternwheeler and rebuilt around 1900. Then she was 31 tons, 78.4' x 22.4' x 5.0'. Crew of three. Owned at one time by George Winans, and used as a bowboat; was in 1905 registry (Memphis). She sank two miles below Cairo, Illinois and had a showboat in tow at the time containing the James C. Moore theatrical company.

FRITZ #120982

Used engines (13" diameter cylinders, 6' piston stroke) from rafter *LUMBERMAN*, which had been dismantled 1893-94. Used as a bowboat, and was 153 tons, 120' x 26' x 4'. Built at Jeffersonville in 1894, 230 h.p. Captain Lon C. Fullis, master in 1894. Exploded a steam line near Cairo on August 19, 1897; nine men died; $6,000 loss to *FRITZ*. Sank in November 1901 in Mississippi River and raised. In Pittsburgh 1906-1907 was rebuilt and renamed *(B) RESCUE*.

FRONTENAC #121018

Sternwheel rafter built 1896 at Wabasha by Samuel Peters for the Laird, Norton Lumber Company of Winona. She was of 146 tons, 138.9' x 29.8' x 5.0'. After the hull was built, it was taken to Winona where the engines and boilers of the *JUNIATA* were transferred to her. The cabin was built at Winona. Her engines were 16" diameter cylinders, 5' piston stroke. Towed for Laird, Norton between West Newton, Stillwater and Winona for eleven years. Henry Slocumb was master; Robert Cassidy pilot; and William McCraney, chief engineer for most of this period.

Around 1906 when the lumber was "sawed out," she was remodeled for the excursion business, working out of St. Paul. As a passenger vessel, had crew of ten and was of 500 h.p. Around 1912 sold to the St. Charles Amusement Company of St. Charles, Minnesota, who converted her into an excursion boat. Captain Henry F. Slocumb, 1912; Captain R. H. Trombley, 1913; Captain Charles White, 1914. Frank Utter was chief engineer those years. She collided with the lower Winona bridge and sank to her middle deck. Raised and sold to Captain Walter Wisherd who renamed her *(B) PRINCE*.

G

GARDIE EASTMAN #88720

Sternwheel rafter. Built 1882 at South Stillwater in 1882 by C. W. Batchelder. 100 tons, 100 tons, 111.5' x 20.7' x 3.7'. Owned by Gardiner Batchelder and Wells of Lyons, Iowa. Engines were 12" diameter cylinders, 6' piston stroke. Joseph Buisson, captain 1882-1889; Captain Joseph Hawthorne, 1890 to 1893; Captain John Moore, 1893-1896 when he went to the Yukon River. Joseph Fuller was chief engineer with Captain Buisson and Palmer Smith of Maiden Rock, Wisconsin, was chief engineer with Captain Hawthorne. In the spring of 1894, she "went through herself" at the Santa Fe Island (near Savanna, Illinois). A wrist pin broke and piston head, piston rod, and pitman went overboard.

She was rebuilt at Rock Island in 1903 and given a new number, #86659. However, she was basically the same size—112' x 22' x 3.7'. Snagged and sunk below Keokuk in July 1913, but soon raised. She was sold to Fetter and Crosby, government contractors, and used in river improvement work in the 1910s and 1920s. She was rebuilt at the Kahlke yard. After Captain Fetter died in July 1920, the *GARDIE EASTMAN* was sold to the McWilliams Dredging Company. In 1922 she was at Shreveport on the Red River. She was rebuilt at Madison, Indiana in 1926 and renamed *McWILLIAMS*.

GAZELLE #86556

Sternwheel towboat/rafter. Built Wabasha, 1901. 87 tons, 87 tons, 124' x 23.2' x 3.9'. Had crew of ten. In June 1904, went to Wheeling, West Virginia to tow transfer barges. On February 12, 1905 while at Wheeling and owned by the Baltimore and Ohio Railroad, she got caught in heavy ice and turned over. She was rebuilt as *(B) CLERIMOND*.

GEORGIE S. #140686

Sternwheel rafter. 37 tons, 37 tons, 82.5' x 18.5' x 3.5'. Built as *(A) LINE HANSON* at Savanna, Illinois. Engines 9" diameter cylinders, 4' piston stroke. In 1911-12, she was towing logs for the Taber Lumber Co. of Keokuk. In 1913 sold to William Lewis of St. Louis, and he in turn sold her in September 1914 to the Meramec Sand Company of St. Louis. In October 1914, towed for the City, Captain John Lewis in command.

GLENMONT #85878

Sternwheel rafter. Built at Dubuque in 1885, using the 15" diameter cylinders, 5' piston stroke engines from the old packet *IDA FULTON*. Van Sant and Musser of Muscatine, Iowa, bought her from the Laird, Norton Company of Winona. She was 92 tons, 92 tons, 128' x 24.6' x 4.6'. In 1892 John O'Connor was master and pilot and Herman Auding was engineer. In 1893 Captain John O'Connor, in attempting to "head out" from the levee at Lacrosse, found he couldn't do it. He should have blown his whistle to open the bridge, but instead turned a "cart wheel" above the bridge. The *GLENMONT* hit the draw bridge pier and the vessel sank in eighteen feet of water. It cost $3,500 to raise her. After years of service as a rafter, she was condemned in 1905. At Eagle Point (Dubuque), the cabin, engines and boilers were transferred to a new hull built by

Captain John Killeen. The combination that resulted was renamed *NORTH STAR* (new registry number).

GOLDEN GATE   #85535

Sternwheel rafter. Built at Dubuque, 1878. 142 tons, 142 tons, 131.4' x 30' x 4'. Her engines, 14" diameter cylinders, 4' piston stroke, were from the packet *JAMES MEANS* (built at Wheeling, West Virginia in 1860). Built by J. H. S. Coleman and his brothers James and Andrew. George Rutherford was also a part owner until 1888 when he sold his interest. He was also master much of this time. The *GOLDEN GATE* was later owned by J. W. Van Sant, Samuel Van Sant and John McCaffrey.

Captain J. M. Turner was on her in 1881–82 running Chippewa Lumber and Boom Company rafts to Hannibal and St. Louis. James and Andrew Coleman were good pilots and also rapids pilots. James Coleman moved to Portland, Oregon in 1909 and died there in 1913, seventy-three years old. Andrew Coleman died at the wheel of the *LIBBIE CONGER* on the Upper Rapids on April 24, 1895. The *GOLDEN GATE* was an elegant looking rafter with cabin skylights and a nice sheer. Under the Colemans, she also ran in the excursion trade between Davenport and Rock Island.

In 1895 the Missouri River Commission bought her at Memphis. In 1899 she was bought by Captain G. M. Sivley of the Illinois River. He ran her a season or two and sold her to Captain W. E. Pratt of Madison, Indiana. She then became a Louisville-Kentucky packet and also ran in the Cincinnati-Madison trade as an independent. She was sold in 1903 for $600 and dismantled on the Kentucky River.

GYPSEY   #141128

Sternwheel rafter. 55 tons, 55 tons, 78.3' x 15.6' x 4.0'. Lost at St. Paul, 1907, (LMV). Formerly *(A) LUMBER BOY*.

GUSSIE GIRDON   #10908

Sternwheel towboat. Built Burlington in 1867. 53 tons, 53 tons. 89.8' x 18.3' x 3.4'. Also erroneously documented as *GUSSIE GORDON* and *GUSSIE GUIDEN*. Named for daughter of Captain George W. Girdon of Galena. In 1874 she was running from Galena to Bellevue and also to Dubuque, Dunleith and Cassville.

In April 1878, it was noted that, "Hanson and Linehan sold the *GUSSIE GIRDON* to H. S. Shultz of Portage, Wisconsin, for $2,000 or thereabout. Rumor is she goes to Wisconsin River to be used by the government in improving that stream." Abandoned in 1889.

H

H. C. BROCKMAN   #96307

Sternwheel towboat. Built in 1895 at Rock Island, Illinois. 75 tons, 75 tons, 90.6' x 22.6' x 3.8'. Had engines of old rafter *NINA*. Bowboat for *F. C. A. DENKMANN* in 1896 when she made her record large raft trip. Sank twenty-five miles below Arkansas City on the Missouri River in December 1911. In records as registered at Memphis in 1913, had crew of ten.

HALLIE   #120445

Sternwheel (ex-rafter). 120' x 32'. Engines were 14" diameter cylinders, 6' piston stroke. Originally *(A) F. C. A. DENKMANN, (B) WABASH, (C) ANNIE H*. Captain Charles Wilcox bought WABASH from the Chicago Mill and Lumber Company of Helena, Arkansas, March 1933. Renamed her *(D) HALLIE* for his wife, wanted to form a barge line. Captain Loyal Wright bought *HALLIE* in October 1934, after losing the *GERARD KLEIN* by fire. *HALLIE* sank at St. Joe below Cincinnati in February 1938.

HARDWOOD   #130850

Originally *(A) NEPTUNE*, built Lyons, Iowa, 1900. 102' x 23' x 4'. Engines 12" diameter cylinders, 4' piston stroke. Renamed *(B) HARDWOOD* in 1910. In 1929 was homeported at Memphis. Worked in log trades shoving barges and possibly handled excursions. Abandoned 1933.

HARTFORD   #95687

Sternwheel packet/rafter. Built 1869, Evansville, Indiana. Local trade packet around Evansville. 94 tons. Sold at U.S. marshal's sale in 1872 to Samuel Van Sant and others. Henry Buisson, master, 1872. Sank in 1873 at LeClaire. In service as a rafter in Beef Slough area. Cabin was placed on *D. A. McDONALD* in 1873, which had lost hers in an explosion. In 1877 she was in operation for Chancy Lamb & Sons, Clinton, Iowa. Rebuilt 1882, Wabasha, Minnesota by M. J. Godfrey. 91 tons, 91 tons, 114' x 22.4' x 4.8'. Owned by Mississippi River Logging Company, Clinton, Iowa. Captain Stephen Hanks was master at one time; Clair C. Fuller and Eugene Fuller were chief engineers. In 1883 Henry Buisson, master. Dismantled at Wabasha in 1896 and machinery put into a new boat, *E. DOUGLASS*.

HELEN MAR   #95332

Sternwheel rafter. Built 1872 Osceola, Wisconsin by Captain William Kent and John Dudley. Captain Kent used her in the packet trade on the St. Croix River, Stillwater to Taylors Falls, 133 tons, 133 tons, 120' x 23' x 4'. Engines were 12" diameter cylinders by 4½' piston stroke. Built by Corming and DePue of Stillwater. Sold to Knapp, Stout and Company in 1880. William R. Slocumb of Albany, Illinois

RAFTING STEAMBOAT HISTORIES

and John Wooders were her captains during this time. In 1890 she was sold to McDonald Brothers. They sold her to the Staples Towing Company of Stillwater in 1894. She was dismantled at North LaCrosse, 1904.

C. N. Edwards reported this incident concerning the *HELEN MAR*. "When Captain W. R. Slocumb, frequently called 'Young Will,' because his uncle, W. W. Slocumb, was known as 'Old Will,' was master and first pilot of the *HELEN MAR* then owned and operated by Knapp, Stout and Company, he had a night watchman by the name of Pete Colby. Pete was Captain William Young's brother-in-law, a good night watchman and fine little fellow and ran with Young Will for years . . . Capt. Slocumb left Reads Landing with the *MAR* hitched to a large lumber raft. I think he had fourteen strings, sixteen cribs long, and the water was low. I clerked on two steamers run by Capt. Slocumb and know he was a fine pilot and very successful, but he was of a nervous temperament and when he hit an island or tried to knock out a bridge pier he would show his temper with a good deal of emphasis and his expressions wouldn't sound good in church.

"So one day on this trip the bow of his raft got too near an island and tore off a chunk, Capt. Will was at the wheel and though he had a wonderful command of language he could not make the men understand what he wanted to do from the pilot house. The ringing of bells and blowing of whistles created such a commotion that it disturbed the slumbers of the watchman, Pete Colby, and he started for the bow. When he got down to check the works he began to get instructions from the pilot house which he could not hear and he turned around and told the captain to go to hell, and he went down to help the boys. They soon got lines across and windlassed up the cribs without loss of lumber in very little time and were again on their way down the river as though nothing had happened, and Colby started back to the boat to get another nap. When he reached the boiler deck Captain Slocumb said, 'Pete, come up here.' Pete started to go up to the pilot house meek as Moses, expecting his discharge, and said, 'Captain, what do you want?' Will said, 'I want to kiss you, You are the only damn man that said a word to me in that mixup.'"

HELENE SCHULENBURG #95297

Sternwheel rafter. Built 1874, Metropolis, Illinois. 107 tons, 107 tons, 130.3' x 35.4' x 3.7'. Owned by Schulenburg & Boeckler of St. Louis. She cost $16,000. Had two boilers, 42" diameter by 26' long. Engines were 15" diameter cylinders, 5' piston stroke. Captain Robert Dodds was the usual master, E. J. Chacey in 1883 and 1890, Charles Brasser, master in 1893. After her rafting days were over, she was in excursion work for Captain John McCaffrey and sons. Sank at Credit Island and dismantled at Rock Island, 1897, or slightly thereafter.

HENRIETTA #76076

Sternwheel. 95 tons, 95 tons. 130' x 24' x 4.3'. Built Stillwater, 1879. Originally *(A) I. E. STAPLES, (B) DAVID BRONSON*, renamed *(C) HENRIETTA*, circa 1889. Owned by Durant and Wheeler, Stillwater, in 1890, Thomas Hoy, master. Captain R. J. Wheeler, master, 1891. Listed as rafter, February 1893. In 1897 she made an excursion to Mankato, indicating she may have been a packet then. Upper river rafting personnel were Captain I. H. Short, 1889; Henry Peavey, captain and pilot, 1890; John Woodburn, captain, 1894; George Brasser and Asa Woodward, captains, 1896; George Carey, captain, 1897. Engineers were A. M. Dansbury in 1889 and Ira Fuller and George Griffin for several seasons. By 1901 in Cairo-Hickman trade in June.

In 1902 she was an excursion boat at Sioux City and Omaha. Captain Shep Greene bought her in winter 1902 for Cumberland River, Dover to Nashville. Captain W. L. Berry of Paducah converted her into a towboat in 1909, ran in the crosstie trade. Dismantled in 1914, machinery used in building the towboat *HIBERNIA*.

HIRAM PRICE #11898

Sternwheel rafter. Built 1867 LeClaire. 26 tons, 35 h.p. Built for C. B. & Q. Railroad. Had a patent upright boiler. On her trial trip to Oquakwa, crew went to dinner and let her steam "to test the boilers." When they returned, she was a wreck. The head of the boiler and upper works were gone as the boiler had exploded. She was brought to Burlington and repaired and put back to work. She was underpowered and sold, being replaced by the *STERLING*. She was purchased by John and James Brewer and put into the Chippewa rafting trade in charge of Captain John Brewer. Later, Decker Dixon was captain, and James Brewer in 1879.

HORACE H. #140457

Sternwheel rafter. Built 1881 in Wabasha as *(A) LITTLE HODDIE*. 40 tons, 40 tons, 83.7' x 13.5' x 2.7'. Thomas Fandree, captain, 1888; Frank Fandree, 1894; John T. Goodrich, 1897; Isaac Brooks, 1898; H. C. Powell, 1901; Pearl Roundy, engineer for a time.

I

I. E. STAPLES #76076

Sternwheel rafter. Built 1879, Stillwater. 95 tons, 95 tons, 130' x 24' x 4.3'. Named for Isaac Edwin Staples. Had part of machinery of *WYMAN X*. I. E. Staples was the son of Isaac Staples. Sold to Matt Clark Towing Company in 1883. Matt Clark was the son-in-law of

Isaac Staples. David Bronson was vice president. John Hoy was master of *I. E. STAPLES* for most of the time she ran for the Staples Lumber Company, 1879-1883. Renamed *(B) DAVID BRONSON* circa 1883. In 1889 renamed *(C) HENRIETTA*. Erroneously listed as *"J. E." STAPLES* for many years.

IDA FULTON   #12146

Sternwheel freight boat/rafter. Built at Cincinnati. Originally was built in 1863 as *(A) CONVOY NO. 2*. 281 tons, 165' x 36' x 4.6'. Engines were 14" diameter cylinders with 4.6' piston stroke. Her two boilers were 42" diameter, 16' long. Sold U.S. Quartermaster Department on January 12, 1864 and redocumented as *(B) IDA FULTON* by January 29, 1867 when sold to private parties. In 1869, 1870, and 1871, she was in charge of Abe Mitchell, Stephen Hanks, pilot. In 1875 the Diamond Jo Line sold her to Captain Charles Meads who used her to tow grain for ten years. Rebuilt by Captain Meads at Dubuque and came out as *GLENMONT*, given new registry number.

INTERSTATE   #219692

Sternwheel. Built from parts of the *OTTUMWA BELLE* at the Kahlke Yard, Rock Island in 1920. 114' x 23' x 3.6'. Engines were 13" diameter cylinders, 3½' piston stroke. She had two boilers. Owned by the Mississippi Sand and Gravel Company of St. Louis in 1923 and chartered to tow a garbage barge. The Jefferson Distributing Company then owned her and sold her in February 1927 to the Burness Construction Company of Carrollton, Missouri. In the spring of 1929, she was sold to H. C. Blaske of Alton, Illinois where she sank in ice, December 21, 1929.

INVERNESS   #100418

Sternwheel rafter. Built 1888, LaCrosse. 121 tons, 121 tons, 129' x 21' x 4.8'. Named for Captain Dan McDonald's Scottish birthplace. Used machinery of rafter *A. REILING*. On May 30, 1888, she collapsed a flue while running the Quincy bridge. Five men were blown overboard, all drowned. Frank Looney, captain; Morrell Looney, second pilot. In 1896 owned by LaCrosse and Mississippi River Towing Company. Commanded by Captain John O'Conner in 1896, 1897, and 1899; George S. Nichols, master, 1898. Peter O'Rourke, captain, pilot in 1895 and George L. Short in 1900. John Burns and Charles Brown were mates at various times. James Tully was chief engineer for some years and Charles Goodbud for some time. Sold to Ayer and Lord Tie Company of Paducah in April 1902, and towed ties on the Tennessee and Cumberland Rivers. Last in 1905 LMV.

IOWA   #12346

Sidewheel rafter. Built 1863, Prairie du Chien. 24 tons. Failed her inspection at Galena in 1876, in Burlington, 1881 and dismantled the same year. Horace Hollingshead was captain and pilot for some years and may have had a financial interest in her.

IOWA   #12155

Sternwheel rafter. Built 1865, Savanna, Illinois. 73 tons, 73 tons, 126' x 20' x 3.7'. Started as sidewheel ferry, ran until 1877 in that capacity. Rebuilt at Bellevue, Iowa, 1877. Tonnage changed in 1877 to 80 tons. Jack and William Young of Reads Landing ran her for several years, towing for Knapp, Stout and Company. On November 5, 1879, Captain Tom Peel bought her as she lay sunk in thirteen feet of water, opposite Dallas City. He floated her using two barges and got steam up on the *IOWA* and brought her to Burlington. Sold to Captain William Davis; his father, Zalus Davis, was engineer, 1883 to 1888. In 1883 owned by Davis and Gardiner, Batchelder and Wells Company of Lyons, Iowa; Frank Wild, master.

Sold to LeClaire Navigation Company (Samuel Van Sant and Walter Blair) in February 1890 by Gardiner, Batchelder and Wells Co. George Carpenter, master, 1893. Later sold to Captain William McKinley who took her to the Illinois River where she towed grain barges. In 1898, 1899 at Evansville. Lytle-Holdcamper says she was lost in 1899. However, a government record shows her at Rock Island, 1903.

IOWA CITY   #12422

Sidewheel rafter. Built Iowa City, Iowa, 1866. 71 or 58 tons. Built at a sawmill near Iowa City on the Iowa River by Graham, Peninger and Sparleder. Captain E. H. Thomas of Ottumwa, Iowa was her first pilot. 90' x 16' x 3', 24 staterooms, 14' wheels. Engines were 8" diameter cylinders, 16" piston stroke, geared with pinions and two large cogwheels. Tubular boiler, 40" x 16'. Joe and William Wolverton of LeClaire were the carpenters who built the hull and cabin during the winter of 1865-66, launching her in the spring of 1866. After a first season on the Iowa and Cedar Rivers, she was placed on the ways and her engines were taken out and replaced by two direct connecting engines, 10" cylinders, 3' piston stroke, and 20' was added to the hull length. Was on Iowa and Cedar Rivers trades for four years and on Mississippi for one year. Seized in Davenport for a $6,000 claim by a Mr. Downs. He chartered her to W. H. Pierce of Rock Island who ran her between there and Clinton. Downs sold her to George Winans, and she soon sank near West Newton, Minnesota while towing a raft.

Captain E. E. Heerman bought her as a complete wreck and rebuilt her into a sternwheeler at Wabasha, brought her out in 1873 and used her on the Chippewa. Captain Heerman wanted to rebuild and bought larger engines that had been taken from a boat lost in the ice gorge at St. Louis in the spring of 1880. In the fall of 1881, he sold the old boiler to W. T. Dugan of Wabasha and the engines to Captain Hays who resold them. In the spring of 1882, the new boat was completed and renamed *MINNIE* after his daughter. He indicated the old bottom was under the steamboat *PERCY SWAIN*. First documented August 1, 1870. Abandoned 1882.

IRENE D.   #100431

Sternwheel rafter. Built 1888, Rock Island, by Dorrance brothers at the Kahlke Yard. 142 tons, 142 tons, 133.5' x 29.6' x 4.8'. Engines 12" diameter cylinders, 8' piston stroke. (*CHANCY LAMB* was the only other rafter with an 8' stroke.) Engines built by Charles Kattenbrocher of LeClaire. Had boilers of old rafter *TIBER*. Named after daughter of Captain D. A. Dorrance of LeClaire. First captain was George Rutherford in 1888. Later used as bowboat for the *LIZZIE GARDNER*, Captain Dorrance, captain.

Captain Walter Blair bought a one-third interest in 1890, McDonald Brothers the rest. (Dorrance needed cash.) In February 1893, owned by Union Towing Company of LeClaire; D. E. Dorrance, master. Sold later to Captain Thomas S. Adams of Quincy, Illinois in 1897 and became the excursion boat *(B) FLYING EAGLE* circa 1902.

ISAAC STAPLES   #100238

Sternwheel rafter. Built 1878, Stillwater, for her namesake. She was 147 tons, 147 tons, 137.8' x 30.4' x 4.7'. Captain Way indicates engines were 13" diameter cylinders, 6' piston stroke. Dyer and Merrick say 14" diameter cylinders, 4½' piston stroke. The vessel cost $18,000 and was built by Captain Morgan of Clinton. Dyer says her engines came off the *JENNIE BROWN*. Captain Hoy was the initial master. Captain John Hoy said, "She can tow as far, and hold a raft as steady, as some of the boats with more power credited to them." In the spring of 1880, she came out with two new steel boilers, carrying 181 pounds of steam. In 1878 and 1879, Charles A. Staples, a son of Isaac Staples, was captain; John Hoy, first pilot and Charles Rhodes, second pilot. In 1880 John Hoy was captain; Ben Shook, chief engineer, and Eugene Carter, second engineer. John Hoy was master again in 1881.

In the fall of 1881, she was sold to Carson and Rand of the Burlington Lumber Company. In 1882-84, Captain Vincent Peel was her master and possibly part owner. *ISAAC STAPLES* was sold in the winter of 1884 to the Matt Clark Towing Company. This company failed in 1886, and Bronson and Folsom bought the *ISAAC STAPLES*. In 1887 Jacob G. Ressor was captain; Ira DeCamp was pilot. John Hoy was captain in 1888. Captain James Pollmer was master in 1889. From 1891 to 1895 Charles B. Roman was master; Sam Lancaster, second pilot; Henry Polis, mate; George Van Beber, chief engineer.

In 1898 Captain William M. Wier chartered the *ISAAC STAPLES* to tow logs from West Newton to LaCrosse. Silas Alexander was second pilot; Harry Dyer, mate; Elmer Stokes, chief engineer. *ISAAC STAPLES* was rebuilt in the winter of 1898 (179 tons, 135' x 26' x 4.5'), and Captain Walter Hunter was in charge when she came out in 1899. He stayed on through 1907. The *ISAAC STAPLES* was sold to the Van Sant Towing Company in the fall of 1907. She burned in early December 1907, while hauled out on the ways at Wabasha along with the *J. W. VAN SANT* and *CYCLONE*.

J

J. C. ATLEE   #76623

Sternwheel towboat. Built in 1886 at Rock Island. 87 tons, 87 tons, 101' x 19.4' x 3.8'. Built by S. and J. C. Atlee of Rock Island and named for the latter. Later traded to Parmalee Brothers for the *OTTUMWA BELLE*. Registered at Burlington, Iowa, until 1895; then sold to Anderson Tully Company of Memphis. She was in their fleet, along with the *L. E. PATTON, JOY PATTON*, and *J. M. LINDER*. In 1904, four crew and 75 h.p. indicated; eleven crew in 1906. Documented at Vicksburg from 1907 until after 1918. Was sold to Jonesville, Louisiana parties and burned there around 1922.

J. G. CHAPMAN (First)—(Number Not Known)

Sternwheel rafter, *iron* hull. Built 1872, Dubuque. 110' x 22'. Engines were 14" diameter cylinders, 6' piston stroke. Walter Blair describes this vessel as a "freak." Her bulkheads were lettered "Eau Claire Lumber Company's Iron Raftboat, J. G. Chapman." Owners were Chapman and Thorpe. Her design was odd—she had "dowler" wheels, somewhat like screw propellers but the wheels were 10' in diameter and only ¼ was submerged. The lowest part of the wheels was not below the bottom of the boat, which only drew 3' of water at the stern. When going ahead, the wheels revolved toward each other and threw a strong current against the balanced rudder, she had good rudder power going forward, but was almost useless in backing and very slow going upstream. Later changed to conventional sternwheel propulsion with same or similar engines.

The iron hull broke in two coming upriver and she sank near Sterling Island ten miles below Hamburg, Illinois. The loss may have been caused by a careless distribution of fuel. A large supply of cheap coal was loaded forward of the boilers, and this weight forward, and the weight of the engines and wheels, parted her hog chains and she broke in two. No lives were lost. The craft was estimated at $12,000. She probably was the second iron-hull steamboat built on the Upper Mississippi. Designed and built by William Hopkins, a Scottish boat builder with the Iowa Iron Works. David Cratte, a cousin of the Buissons, was master for second season, followed by Dan Davison. Not in 1877 LMV.

J. G. CHAPMAN (Second) #76217

Sternwheel rafter. Built 1881, Metropolis, Illinois. Built for the Eau Claire (Wisconsin) Lumber Company and was a big powerful boat. 146 tons, 106 tons, 141' x 28' x 4'. Engines had 14" diameter cylinders, 6' piston stroke (from the prior vessel of this name). Also owned by Captain Peter Kirns of St. Louis and the Jellison Towing Company of Wabasha. According to Dyer, she burned at Wabasha September 16 or 19, 1893. She was valued at $10,000 and insured for $8,500. According to Way, she burned in August 1894. This vessel was quite ornamental with a pilot house on the roof. Masters at various times were: Dan Davison, John O'Connor (1883), Peter Kirns, George Martin and Ira DeCamp. Clair C. Fuller was chief engineer for a time.

J. H. BALDWIN #4658

Sidewheel packet. Built at Louisville, 1861. 173 tons. On Louisville-Cumberland River route. Captured by U.S. forces on the Cumberland River in the spring of 1862 and sold to Wiley Simms and A. Hamilton Company, steamboat agents at Nashville, for $12,000. Sold at Nashville to the U.S. Quartermaster Department on March 21, 1864. Redocumented October 4, 1865 as *C. J. CAFFREY*. Sold to U. S. Army Corps of Engineers as a snagboat on August 31, 1867.

J. K. GRAVES #78589

Sternwheel rafter, *steel* hull. Built at Dubuque in 1885 for the Matt Clark Towing Company. Named for the Honorable J. K. Graves of Dubuque. 96 tons, 96 tons, 117' x 20' x 4'. Engines 12" diameter cylinders, 6½' piston stroke. She had three boilers. The Matt Clark Company "collapsed" in 1886, and she was sold to Weyerhaeuser and Denkmann. George Trombley, Jr. ran her in 1886. Ira Fuller was master in 1880s. John Huginin was master 1893; James Lyon, mate. In 1894, Ben Metzger was captain and Harry Dyer was mate.

In August 1894, while running the Upper Rapids with a raft, Captain Dana Dorrance in charge, she hit a rock and sank near Cat Island below LeClaire in ten feet of water. Raised and repaired and ran the next season (1895) in charge of Captain John O'Conner, George Knapp, second pilot. Chief engineers during her Upper Mississippi River career were Edward Bergen, Sol Fuller and Hiram Fuller.

J. M. #20428

Sternwheel towboat. Built Diamond Bluff, Wisconsin in 1907. 39 tons, 26 tons, 81.6' x 16.0' x 3'. Still listed in 1920 LMV.

J. M. RICHTMAN #77345

Sternwheel rafter. Built Sterling Island, Illinois in 1899. 121' x 23.5' x 3.9'. Engines 12" diameter cylinders, 6' piston stroke. She had two boilers. Built by John Rohn and Sons, St. Louis, Missouri. Owned by Jacob Richtman and Sons (James and Jack). Captain James J. Richtman, master. Several passengers were scalded when her starboard boiler let go on September 13, 1900. She was on the Missouri River near Florence, Nebraska at the time. Renamed *(B) CONQUEST* in June 1904.

J. S. KEATOR #110177

Sternwheel rafter. Perhaps rebuilt at LaCrosse, 1878. 172 tons, 123' x 24.5' x 4.5'. Originally *(A) ROBERT ROSS*, built in LaCrosse in 1873. Sold to Keaton Lumber Company of Moline and name changed to *(B) J. S. KEATOR* in 1880. The *ROBERT ROSS* was built from the remains of the *JAMES MALBON* which had exploded her boilers at McGregor, Iowa in 1872. The later engines had 14" diameter cylinders, 6' piston stroke; earlier ones had 4' stroke. Dyer says, "She was a good raft boat. Had good power." Captain L. H. Day was master for a long time; L. P. Maxfield was chief engineer. When the Keaton mill burned, she was laid up and later sold to Captain L. E. Patton of Memphis in 1900.

J. W. MILLS #75563

Sternwheel rafter. Built in 1872 at Paducah, Kentucky by Captain T. L. Lee as a coal towboat. He sold her in 1873 to the William J. Young Company, Clinton, Iowa. 86 tons, 86 tons, 109.7' x 22.2' x 3'. Engines 13" diameter cylinders, 3½' piston stroke. Captain Paul Kerz was the usual master for the Young Company. Chief Engineer was Conrad Kraus, both continued until 1880; Captain James Bellis was master for the next three years. The *J. W. MILLS* was the "family boat" of the firm until the *DOUGLAS BOARDMAN* was built.

The LeClaire Navigation Company (Samuel Van Sant and Walter Blair) purchased the *J. W. MILLS* from the Young firm in 1883 for $7,000. Captain Walter A. Blair was the usual captain. The *J. W. MILLS* "paid out" in two years. Van Sant and Blair traded her to the Parmalee Brothers of Canton, Missouri in the spring of 1894 for the *CITY OF QUINCY*. Parmalee dismantled *J. W. MILLS* that summer and used the engines, shaft, etc., in building the *OTTUMWA BELLE* in Canton.

J. W. VAN SANT (First) #75628

Sternwheel rafter. Built 1869 at LeClaire by J. W. and Samuel Van Sant. Named for Captain Sam Van Sant's father. 71 tons, 100' x 20' x 4'. Engines 12" diameter cylinders, 4' piston stroke, manufactured by the Niles Works at Cincinnati. One boiler, 10" flues. Owned by J. W. Van Sant and Son. Specially built for rafting; first vessel so designed. She was built to lower her stacks and pilothouse to get under the

Rock Island bridge. A passenger on her first trip was Frederick Weyerhaeuser, at that time of Rock Island. Her first tow was from Cat Tail Slough to Rockford for Weyerhaeuser and Denkmann. She was chartered to George Winans in 1870 and was sold early in 1872 to the Eau Claire Lumber Company, Peter Kirns was her master. She was sunk at the rapids at Keokuk, November 1, 1876. Her engines went to the PETE KIRNS which replaced her.

J. W. VAN SANT (Second)   #76871

Sternwheel rafter. Second of the name. Built at LeClaire in 1890 for the Van Sant and Musser Transportation Company of Muscatine, Iowa to take place of the worn-out SILVER WAVE. 228 tons, 228 tons, 140′ x 30′ x 4.5′, 324 h.p., 17 crew. Engines were 14″ diameter cylinders, 6′ piston stroke. "One of the best raft boats on the river." George Tromley, Jr. came out as Captain (had her for thirteen seasons); James Lyons was mate. James Steadman was chief engineer for some time. Other occasional officers were Robert Mitchell and John O'Connor as masters; Charles Tromley as second pilot; Ben Metzger as mate; and Frank A. Whitney as assistant engineer. "She, with the LYDIA VAN SANT for a bowboat, made an outfit hard to beat," according to Harry Dyer. She burned at the Wabasha Yard in December 1907 along with the CYCLONE and ISAAC STAPLES.

JAMES FISK, JR.   #75639

Sternwheel towboat/rafter. Built at Ironton, Ohio in 1870. 160 tons, 126.6′ x 24′ x 8.7′. Engines 13″ diameter cylinders, 5′ piston stroke. In Cairo-Paducah trade until 1880 when she was sold to the Van Sants. Captain Dan Davison in charge followed by Tom Dolson the next few years until she was dismantled at LeClaire in 1886. Henry Bell was mate in 1881, and John Burns was mate in 1885. Her machinery was placed in a new boat, the G. J. SIVLEY, built for the Illinois River trade.

JAMES MALBON   #75473

Sternwheel rafter. Built at LaCrosse in 1872 for Captain James Malbon. 120 tons. Very early in her brief career, she exploded her boilers in late July 1872 near North McGregor, Iowa. She was upbound on her fourth trip and had just placed twelve raft hands ashore at McGregor. According to the official inspector's report, eight of the crew, including Captain Malbon, were killed and five injured. A spoke of the pilotwheel was driven through his neck and his body was blown onto a nearby island. The CITY OF McGREGOR and ALLAMAKEE were nearby and rendered aid. The LUMBERMAN came down river from LaCrosse with a Dr. Anderson and members of the Malbon family aboard. After looking over the wreck, which sank in seventeen feet of water, and interviewing survivors, the inspectors decided that the accident was caused by great recklessness and carelessness on the part of W. Harvey Pierce, second engineer on watch at the time. "Pierce was charged with carrying high steam and not paying attention to the new boilers which he knew were foaming." His license was revoked.

Ironically, the accident occurred within a mile of the spot where the D. A. McDONALD had exploded her boilers on June 10, 1872. She was also a new boat with new boilers built to newly adopted standards, same as the JAMES MALBON. The JAMES MALBON's engines were placed in the rafter ROBERT ROSS which was built in 1873.

JAMES MEANS   #13032

Sternwheel rafter. Built Wheeling, West Virginia, 1860. 99 tons, 140′ x 31.5′ x 4.5′. Engines 14″ diameter cylinders, 4′ piston stroke. Originally a short trade packet on the Ohio River. By 1865 she was on the Upper Mississippi as a packet or towboat. In 1868 was in the wheat trade pushing barges. She was sold in 1871 to J. W. Van Sant and Son and converted into a rafter. Captain John McCaffrey was half owner in 1871 and ran her for five years. She was dismantled in 1877; her engines went into the GOLDEN GATE.

JENNIE HAYES   #76083

Sternwheel packet initially. Built 1879, Franconia, Minnesota for Captain Oscar F. Knapp and sons, Ben and George B. 87 tons, 87 tons. 117.4′ x 14.5′ x 2.6′. Original engines were 10″ diameter cylinders, 6′ piston stroke. These engines were taken out and those of the CLEON used instead. In 1889 engines of the PAULINE were installed and she was cut down from a packet into a rafter. Sold to Captain William Davis of Rock Island (master in 1890). Captain Russ Ruley was her master for several seasons while owned by the Knapps.

On June 22, 1892, she was about to go through the open swing span of the Dubuque bridge when a sudden gust of wind caught the swing bridge and partially closed it. In doing so, both boat stacks were knocked off as was the pilot house and forward end of the cabin, hog chain braces, etc., totalling $4,500. Sold by Captain Davis to Captain Thomas Parker of St. Louis in 1892 and he dismantled her in 1893, putting the machinery in a new boat, THOMAS PARKER, (burned at St. Louis in 1897).

JEFFERSON   #161681

Sternwheel. Was built as (A) VERNIE MAC at Wabasha, 1892. Later (B) BESSIE KATZ. Was a towing vessel until the end of the 1920s operating out of St. Louis. Had a crew of eighteen in 1929, 350 h.p., 91 tons, 91 tons, 124.3′ x 22′ x 3.8′. Sold to Captain Hugh C. Blaske in September 1928. Dismantled in 1931, machinery went to the FLOYD H. BLASKE which burned in October 1940 at Alton, Illinois.

Jessie B. #76934

Sternwheel rafter. Built 1891, Dubuque. 78 tons, 78 tons, 121' x 21.6' x 4.3'. Built for Captain Volney Bigelow at LaCrosse and named for his daughter Jessie. Had engines of old rafter *NATRONA*, two boilers 20' long by 36" diameter, engines were 12" diameter cylinders, 4' piston stroke. Sold to the Staples Towing Company of Stillwater. They used her to drop logs from the St. Paul boom to Prescott, Wisconsin. In 1900 Dan Rice was captain; Amel Knipburg, pilot. Often used as excursion vessel, St. Paul and Stillwater area. The Staples Company sold her to Captain E. Picksley who took her to the Tennessee River. Registered three years at Paducah (1904–1907). Dismantled 1907.

Jessie Bill #76308

Sternwheel rafter. Built 1882, Wabasha. 60 tons, 60 tons, 90.9' x 15' x 3.5'. Named after Captain Fred A. Bill's daughter, Jessie. Captain E. C. Bill, master, 1883 (also owned the *BUCKEYE*); Henry Buisson in 1888, and also Eli Minder. Clair C. Fuller was chief engineer for several seasons. Worked in Beef Slough, Captain Lew Malin, master. Frank Weir, chief engineer, 1899. Owned by Freeman Bacher and Frank Smith in 1902 who had purchased her from Knapp Brothers, Dubuque. Last year in LMV was 1907.

John H. Douglass #157126

Sternwheel rafter. Built from the *DAN THAYER* at LaCrosse in 1884. 145.5' x 26' x 4.3'. Rebuilt as *JOHN H. DOUGLASS* in 1899 at Rock Island; assigned new registry number. Purchased by Captain George Winans of Waukesha who had the cabin and superstructure enlarged at the Kahlke Yard. In August 1900, the *JOHN H. DOUGLASS* pushed a lumber raft 768 feet long by 256 feet wide containing nine million board feet and sixty carloads of shingles and lath on top. A month later, assisted by *SATELLITE* as the bow boat, *JOHN H. DOUGLASS* went by Rock Island pushing a raft 128 feet wide and 1,400 feet long with a deck load of shingles, Captain Napoleon Lucas, master; John O'Connor, pilot; Levi M. King, chief engineer.

In 1901 she was given a new larger hull at the Kahlke yard, given a new registry number and renamed *SATURN*. The first *SATURN* had burned at the Kahlke yard in April 1900 along with the *VOLUNTEER* and *MASCOT*.

John H. Rich #136270

Sternwheel rafter. Built in 1892, Rock Island as *(A) E. RUTLEDGE*. 132.7' x 30.5' x 4.7'. Engines 15" diameter cylinders, 5' piston stroke. Renamed *(B) JOHN H. RICH* in 1910 for John H. Rich, president of Woods Produce Company of Red Wing, Minnesota. The celebrated doctors Mayo, Charles Horace and William James, had invested in a lumber company which went into receivership. Their share of the proceeds was the *JOHN M. RICH*. They converted her into the pleasure vessel, *(C) ORONOCO*. The latter was commanded for several years by Captain Robert N. Cassidy of Winona who retired due to failing eye sight after fifty years of continuous service (fall 1915). Other officers of the *JOHN H. RICH* and *ORONOCO* were Pearl Roundy and John R. Wiley, engineers and James Lyon, mate.

Jo Long #77214

Sternwheel rafter. Built 1887, Stillwater, by D. M. Swain for John McCaffrey and Jo. N. Long of LeClaire. 130 tons, 120' x 22' x 4.4'. Had two large boilers; engines were 12" diameter cylinders, 6' piston stroke. In the 1890s, she was one of the three fastest boats on river (others were the *JUNIATA* and *CLYDE*). Used as a helper on the rapids for several years. Captain Long put her on run between Rock Island and Clinton in 1895 in competition to Captain Streckfus' *VERNE SWAIN*. Streckfus bought the *CITY OF WINONA* to meet the *JO LONG* competition in the spring of 1896. Many daily races and keen rivalry culminated when Captain Jo Long lost self-control and stabbed James Osborne, an agent of Streckfus at Davenport. Long was arrested and fined and withdrew the *JO LONG* from the trade. Later in 1898 sold to Captains Yerger and Morgan of Vicksburg. Her name was changed to *(B) PROVIDENCE*. She was caught in a storm on Lake Providence circa 1909, capsized and sank with loss of many lives.

John Rumsey—(No Number)

Sternwheel. Built 1862, Waubeck, Wisconsin. Operated on Chippewa River by Captain Nathaniel Harris. The *JOHN RUMSEY* was built out of the *FLORA TEMPLE*. The latter had been on the Chippewa River looking for business and then was laid up. Colonel H. T. Rumsey bought her and rebuilt her into a sternwheeler. Of 39 tons and on the Chippewa River to the fall of 1864. Named for John Rumsey, a relative of Colonel H. T. Rumsey.

She is best known due to her demise on November 4, 1864. Towing two barges of freight, she raced the *ALBANY*, also with two barges. The *JOHN RUMSEY* exploded near St. Paul, killing four men of her crew and three of the *ALBANY*'s crew. Captain M. M. Harris was badly injured. He was standing in front of the *JOHN RUMSEY*'s cabin and went up in the air and came down in the wreck of the cabin. The pilot, D. W. Heylman, went up in the air and came down uninjured with his hands still on the spokes. Hearing the groans of Captain Harris, he reached him just in time to save him as the wreck sank. Only the engines were salvaged and put into the *ALICE*, owned by Colonel Rumsey.

Johnny Schmoker #13521

Sidewheel rafter. Built at LaCrosse, 1866. 27 tons. Geared sidewheeler,

70′ x 12′. Hull built by Captain Ben Seevey at Waubeck, Wisconsin (on the Chippewa River). Taken to La-Crosse and sold to Colonel H. T. Rumsey who put the machinery in. (Also spelled JOHNNY SMOKER.) Used in grain trade on Chippewa and sawmills and probably in rafting. While owned by Rumsey, James Healy was captain; later William Dustin; Al Carpenter was master in 1874. In 1872 chartered to Captain E. E. Heerman; Captain Chet Dunn; James Shaw, engineer. "Smart little boat, fastest on the Chippewa in her day."

Reported to have burned along with the CHIPPEWA at Rumsey's Landing on the Chippewa River on January 21, 1871. Both vessels were owned by H. T. Rumsey of La-Crosse. The fire was set by arsonists. However, according to Captain E. E. Heerman, she was not burned. Captain Dustin libeled the boat in 1872 when Colonel H. T. Rumsey died and then owned her. She may have been sold down river later.

JOSEPHINE LOVIZA #105974

Sternwheel rafter originally built at Cincinnati in 1880 as *(A) A. T. JENKS*. 113.6′ x 22′ x 3.7′. Engines 10″ diameter cylinders, 6′ piston stroke. Two boilers, 34″ diameter, 20′ long. Was renamed *(B) ED DURANT, JR.* and *(C) JOSEPHINE LOVIZA* in 1897. Sold Vicksburg 1896. Came to rescue of IRON AGE at Island #95 December 3, 1898. In 1901 she was purchased by Captain H. R. Higbee and rebuilt at Patterson, Louisiana as new towboat HARRY HIGBEE.

JULIA #75471

Sternwheel rafter. Built 1871, Winona. 58 tons, 58 tons, 107′ x 22.3′ x 3.5′. Built and owned by Laird, Norton Company of Winona. Rebuilt 1876, Dubuque. 47 tons. Sold to George Winans in 1884. Captains were William and Henry Slocumb. Cut down by ice at Rock Island, March 24, 1893. Total loss of $3,500. Dismantled where she lay. (May have been sidewheel originally, rebuilt into sternwheel.)

Late in the fall of 1890, the JULIA was bound for St. Louis with twelve strings of lumber, thirty-two cribs long. She landed at Lyons and split her raft to run the Clinton bridge. Dan Davison was captain and first pilot and Peter O'Rourke was second pilot. Captain Davison went on watch at 2 A.M., and about 3 A.M., he called O'Rourke who promptly came on watch and took the wheel. Harry G. Dyer was mate on the nearby PAULINE and gave the following details. "We had to land above Clinton that afternoon about two o'clock as the JULIA and her raft had the channel blocked on the draw side of the river. Captain O'Rourke told me if he had taken a second thought, he would have refused to relieve Captain Davison until he got through the bridge. When Pete came on watch they were almost into the bridge, and he said that Captain Dan had the raft in such shape it was impossible to get it 'straightened' up for the bridge. The JULIA had the steamer SATELLITE for a bowboat and before Captain O'Rourke could get 'straightened out,' the bow of the raft was almost against the pier at the left of the draw. The SATELLITE hit the pier and the raft ran under her so as to force her up the pier, and when the headway was finally checked the bowboat's wheel was level with the railroad track on the bridge, while about half of her forecastle was under water, the boat standing on her head on the raft which was somewhat submerged but held together so as to carry the weight of the boat. The stern of the raft was against the bank, just above the warehouse at Clinton. LITE, got lines around her and pulled the raft back a few feet and slid the SATELLITE back into the river without much damage. Captain George Winans owned the boats at that time, and he arrived at Clinton in time to take charge of the work of getting the SATELLITE out of the railroad business and back into the lumber trade."

Captain Jack Hanford, one of the early pilots dating back to the 1840s lost his life accidentally on the JULIA. It occurred when he was re-

"They took the engines and everything moveable off the SATEL-turning after delivering a raft at St. Louis.

JULIA HADLEY #13518

Sidewheel rafter. According to LMV, built Stillwater, 1866. According to LH, built Eau Claire, 1866. 47 tons, 47 tons, 114′ x 14.5′ x 26′. In the spring of 1867, hauled out and lengthened 20′. Operated as a packet between Eau Claire and La-Crosse. Owned by Colonel Ed W. Durant and Captain Jack Hanford. JULIA HADLEY was a stiff shaft boat with a geared drive, one of the last three sidewheelers built for rafting. (The other two were the MINNIE WILL and the CLYDE). R. J. Wheeler later became Durant's partner. Dismantled 1890.

JUMBO #76398

Sternwheel rafter. Built 1889, Winona. 21 tons, 58.6′ x 20′ x 3′. Small boat, owned in Hastings, Minnesota and LaCrosse. Burned at Winona and lost in late May 1901.

JUNIATA #76793

Sternwheel rafter. Built 1889, Winona, by the Laird, Norton Company. 98 tons, 134′ x 22.5′ x 4.2′. Engines 16″ diameter cylinders, 5′ piston stroke, 150 h.p. Sold to Bronson and Folsom in 1895, but her engines were too large and were taken out before the sale and put in the FRONTENAC, a new Laird and Norton craft. Bronson and Folsom then placed the old engines of the MENOMONIE (12″ diameter cylinders, 6′ piston stroke) into the JUNIATA. Isaac Newcomb was her master in 1896 and 1897. From 1899 to 1903, William Wier was master, and Edward Huttenhow was second pilot. Harry Dyer was mate in 1898 and 1899 and also in 1902. Henry Slocumb was captain and Robert

Cassidy second pilot all the time the *JUNIATA* was owned by Laird and Norton.

In 1907 Bronson and Folsom sold the *JUNIATA* to Captain Milt Newcomb and Charles Frances of Pepin, Wisconsin. They changed her name to *RED WING* and put her in the packet trade between St. Paul and Wabasha. Dyer observed, "Bronson and Folsom were fine men to work for, paid good wages, their boats were always well furnished, but if a man wouldn't do his work he would last as long as a white shirt in a coal pile."

K

KATHERINE   #145502

Sternwheel. Built 1889 in Jeffersonville. Built as *(A) THE NEW IDEA*. 146 tons, 146 tons, 125' x 28' x 4'. Taken to Cairo for ferry service. On May 26, 1896, the *KATHERINE* capsized in a severe cyclone, drowning eleven persons. Sold to Barrett Line; then in October 1907, taken to Point Pleasant and parts of her used in building a towboat named the *I. N. FLESHER*. Last at Cairo, 1907 LMV.

KIRNS

Sternwheel towboat. Built *(A)* as rafter *PETE KIRNS* in 1879 at St. Louis. 122' xx 24' x 4'. Engines 12" diameter cylinders, 4' piston stroke. The Mississippi River Commission bought the *PETE KIRNS* from the Eau Claire Lumber Company at Hannibal, Missouri and renamed her *(B) KIRNS*. Off the list by June 30, 1893.

KIT CARSON   #14386

Sternwheel rafter. Built in 1880 at South Stillwater by Josiah Batchelder for Captain Augustus R. Young and the Carson and Rand Lumber Company of Eau Claire. 96 tons, 96 tons, 138.3' x 28' x 4'. Engines 16" diameter cylinders, 6' piston stroke. Had three boilers, 41" diameter, 22' long. Her boilers and engines were first in the sidewheel packet *HAMBURG* and then the towboat *MINNESOTA*. Harry Dyer indicates that "the *KIT CARSON* was one of the most powerful rafters on the river, but was not moulded for speed, being too blunt at her quarters." She was most successful in towing lumber, being too heavy for logs. She was named for one of Mr. Carson's daughters, *not* for the famed scout of the frontier.

The *KIT CARSON* was sold to the Burlington lumber Company in 1885 and to J. C. Daniels, Keokuk in 1889. Daniels sold her to McDonald Brothers in 1891. As a rafter, she had no unnecessary upper works to catch the wind. Sam Hitchcock was pilot on her for several years, and Gary Denberg was master and pilot for Daniels. McDonald sold her to Lower River parties in 1904 and she was dismantled in 1916 at Memphis after being condemned by inspectors. Her machinery was then used in a steel hull towboat built by Dubuque Boat and Boiler Works for Patton-Tully of Memphis.

Captains were: A. R. Young, 1880 to 1885; Robert N. Cassidy, 1886 to 1889; William Slocumb, 1890 to 1894; John C. Daniels, 1897; William Dobler, 1900 to 1904. Others may have been George S. Nichols, Henry C. Walker and Cornelius Knapp. Some of the pilots were William Wooders, four seasons; John Bradley, two seasons; John Smith or Schmidt, four seasons; Frank Wettenhall and N. B. Lucas. Engineers were: Charles H. Meads, 1896 and 1889; Sol. Fuller, 1888 and 1889; Henry Garrett; Charles Lumley.

L

L. W. BARDEN   #15736

Sidewheel rafter. Built 1864, Berlin, Wisconsin on the Wolf River. Brought to the Mississippi via the Wolf River, Portage Canal and Wisconsin River. Engines were 12" diameter cylinders, 26" piston stroke and were geared directly to the shaft, 102 tons (1871). Captains Joseph Buisson and Cyprian Buisson were mates for a long time. Registered at Prairie du Chien, 1877. Dismantled 1881 at Dubuque. Engines and other material put in new boat *P. O. LAWSON*. The *L. W. BARDEN* was similar to the *L. W. CRANE* built in 1865 at Berlin.

L. W. CRANE   #15877

Sidewheel rafter. Built 1865, Berlin, Wisconsin on the Wolf River. 101 tons. Brought to the Mississippi via the Wolf River, the Portage Canal and the Wisconsin River. George Rutherford was master for several seasons, and Joseph Buisson also. John Sealing chartered her and towed lumber from Reads Landing to St. Louis. Dismantled 1881. Similar to the *L. W. BARDEN*.

LADY GRACE   #140473

Sternwheel rafter. Built 1881, Clinton. 190 tons, 144 tons circa 1904. 134.5' x 28.4' x 4.6'. Engines 15" diameter cylinders, 6' piston stroke. The engines were made by C. T. Dumont, Cincinnati. The three boilers were each 24 feet long and were made in Clinton. Owned by Chancy Lamb and Sons. Dyer says "she was one of the finest and most powerful raft boats." She was named for Chancy Lamb's little granddaughter and one of her fourteen staterooms was set aside for her use only. The main cabin was 68 feet long and was decorated by Henry Rumble, a top artisan. The entrance was floored with oak and walnut, and there were Brussels carpets in the cabin. Across the front of the cabin, the name of the boat was painted in large block letters against a river background scene. The pilothouse had fancy scrollwork for her cupola, and when she came out on her initial trip in

1881, a large blue flag, 26 feet long, flew from her jackstaff.

Captain in 1883 was Toliver McDonald. In 1890, her captain was Cyrus King. In 1892, Stephen B. Hanks was captain, and John G. Moore in 1893. Others who served were Henry Fuller, Alvin Collier, James P. Boland, Cornelius Knapp and John W. Betz. Barnard Rockwood was chief engineer for several seasons.

In 1896 the Lambs sold her to Captain William Davis of Rock Island. He sold her in 1897 to Stewart and Company, government contractors on the river. At the Plaquemine Lock in June 1901, she collapsed a flue, killing one crew member and injuring others. She was repaired, and on September 17, 1906, sank near Mobile, Alabama on account of a hurricane. In 1915 her hull was cut in two and the parts used as hulls for a couple of quarter boats.

LAFAYETTE LAMB #15985

Sternwheel rafter. Built in 1874 in Clinton for Chancy Lamb and Sons. 118 tons, 118 tons, 100' x 22' x 3.6'. Engines had 10" diameter cylinders, 6½' piston stroke. Named after Lafayette Lamb, son of Chancy. The Lambs used her in their business until 1891 and then sold her to Captain J. E. Kaiser (Valley Navigation Company of Wabasha). In 1899 she was sold to Bronson and Folsom, Stillwater, for $2,500. They used her one season as a bowboat for the *ISAAC STAPLES*, then dismantled her and her machinery went into a new boat, *FOUNTAIN CITY*.

Harry Dyer indicates, "The Lambs were nice people to work for and paid good wages. The food was of the best and plenty of it. Their boats were always well kept up and well equipped." Some of the *LAFAYETTE LAMB*'s captains were Cyrus King (1883), followed by Stephen B. Hanks, John Monroe (1890), John G. Moore, Abe Mitchell (1893), and George Carpenter (1898). Lafayette Lamb died in a train wreck in 1901 and left an estate of $7 million.

LAST CHANCE #15653

Sternwheel rafter. Built in 1870 at Burlington, Iowa for Geiger Brothers and used for towing grain and wood barges initially. 50 tons, 50 tons, 98.2' x 17.8' x 3.0'. Original engines were 10" diameter cylinders, 3½' piston stroke. One iron boiler. Used in towing in 1881. Captain Walter Blair relates, "In 1880, the *LAST CHANCE* was owned at LeClaire and used to assist in taking rafts over the Rock Island rapids. In 1881, Captain Sam Van Sant bought a half interest in her, (Captain) John McCaffrey owning the other half. Captain Van Sant sold me a sixth interest in her for $583.33. She had a good season and divided what looked to me like a handsome profit, and made me anxious to increase my holdings.

"During the winter of 1881-82 while she was on the LeClaire ways Captain Van Sant and I bought out Captain McCaffrey. We then organized the LeClaire Navigation Company and sold the boat to this company, dividing the stock equally between us. We made suitable repairs and added a few improvements, including new cylinders, eleven inches by three feet, one inch larger than the old ones . . . The *LAST CHANCE* was my first command. Vitel Burrow was my pilot, Robert Shannon and George Lancaster, engineers, and Oliver White, mate. When low water came we used her at the rapids. J. N. Long and J. W. Rambo used her to 'follow down the shore' or to go on the bow when we had to double trip the steamboat channel . . . Tromley was my successor on the *LAST CHANCE* followed by John Monroe. We finally sold her . . ." in August 1884 to Captain H. J. King who took her to Chamberlain, S.D. where she was in the ferry and grain business.

Captain Blair goes on, "(she was) homely in appearance, slow of speed and of light power, never had a bad accident, and nearly always made good money for her owners. She was favorably regarded as a leading boat and we never had any trouble to ship a crew for her." She was on her third set of engines by this time and her second cabin. One winter she carried a circus, went as far as New Orleans. In 1898 she ran between Sioux City and Chamberlain, South Dakota. Snagged near Omaha circa 1899.

LECLAIRE #15335

Sidewheel rafter. Built at Dubuque in 1866 for Captain Thomas Doughty by Jonathan Zelby. The cost was $8,000. Walter Blair indicated she was the first boat to tow rafters. 70 tons or 25 tons. One source says dimensions were 80.3' x 15' x 3.1' (LMV); another says 75' x 16' x 3.5'. Tom Doughty was an engineer, and during the Civil War was in charge of the machinery of the *U.S. OSAGE*, a river monitor. He devised a periscope for peering out of a turret, crude, but the first of its kind. Captain Doughty came to LeClaire in the late 1850s. In 1859 he was engineer on the *KENTUCKY NO. 2* towing rafts through lakes St. Croix and Pepin. After the Civil War, he had Jonathan Zelby build a rafter for him in the winter of 1865-66.

The *LECLAIRE* made her maiden trip from LeClaire to Stillwater in May 1866. The water was high, the engines new and untried and too light for the work they were to do. The trip was quite disappointing. George Tromley, Jr. gave Doughty and the *LECLAIRE* a chance at towing one of his rafts, but the venture was not a financial success and the plan of towing by steamboat was abandoned by Doughty. He sold the *LECLAIRE* and went to work for others in engine rooms. She was sold after a spell to C. G. Case and Company, upper rapids contractors, and used for towing in deepening and improving the channel between Le-

Claire and Davenport. One winter she sunk opposite Hampton in the middle of the river. J. W. Van Sant and Company was asked to bid on raising and repairing the boat and bid $1,500. This company raised the boat and sold her back to the former owners at a price of $4,000. In 1876 she was thoroughly overhauled, had a new boiler and a pair of Tremain piston valves installed. They were a great success and that spring she made a trip from Rock Island to Florence, Alabama on the Tennessee River. Returning that fall, Captain Andrew J. Whitney bought her for towing with his dredge fleet.

In September 1879, when on a trip from Muscatine to Rock Island, about twelve miles above Muscatine, she was in a collision with the *VICTORY* and sank in twenty-two feet of water. No lives were lost, all were rescued by the *VICTORY*, but the *LECLAIRE* was a total loss. She was towed to Rock Island and dismantled at the Kahlke yard and the machinery was placed in the new steamboat *A. J. WHITNEY* in the winter of 1879–80. Captain Shell Russell was pilot and Frank A. Whitney was chief engineer on the *LECLAIRE* at the time of the sinking; no blame was attached to anyone on either vessel.

LECLAIRE BELLE   #15986

Sternwheel rafter. Built in 1873 at LeClaire. 171 tons, 171 tons. 125′ x 22.5′ x 4.0′. Later, 126.5′ x 31′ x 4′. According to Sam Van Sant, one of his best boats. Engines 14″ diameter cylinders, 4′ piston stroke, two boilers. I. H. "Windy" Short was captain in 1882 and 1883; George Rutherford in 1880. Towed to Fort Madison, Iowa in 1880 and dismantled at LeClaire in 1890. First boat Captain Walter Blair worked on. The *LECLAIRE BELLE, D. A. McDONALD* and *HARTFORD* were owned by J. W. Van Sant and Sons and "brought them out of the red." This vessel was built at the Van Sant boat yard during the fall and winter of 1872–73. She entered the rafting business in the early spring of 1873. The promoters and builders of the vessel were Van Sant and Son, Captain John McCaffrey and Robert Isherwood and Jonathan Zelby. She was built after two other vessels, the *JAMES FISK, JR.* and the *SILVER WAVE* and was called a "clean up" boat as it was intimated she was built from the scraps and leavings of the other boats. Mrs. Ruth Van Sant named her.

Sam Van Sant relates, "She was a most successful craft and always 'brought home the bacon' for her owners. By the time the boat was completed, her owners had been reduced to Van Sant and McCaffrey. Her engines and doctor came out of the sunken ferryboat *BENTON* at Alton. [She had] two boilers with two flues twenty-four feet long, forty inches in diameter, with cylinders fourteen inches by four feet stroke . . .

"As Captain McCaffrey managed the *LECLAIRE BELLE* I cannot speak of her first seasons's profits; but I know when fall came she owed no man a dollar. The *McDONALD*'s first trip with the new boilers was the most successful trip, financially, ever made by her or any other boat we ever owned. She made enough to pay for both boilers and a handsome surplus left over . . . she practically paid for herself every season she ran. She was dismantled at LeClaire after seventeen years of active service. Her machinery, engines, etc., were in operation fully fifty years, and perhaps more. Her engines were broken up for old iron but her hull was in such a state it was converted to a coal barge and a few years later sank on the Illinois shore, near the Rapids City coal mines.

"Our company in connection with Captain McCaffrey used the *LECLAIRE BELLE* in towing rafts until 1877 or 1879 when the S. and J. C. Atlee Co. bought Captain McCaffrey's half. The boat made such a good season running Atlee's logs that he wanted the entire boat, so the only thing we could do was to let her go. A year or so later, Atlee and Co. built the *SAM ATLEE*. They soon found that they had too many boats and our company again purchased the *LECLAIRE BELLE* and kept her until she was dismantled. Most of the time Captain J. H. Short commanded while we owned her. She was one of the first boats to have electric light . . . She was affectionately known as the 'Midnight Belle.'" She was also nicknamed the Blue Ribbon Belle. "This boat made the most marvelous record on seven consecutive trips from Beef Slough to Muscatine. When the *McDONALD* sank at Keokuk, the *BELLE* took her place on the run with Captain Rutherford at the wheel. The seven trips were made in forty-two days. Captain George Rutherford was second to no other raft pilot."

LILY TURNER   #140612

Sternwheel rafter. Built 1883, Dubuque. 154 tons, 115 tons, 110′ x 18′ x 3.8′. Owned by Turner and Hollingshead, Lansing, Iowa. Captain J. M. Turner, master. In 1890 Chris C. Carpenter was master; in 1895 Horace Hollister commanded; later William Davis was master. Edward Hollingshead was chief engineer, 1885–1887. Ira Fuller was chief engineer for several seasons. In 1888 the *LILY TURNER* was in a collision with the *C. W. COWLES* and was sunk with the loss of two lives. She was raised and later sold to Dimmock Gould and Company of Moline, who used her as a bowboat for the rafter *MOLINE*. By 1890 owned by Edward Hollingshead, Ida S. Lachmund and George Ashton of Lyons, Iowa. Dismantled at Rock Island in 1896, some parts used in building the *MASCOT*.

LINE HANSON   #140686

Sternwheel. 54 tons, 54 tons, 82.5′ x 18.5′ x 3.5′. Built 1884, Savanna, Illinois. She was owned and commanded by Captain William Kimball who used her in job work around the harbor at Dubuque and she also towed barges of clam shells for button factories at Dubuque. Dismantled and rebuilt as *(B) GEORGIE S.*

LION   #140022

Sternwheel rafter/packet. Built in 1875 at Lyons, Iowa. Originally 86' x 15.6' x 3'. Engines 10" diameter cylinders, 4' piston stroke, one boiler. In 1888, rebuilt and enlarged to 101.5' x 19.5' x 2.6'. Up to 1886 *LION* was in the Wabasha, Minnesota to Alma, Wisconsin trade, two round trips per day. The Burlington Railroad was located on the east side of the Mississippi River, however, and *LION* then served three years as a rafter. Owned in 1888 by Captain Hiram C. Wilcox who was also engineer and ran in that capacity on the LION. James Fullmer was captain in 1890. She then went to the Wabasha-LaCrosse trade until after the 1906 season. Dismantled at the Kahlke yard in 1907. Her engines were purchased by the Marine Iron Works of Chicago and then went to Honduras for use on the Ulna River.

LITTLE EAGLE   #10317

Sternwheel towboat. Built in 1868 at Madison, Indiana. Came to the Upper Mississippi around 1870. Purchased by McDonald Brothers in 1875. N. B. Lucas was captain and pilot for a time. In the spring of 1882, she was on her way up river after laying over at St. Louis all winter and stopped at Hannibal to drop a raft. The *LITTLE EAGLE* was not properly "hitched in" to the raft and did not have guy lines out. She struck the draw pier of the bridge and was a total loss, drowning three men. Dyer attributes the loss to the carelessness of Captain Dan Davison. Valued at $10,000 at the time.

LITTLE HODDIE   #140457

Sternwheel. Built 1881, Wabasha. 40 tons, 40 tons, 83.7' x 13.5' x 2.7'. Used for dropping brails at Beef Slough rafting works and in 1888 and 1889, as a bowboat for the rafter *LUELLA*. Rebuilt and renamed *(B) HORACE H.* circa 1898 (at Wabasha).

LIZZIE GARDNER   #15827

Sternwheel rafter. Built in Cincinnati in 1871. 82 tons, 82 tons, 143.6' x 21.0' x 3.6'. She left Parkersburg, West Virginia on March 30, 1878 "with a magnificent fleet of timber for Thacker and Jackson, Cincinnati, the largest and finest fleet ever brought out of the Little Kanawha River." Owned by Drury and Kirns of St. Louis. The Eau Claire Lumber Company also owned her for several seasons and ran lumber from Read's Landing to St. Louis, Jacob Ressor, captain. William Kratka of Lansing, Iowa bought her and ran her a few seasons, selling her to Captain Al Ehart in 1898. His brother, J. E. Short, and he ran logs with her until 1908 to the S. & J. C. Atlee Company, Fort Madison, Iowa. Owned in 1883 by M. E. Drury of Wabasha, Asa Woodward, master. In 1890 owned by Sawyer and Austin, LaCrosse, Ed Kratka, master. The *LIZZIE GARDNER* and *THISTLE* (Gateway Packet Company) were operated in the St. Paul-LaCrosse trade in July 1894. In the fall of 1908 or 1909, while laid up in Rockingham Slough, Captain Short was heating some roof paint to make repairs and the *LIZZIE GARDNER* caught fire and burned.

LONE STAR   #15524

Sidewheel towboat. Built 1868, Lyons, Iowa. 27 tons, 27 tons, 68.4' x 19.3' x 3.2'. George Winans had her chartered at one time towing logs for the Mississippi Logging and Lumber Company. Lome Short was captain for several seasons. Blair remembers her in packet service between Davenport and Buffalo, Iowa, in the late 1860s operated by Captain Sam Mitchell. "Not very fast and limited accommodations." In November 1876, she went into winter quarters and was to be made into a towboat. Captain Mitchell sold her to Goss and Company, sand dealers, for $1,050 at that time. She was dismantled in 1890 in Rock Island, being owned by the Davenport Sand and Gravel Company and rebuilt as a new *LONE STAR*, different registry number.

LOTUS   #141319

Sternwheel rafter. Built Rock Island, 1893. 28 tons, 28 tons, 78' x 16' x 3'. Operated as a rafter until 1903. In 1904 operated out of Paducah on the Green River. Last in service around 1905.

LOUISVILLE   #15863

Sternwheel rafter. Built at Freedom, Pennsylvania in 1864. 191 tons, 191 tons, 125' x 23.3' x 3.6'. Engines either 14" or 15" diameter cylinders by 5' piston stroke. Two boilers. Initially owned by Cyrus Miller, captain Robert M. Boles. Bought in 1865 by R. D. and G. W. Cochran to furnish oil to Pittsburgh from the upper Allegheny River. Brought to the Upper Mississippi in 1868 or 1869 by Durant and Wheeler of Stillwater. Knapp, Stout and Company bought her in 1879. She towed lumber from Reads Landing to St. Louis. Sold to McDonald Brothers, LaCrosse, and they dismantled her there in 1894. Andrew Larkin, I. N. "John" Wooders, and Henry Walker were Knapp, Stout captains. L. A. Day and Robert Cassidy were McDonald captains.

A Knapp, Stout clerk, C. N. Edwards, relates, "Capt. Robert Irving of Alton, Illinois was pilot one summer, as well as Capt. Andrew Larkin. We made one trip from Reads Landing to St. Louis on a good, fair stage of water with fourteen strings of lumber, fifteen cribs long and returned to Reads Landing in fourteen days and we never wet a line on the trip, never landed either the whole or part of our raft, till we landed at St. Louis . . . We were running a raft over the upper rapids once in low water, had a rapids pilot with us, got into the rocks, broke twenty-six deck timbers and tore a hole in her sixteen feet long and eleven inches wide and she sank in six minutes; her main deck was dry, fore and aft, but midships had about two feet of water on it. A friendly boat took care of our raft. I wired St. Louis for a diver, who came at once and built a bulkhead around the break under water. We got up steam, and [with] two barges floated her, and in fifty-five hours from the time she went down, we had her on Kahlke Brothers ways at Rock Island for repair. "At another time, we twisted off the main shaft just over the Rock Island bridge; two boats came to the rescue. One took the raft, the other the boat, and we got out of that scrape without much harm, had to send to Chicago for a new shaft which delayed us a number of days before getting out again."

LUELLA   #140706

Sternwheel rafter built in 1884 at Prescott, Wisconsin. 100 tons, 100' x 19' x 3.8'. Used engines of old rafter *STERLING*, dismantled in 1883 at Hastings. She was built by Ham, West and Truex for the John Dudley Lumber Company of Prescott. In 1890 owned by C. Jellison Towing Company of Wabasha, Captain Jack S. Walker. In 1892, may have been owned by the Valley Navigation Company (Buisson Brothers), Antoine LaRoque, captain for several seasons. In 1892, 93, 94, Jack Walker was master, son Arnell, mate. The *LUELLA* and companion rafter *J. G. CHAPMAN* burned in August 1894 at Wabasha.

LUMBER BOY   #141128

Sternwheel towboat. Built 1891, LeClaire. 55 tons, 55 tons, 78.3' x 15.6' x 4'. Built for Captain J. C. Daniels of Keokuk. Engines were 7" diameter cylinders, 3-1/2' piston stroke. Captain Daniels used her as a bowboat for the rafter *LUMBERMAN* for several seasons and then sold her to McDonald Brothers who used her as a bowboat for their *CLYDE*. Rebuilt at LaCrosse and renamed *(B) GYPSEY* in 1900. Sold to Bronson and Folsom of Stillwater, still running in 1903. Captain Charles W. Conant was master in 1894 and Captain George Senthouse in 1895.

LUMBERMAN   #15804

Sternwheel rafter. Built at Oshkosh, Wisconsin in 1866. 73 tons, 73 tons, 127.5' x 27.7' x 4.4', 50 h.p. First documented April 1871. Owned by S. L. Nevens of LaCrosse in summer 1872. Came from LaCrosse with a doctor to North McGregor, Iowa in July 1872 when the *JAMES MALBON* exploded. Owned in 1883 by J. C. Daniels of Keokuk, Captain Hiram Brazee, master. In 1880 Captain Gary Denberg, master. Sold to Captain B. B. Bradley, Cairo, who used her for towing lumber by barge to that port. Dismantled in 1893 at Jeffersonville. Her machinery went into the towboat *FRITZ*, which was built for Captain Bradley at the Howard shipyard, Jeffersonville, Indiana in 1894.

LYDIA VAN SANT   #144522

Sternwheel rafter. Built 1898, LeClaire as *(A) NETTA DURANT*. 93 tons, 93 tons, 102' x 23' x 4'. Engines 12" diameter cylinder, 6' piston stroke. Built and owned by the Van Sants. The *NETTA DURANT* was hauled out at LeClaire, and it was found best to rebuild rather than repair her, so in 1899 she was made into a bowboat. She was used with the *J. W. VAN SANT*. John Warren was engineer for a time; George Tromley, Sr. was captain just before his death in 1902. Chartered for ten years to the Taber Lumber Company of Keokuk, then bought by Taber and dismantled, rebuilt, and renamed *TABER* (given new registry number).

M

M. WHITMORE   #90019

Sternwheel towboat. Built Pittsburgh, 1868. 97 tons, engines 13" diameter cylinders, 5' piston stroke. Owned by William Hodgson, Captain Willis Hodgson, master. In rafting trade by 1874, then owned by Schulenburg and Boeckler and documented at St. Louis. Still there in 1877, gone by 1881, as she was dismantled and machinery put into a new boat, the *ROBERT DODDS*. George Brasser was her captain for several years. Ezra Schacey was captain and pilot in 1878, followed by Captain Robert Dodds. James Henry Harris was chief engineer for a time.

MARK BRADLEY   #90698

Sternwheel rafter. Built 1872, Prescott, Wisconsin for Captain Cyrus Bradley of Osceola, Wisconsin. 111 tons. Alfred Fuller installed her machinery. Ira Fuller was captain for Bradley in the rafting trade. Dismantled in 1881 at South Stillwater, machinery was put in the *TEN BROECK*, a Gillespie and Harper boat.

MARS   #93315

Sternwheel rafter. Built 1902 at Lyons, Iowa. 132 tons, 120' x 18' x 4'. Engines 10" diameter cylinders, 6' piston stroke. Towed logs from St. Paul to lower river points for many years. On August 30, 1910, she struck a snag at St. Paul and sank in shallow water, but was raised in a few days. Levi King, Sr., chief engineer, 1904 to 1908; Levi King, Jr., his assistant. Owned by Captain George Winans for a time. Foundered August 5, 1912 at Winona; eleven on board, no lives lost.

During his long career of owning

rafting vessels, George Winans liked to name his vessels after the planets. He started a sequence of boats, including *MARS, NEPTUNE,* and *SATURN* (twice). Had not the lumber trade played out, he would have built and commanded many others similarly named.

MARY B.   #136134

Sternwheel towboat. Built *(A) ETHEL HOWARD* at Lake City, Minnesota in 1890. 90 tons, 90 tons, 95.4′ x 22.9′ x 4.2′. Single deck towboat. Bowboat for the *BART E. LINEHAN*. While on ways in winter (December 2, 1907) at Wabasha, fire broke out on the rafter *ISAAC STAPLES* resulting in damage to *MARY B.* and a total loss of the *ISAAC STAPLES, J. W. VAN SANT* and *CYCLONE*. Damage to *MARY B.* $2,600. *MARY B.* burned Wolf River, Tennessee, August 5, 1915.

MASCOT   #927937

Sternwheel rafter. Built Galland, Iowa, 1896. 56 tons, 38 tons, 81′ x 19′ x 3.6′. Engines 10″ diameter cylinders, 6′ piston stroke. Had machinery from the *LILY TURNER*. Sold to C. H. Deere of Moline in 1899 who converted her to a pleasure craft. Another source says she was built at the Kahlke yard at Rock Island for Dimmock, Gould & Company. Burned at Kahlke yard, Rock Island, April 10, 1900 in the same fire that destroyed the rafter *SATURN* (#1) and packet *VOLUNTEER*. *MASCOT* was valued at $8,000.

MAUD   #92212

Sternwheel rafter. Built Wabasha, 1890. 23 tons, 79′ x 16.5′ x 3.2′. Captain Ira DeCamp part owner. Owned by Jellison Towing Company, Wabasha; they also operated rafters *J. G. CHAPMAN* and *LUELLA*. Sold to Tennessee River, circa 1896.

MAY LIBBY   #91610

Sternwheel rafter. 58 tons, 58 tons, 102′ x 13′ x 3.2′. Built 1883 in Hastings, Minnesota by Captain Libby. Used in general towing at Hastings and vicinity and later as a bowboat for the *DAN THAYER* and *SAM ATLEE*. George Dansbury was engineer for a time. Captain Elmer Brown was master in 1893. Dismantled in Lyons, Iowa, 1898.

MENOMONIE   #91259

Sternwheel rafter. Built 1880, Madison, Indiana. 89 tons, 89 tons, 119′ x 25.5′ x 4′. Engines had 10-1/2″ diameter cylinders, 6′ piston stroke. Knapp, Stout owned her initially and ran her in their harbor business out of the Red Cedar and Chippewa Rivers until 1886 and then sold her to the Matt Clark Towing Company of Stillwater. She was in the Reads Landing-St. Louis trade. About 1883 sold to Bronson and Folsom of Stillwater. Captain I. H. Miliron, master, 1883. In May 1883, Captain Stephen B. Withrow raced *MENOMONIE* against *LOUISVILLE* from Reads Landing to St. Louis. Both vessels had lumber rafts about 200 by 600 feet. Also in 1883, *MENOMONIE* took a 192 foot x 576 foot lumber raft from Reads Landing to Alton, Illinois in six days, four hours, non-stop. Captain D. Dorrance, a LeClaire rapids pilot, took her through the Davenport Bridge without double-tripping. He had about four feet each side to spare, never touched a bridge pier. One of the great raft exploits of all times. Sunk in Sturgeon Bay, July 31, 1894. Raised and dismantled at Stillwater, 1895, machinery placed in *JUNIATA*.

Stephen B. Withrow was master, 1882 and 1885. Robert N. Cassidy, pilot; Tyler Rowe, engineer; "Deck" Dixon was captain in 1892 or 1893; Charles Davison, 1895. Ben Hanks was chief engineer, 1892-95; Arthur Fayerweather, assistant. Mates were Owen Corcoran, 1882 and 1883; Henry Seifert, 1885; and Felix Bruner, 1893 and 1894.

MINNESOTA   #17309

Sternwheel rafter. Built 1865, Wacouta, Minnesota by Captain Obadiah Ames. 218 tons. Her engines were 16″ diameter cylinders, 6′ piston stroke and came from sidewheel packet *HAMBURG*, a vessel that 'scaped louder than she whistled. Her boilers were of 44″ diameter and 22′ length. Ran as a towboat on the St. Croix and Pepin lakes, in command of Captain Albert Ames, brother of Obadiah. Around 1870 sold to Captain Augustus R. Young who used her in rafting for several seasons, then sold a half interest to Carson and Rand Company of Eau Claire. Captain Robert N. Cassidy was master in 1876. Owned in 1878 by Durant and Wheeler, operated out of Stillwater on the St. Croix River. W. R. Young, master. Described as the largest and most powerful rafter of the time. Captain Samuel Hitchcock, pilot with Captain Young for several years. Dismantled in 1879 at South Stillwater.

MINNIETTA   #90453

Sidewheel rafter/packet. Built 1871 at LaCrosse. 70 or 79 tons. May have been sternwheel (or converted). Captain E. E. Heerman was very fond of his daughter, so he named the *MINNIETTA* after her, a combination of her two names. The hull was built in the winter of 1869 on the bank of the Chippewa River opposite the village of Marksville. The hull was towed to LaCrosse in the summer of 1870 and the upper works were placed upon her. She was completed the following winter and came out in 1871. The Michael Funks Boiler Works at LaCrosse built the boiler. The engines were 10″ diameter cylinders with a 3′ piston stroke. At times of favorable water, she made a trip from Reads Landing to Eau Claire daily. The *MINNIETTA* was also employed in rafting from Beef Slough to St. Louis and places in between.

Captain Heerman describes a trip on the *MINNIETTA*. "I was . . . taking a log raft down the great river in 1873 or 74, I think, in July of that year the water got low on the Chippewa and I put a lighter boat on the *MINNIETTA*'s run and put her to towing logs and lumber . . . I started the MINNIETTA out from Beef Slough with thirteen strings of logs, the usual raft. . . . Arriving at the Clinton bridge, the raft was split in half . . . The *MINNIETTA* took one piece through the bridge and the other piece was floated through the easterly span, both parts passing the bridge safely. After passing the bridge, we usually got together as soon as practicable. We had scarcely got our raft together when we observed that a cyclone was bearing down directly upon us. Lashing the two parts of the raft together as speedily as possible, I placed my young son under the snubbing works, putting his little hands around a grub pin, telling him to hang on for his life, that the snubbing works could not break up; that he might get wet, but to stay there, regardless of what might happen.

"I then made my way to the hurricane roof in order to get the pilot, but I met him at the foot of the stairs shouting, 'I am going for the raft; the boat cannot live in this storm.' I crawled into the pilothouse, opened the windward window and straddled the window sill. I got the engineer who was my faithful man [Louis] Duscher. I asked him if he were going to stick to his post, he replied that he was, but that the boat would go down. The water was already up to the sheet iron on the boiler in the ash pan, I asked him to encourage the fireman, who also was sticking to his post, and told him that I would save the boat if they would stay by. That left the three of us on the boat, the rest of the crew having escaped to the raft. All of this time the logs were separating from the raft like knocking down ten pins with a big ball. The logs were scattering in every direction, and seemingly in a few minutes all that was left of the raft was about forty logs where the snubbing works were and those forty logs carried all the crew, except the three on the boat to safety. Both the boat and the pieces of raft remaining were driven ashore on the Illinois side not far below the bridge. The little boy had obeyed his father to the letter and was still holding on to the grub pin.

"Right here the men refused to do further duty, not even to help make the boat fast to the bank, or to save a log. I ordered the cook to get a good dinner for the men, which he did with good effect. It so happened that the boom at Lyons broke in the storm and many logs came floating down the river. Most of them came from Beef Slough, with the same marks as those in my raft, so that no one could tell which was which. After the men were fed, I said: 'Come with me boys; we will soon have our logs together again.' I have often thought, since, that these were the most doubtful words I ever uttered, for the reason that it seemed impossible to save one half of them. I was thankful that it was not worse, and that there had been no loss of life in the storm . . . Had the *MINNIETTA* been caught broadside she would have turned over in half a minute and have been in the bottom of the river quicker than it takes to tell it. As it was it caught her stern to the storm, with the guy lines out. When the first gust passed it was a great wind, which held the boat almost on her beam ends until the raft was destroyed and separated except the few logs pinned together for the snubbing works.

"It took us about eight days to gather up and put together the raft. The logs had gone in all directions, with but a few in one place, scattered on the shore and tangled in the brush and willows. Before we got through the whole crew was destitute of clothing. The whole crew could not muster enough to decently clothe one person. One can readily understand the result to one's clothing of handspiking logs from the shore and picking them out of the willows, for eight days running.

"I took the best dressed man of the crew with me and went to Albany, I staying outside the town and sending the man to the store. The pants he brought me were so small that I could not button them around me, although I am not a large man and could not have weighed over 180 pounds at the time. A steamboat had landed on the Iowa shore and I pulled to it in the skiff. I landed alongside just as the engineer opened the mud valve, I being unobserved by him. Had I been six inches further aft, I would have been badly scalded. . . .

"I then went to Cordova in search of clothing, hiding out in a little grove outside the town, fearing the police would pick me up if I appeared on the streets in such a destitute condition. The man brought me the largest pants he could find, and on putting them on there was at least five inches between the tops of my shoes and the bottom of the trouser legs; but I finally found some clothing and proceeded on the trip, delivering the raft with but three logs short."

The *MINNIETTA* was completely rebuilt, coming out in April 1880 as the *MINNIE H.* and took a colony to the upper Missouri to Judith Basin in Montana. She wintered at Sioux City the following winter, and in 1881, was sold to the government and her name changed to *LITTLE MISSOURI*. Some years later, she was destroyed in an ice gorge near Bismarck, North Dakota.

MINNIE WILL   #17312

Sidewheel rafter. Built Osceola, Wisconsin in 1865 by Captain Cyrus G. Bradley. 51 tons. Typical "stiff" cogwheel engine system. One of first rafters on the St. Croix River. Named after Captain Bradley's 8-year-old niece. The *MINNIE WILL* was built from the salvaged remnants of the *ACTIVE*, a similar craft. Captain Cyrus Bradley successfully towed logs using the

RAFTING STEAMBOAT HISTORIES

MINNIE WILL from the St. Croix river area to Clinton for the W. J. Young Company of that town. Masters of the *MINNIE WILL* were: Hiram Baise, 1865; Hugh O'Neal, 1867; Abe Gilpatrick, 1868; and William M. "Noisy" Smith, 1868. Lost (snagged or sunk) November 1, 1877, mouth of Edwards River, Illinois, on Mississippi River. Sold to government for river improvement work.

MOLINE   #91248

Sternwheel rafter, built 1880, Cincinnati, by C. T. Dumont for Dimmock, Gould and Company of Moline. 192 tons, 192 tons. 126.2′ x 26.2′ x 4.0′. Engines had 14″ diameter cylinders by 5′ piston stroke. She had two steel boilers, 42″ diameter and 24′ long with six 8″ flues, 120 h.p. One of best raft boats on river according to Dyer. Isaac (Isaiah) N. Wasson of LeClaire (one-tenth owner) took charge of her when she came out and was on her until 1889. Mate for Captain Wasson was Ben Metzger, and Thomas Cody in 1882; chief engineer for a long time was Conrad Kraus. Sank near LaCrosse in 1896 but was soon raised and placed back in service. The Kansas City Navigation Company bought her in 1900 and used her as an excursion boat on the Missouri.

Rebuilt at Pikeville, Missouri in 1904. Sold at auction, October 10, 1904 to Thomas and Harry Parker, St. Louis. On December 10, 1907, sold to Captain Ralph Emerson Gaches of Letart Falls, Ohio and Edwin A. Price, Newport, Kentucky (50/50). Renamed *(B) EMERSON* on February 7, 1908 and towed the Emerson showboat *GRAND FLOATING PALACE*. Caught in a cyclone near Kansas City and sunk, a total loss.

MOLLIE MOHLER   #17310

Sidewheel rafter. Built at Carver, Minnesota on the Minnesota River, 1865 by Captain George Houghton, James Houghton and William F. Davidson. 135 tons, 135 tons, 121′ x 21′ x 4′. Built for Minnesota River trade, later a low water boat, running between LaCrosse and Chippewa River points. Named for the sister of an old steamboat clerk, William B. Mohler. In 1872 commanded by Captain J. M. Whistler; Robert N. Cassidy, pilot; J. M. Tully, chief engineer. Bought by McDonald Brothers about 1872. Charles M. Short, master in 1881 (his first boat as master), pilot was Frank Looney. George Dansbury and Charles Higbee were chief engineers. In late November 1880, frozen in for the winter at New Boston. Captain N. B. Lucas was her master in 1883. Dismantled at LaCrosse circa 1889 and machinery placed in *NELLIE KENT*.

MONITOR   #90455

Sidewheel freight-rafter. Built 1863, Reads Landing, Minnesota by a Mr. Thorpe in association with Captain Ben Seavey. 16 tons. Had single engine 6″ diameter cylinder by 12″ piston stroke, geared one to four with maple cogs; engine made four revolutions for every one of the wheels. Opposite the crank was a good sized balance wheel which helped to carry the wheel over the center. Had locomotive boiler, 36″ diameter by 7′ length. Ran Chippewa River most of her career between Durand and Reads Landing, making daily trips. One of the smartest little boats on the Chippewa. Changed hands many times; i.e., Seavey and Thorpe, Seavey and Carlisle, Carlisle Brothers (Henry W. and James). Owned or chartered by Henry Ash, a livery man at Wabasha who ran her to Durand in conjunction with a stage line between Durand and Eau Claire. Also owned by the Eau Claire Lumber Company, which was owned by the Thorpes. Captain E. E. Heerman had her at Reads Landing where he picked up raft crews and got them to Eau Claire on one of his other boats. In March 1881, sold by U. S. marshal to Captain E. C. Bill at Reads Landing for $500 and dismantled there.

MOONSTONE   #17964

Sidewheel rafter. Built 1864, Liverpool, Illinois. 194 tons, 6 h.p. Used by Captain Joseph "Big Joe" Perro to tow rafts. It took fifteen days to go from Stillwater to St. Louis and eighteen days to return so Perro found a more suitable boat. Probably dismantled 1873.

MOUNTAIN BELLE   #90374

Sternwheel packet/rafter. Built 1869, Pittsburgh (Brownsville). 193 tons, 193 tons, 140′ x 22′ x 4.8′. Originally a packet on the Kanawha River. Brought to the Mississippi in March 1873 (sold to Hewitt and Wood, LaCrosse), converted into a rafter. McDonald Brothers had her in their fleet from 1878 on. Sold to the Gem City Sawmill Company of Quincy, Illinois, who used her until 1892 in milling operations. Repurchased by the McDonalds and used until 1904 when they sold her to Captain Anthony. Captains were John Lancaster, 1870; Morrell M. Looney, 1883; Henry (Hank) Walker, 1890; Robert Irvine, pilot; Harry G. Dyer, mate; Andrew P. Lambert, master, 1898-1900. Peter O'Rourke and Andy Lambert mates under McDonald ownership. Chief engineers were Joe Stombs, Henry Tully and Frank Dillon; George Hild was assistant engineer.

Renamed *(B) THE PURCHASE*, circa 1902 to 1904. In June 1903, she was towing an excursion barge between St. Paul and the St. Louis World's Fair (Louisiana Purchase Exposition). The barge was a hotel at St. Louis during the fair. She was condemned and dismantled at Wabasha in 1911 by Peters and Son. Blair says she never had a bad mishap causing any great loss.

An old river man, A. D. Summers, wrote to George Merrick in May 1916 and related this story of a trip on the *MOUNTAIN BELLE*. "At one time during the later seventies I found myself . . . with a very small nest egg and a hard winter ahead, so making the best of a bad situation I shipped out as linesman on the *MOUNTAIN BELLE* with Captain E. J. Lancaster.

". . . Henry Horton was in charge of the engines . . . B.P. Lancaster, mate; Jack Lyons and Johnny Coyne, firemen; Mike and Mary in the cook house.

"We were to deliver at Hannibal and as we were shorthanded, only having five men on deck we took aboard several lower river towboatmen to work their way down.

"One of them could pull a skiff a little and being the only man on deck besides myself who could, he was given to me as assistant. He was considerably older than I and he was in bad shape physically and feeling sorry for him I did him several favors which I have reason to believe he more than repaid some years later when I was night clerk at Disney's coal yard on the LeClaire levee.

"I think Mike (not his real name) was in LeClaire the night Snow was held up in the McCaffrey coal yard and was missing the next day or two, although I didn't connect these happenings until a long time later.

"About all I remember of that trip down was that we were very busy and that we had a re-rafted raft which we cut into eight pieces and cordelied thru the canal, that being the only boat I ever run on where we kept constantly busy boring and plugging down binders . . . another thing I recall was the fact that I ruined a quart of the best liquor I could get at Keokuk. Some one told me that pulverized rhubarb dissolved in whiskey would cure malaria and as I was ailing a little I tried it. I afterwards tried to salvage that quart and would let it settle and pour off. I expect I worked a week at that but that booze was a lost asset.

"After delivering the raft at Hannibal about the last of September we went back up, I believe to Reads Landing where we found a few strings of rafted logs which we dropped down with, and tied up, at the cutoff into Buffalo City. When we went into the cutoff we found several strings of pick-ups waiting for us. It was pretty cold by this time and we took it pretty easy, not working or running at night. As these logs were badly aground it took us several days to get them out to the river and we had time to see a good deal of Buffalo City which I should imagine was a counterpart of a village in the 'Fatherland.'

"While there we stocked up on homespun and home knit mittens and socks, they were great too.

"We then dropped down to LaCrosse with our raft and taking the boat we went up Black River and picked up several more strings of logs. These we had to cut out of the ice with axes and saws, it having turned quite cold and we also had a snowfall of about four inches the day we dropped this piece out.

"I wonder if any of my readers ever ran with Captain B. P. Lancaster. It always seemed to me that Parm (as he was called in those days before he acquired the title of captain) was afraid that if he didn't keep us moving all of our working hours, and seeing that we didn't have too many sleeping hours, we might forget to move at all and what do you suppose he found for us to do that snowy day after we finished our regular lining up? He sent us down in the willows and had us cut a couple of loads of windlass poles and then out to LaCrosse for a coil of brail line (mind you, this was after we had the raft lined up and were ready to start down the river), and had us tacking around in the snow and ice covering the raft all over with brail lines.

"And what do you think happened the next day when the Old Man looked out and saw that network of lines and poles?

"It was reported that he called Parm up and wanted to know what all that was and when Parm explained he said, "Well you go down and take them all off. Do you suppose I am going to have all the men on the river joshing me about the crow's nest?' and we put in another day taking those brail lines off.

"What made it appear harder to us was the fact that 'Curly,' who was mating the *ABNER GILE* offered us $60.00 per, while we were laying at LaCrosse, while we had shipped out at $25.00.

"On the *MOUNTAIN BELLE* we all dined in the main cabin. The men's table was forward and the officer's aft. The men coming in by the officer's table and the officers came by the men's table and I have seen Captain John look over our table and then go down and look over his own, and then call Mike and ask him why such and such a dish wasn't on the men's table and once Mike's explaining that there wasn't enough for both tables he would tell him to put what there was on the men's table then.

"Another thing that was out of the ordinary was that the firemen sat at the officer's table and a further most remarkable fact that captain, mate and both firemen were all engaged in the same battle during the Civil War. I think it was on Lookout Mountain. Captain and mate [were] on the Union side, and the firemen on the Confederate side.

"I don't believe there was a time when all four were seated together at table that the Old Man didn't stir Parm and the firemen up with some slighting remark and then sit back and chuckle until they became so bloodthirsty that he would be obliged to choke them off. Of course as the tables were so close together we got as much fun out of it as the Old Man did, but it was quite a serious matter with Parm as those of you who remember him about that time may imagine.

"It was rather hard to realize it but Captain John told me he only weighed 115 pounds when he came out of Andersonville and he was one of the very few actual fighting soldiers I have ever met on either side who came out of the war with a grouch.

"When we got down to Cat Tail Slough it was getting so late that the company was afraid to risk our going on down as we had nineteen strings and were double tripping so we laid up both boat and raft up in Cat Tail and took the train home. The day we laid up was a beautiful day, I remember."

MUSSER   #91829

Sternwheel towboat/rafter. Built at LeClaire, 1886 for the Van Sant and Musser Towing Company. 163 tons, 163 tons, 137' x 24' x 4.6'. Engines 13" diameter cylinders, 6' piston stroke. Captain Thomas Dolson, master, 1890. In 1890 Stephen B. Withrow was master, I. H. Short, pilot and Harry G. Dyer was mate. Sold in 1907 to Captain Walter Blair. He had the MUSSER hauled out at Wabasha; her cabin, machinery and boilers were raised and a new and larger hull constructed underneath. She was then the packet KEOKUK and ran between Burlington, Keokuk and Quincy as part of the White Collar Line and Carnival City Lumber Company, 1908 to 1923, when roads, trains and buses put her out of business. The KEOKUK burned at Davenport, August 1926.

N

NATRONA   #18453

Sternwheel towboat/packet rafter. Built Pittsburgh, 1863. 193 tons, 193 tons, 120' x 24' x 4'. Engines 12" diameter cylinders, 4' piston stroke, 48 h.p., and originally owned by the Pennsylvania Salt Manufacturing Company of Natrona, Pennsylvania and operated on the Allegheny River. This company sold "Natrona Oil," and once was the largest refiner in the country. NATRONA was bought by the Allegheny Valley Railroad in 1867 who used her to help build that line. NATRONA arrived in Memphis May 31, 1868. Captain James Lee of Memphis owned half of her in April, 1868. She had fifty Pennsylvanians aboard who were going to be "colonists." They had a portable sawmill with them to cut lumber for the New Orleans market. Captain Lee ran her Memphis-St. Francis River (start of his Lee Line).

She was purchased by the McDonald brothers in the early 1870s and brought to the upper Mississippi River for the rafting trade. Pilot was Bill Desmond; Jim Bulls, master for many years. Owned by Captain Volney A. Bigelow in 1883, who was also her master. Sunk in 1891 near East Dubuque, Iowa. U.S. snagboats removed her wreck in 1892. Her engines and machinery were placed in the rafter, JESSIE B., built by Captain Volney A. Bigelow.

NELLIE   #130177

Sternwheel rafter. Built 1880 at Wabasha for Captains Jerry M. Turner and Al Hollingshead of Lansing, Iowa. They used her in the rafting trade until at least 1886. She was 76 tons, 86.9' x 16' x 3'. Horace Hollingshead was captain and pilot for a time.

NELLIE THOMAS   #18742

Sternwheel rafter. Built LaCrosse circa 1870. Had machinery of CHIPPEWA FALLS; i.e., engines were 10" diameter cylinders with a 3½' piston stroke. Abe Looney was part owner and pilot for several seasons. Alex Gordon was her first captain. She was sold to the Davidsons who changed her name to ALFRED TOLL. She received a new registry number, so she must have also been extensively rebuilt.

NEPTUNE   #130854

Sternwheel rafter. Built 1900 in Lyons, Iowa at Godfrey's Marine Ways. 80 tons, 80 tons, 102' x 23.6' x 4.0'. Engines were 12" diameter cylinders, 4' piston stroke and were from the WILDWOOD. Owned by Captain George Winans; Robert Mitchell, first skipper; Captain Joseph Hawthorne, pilot; Harry G. Dyer, mate; John McKeever and Charles Lumley, engineers. In 1901–1904, her master was Captain Charles Trombley. Registered at Evansville, Indiana, circa 1903 and towed out of the Green River. In 1910 she was renamed (B) HARDWOOD.

NETTA DURANT   #130204

Sternwheel rafter. Built 1881, Baytown, Minnesota. 64 tons, 64 tons, 100' x 18.5' x 3.5'. Built by Durant, Wheeler and Company. By 1883 was owned by the Clinton Lumber Company and Captain Al E. Duncan. Frank Wilds was her captain in 1884 when he piled a log raft all over an island above Winona, giving it forever the name of Wilds' Island. In 1890 she was owned by the LeClaire Navigation Company, and they sold her to the Van Sant and Musser Company. Dismantled or rebuilt in 1898 to become the LYDIA VAN SANT.

NINA   #130197

Sternwheel rafter. Built in 1881 near Stillwater in a yard on the Wisconsin side. 86 tons, 86 tons, 114' x 19' x 3'. M. J. Godfrey, an old Scottish shipbuilder, was her architect and builder. Engines were 10" diameter cylinders, 6' piston stroke. Built for Gillespie and Harper who, after a few years, sold her to Hollingshead and Sterling, Lyons, Iowa. Horace Hollingshead was master, 1883. Tom Witherow, captain, 1882. In 1888 mate John Haines was landing a raft at Hannibal, Missouri and dropped between the logs and was drowned.

In 1890 she was owned by Ida S. Lachmund, George W. Washton and the Lyons Lumber Company; Captain Hiram Breeze, master. In 1893 owned by Lowell Sterling and Ida S. Lachmund of Lyons, Iowa. Ira Fuller was master for a few seasons. She burned on the Godfrey Marine Ways, Clinton, on June 16, 1894. Her machinery was salvaged and placed in the *H. C. BROCKMAN*, bowboat for the *F. WEYERHAEUSER.*

NORTH STAR   #202938

Sternwheel rafter. Built 1906 at Dubuque. 138 tons, 138 tons, 140' x 32' x 4.2'. The *NORTH STAR* received the cabin, engines and boilers from the *GLENMONT*. Captain William Dobler was her initial master and James Adams, chief engineer. Owned initially by Sam Van Sant and Captain Elmer McCraney. She had three boilers 38" diameter and 20' long, each with six 6" flues. She was allowed 214 psi and had a 5' piston stroke.

She was one of the last rafters built. She was sold to the Burlington Railroad, October 1911 and went to Metropolis, Illinois and served several years until bought by the Patton-Tully Transportation Company of Memphis and renamed *(B) EUGENIA TULLY.*

NOVELTY—(No Number Found)

Sidewheel towboat/rafter. Built 1868, Lansing, Iowa by a Mr. Robinson of Wabasha. 17 tons. Probably a small log tug around sawmills. She was the first steamboat Captain Cyprian Buisson piloted with Captain John Trudo. She was chartered by Buisson and Jack Walker to run rafts. No record found after 1869.

An unknown river man at Reads Landing told George Merrick that the *NOVELTY* "was the slowest boat ever known—in fact that she was champion of the world for slowness." He said she took a string of lumber from Reads to Burlington in nine days, by the help of the current, of course; and it took her eleven days to get back to Reads running "flying" light—that is if you could imagine her flying under any condition. Perhaps that is where she got her name?

O

ORONOCO   #136270

Originally rafter *(A) E. RUTLEDGE*, built 1892 at Rock Island. Bought by Doctors Charles and William Mayo of Rochester, Minnesota as *(B) JOHN H. RICH*, and she was converted into a pleasure boat by them. 212 tons, 132.7' x 35.5' x 5.4', 375 h.p. Captain Robert N. Cassidy was master and John Wiley, engineer from 1910 to 1914. Captain James J. Richtman replaced Captain Cassidy when the latter retired in 1915. She was registered as a towboat in 1914 and, by 1918, was owned by the St. Louis and Memphis Steamboat Company. In 1920 her home port was New Orleans. Owned by Frank, Williams, and Harry Lyon. Sold to the Ben Franklin Coal Company in November 1921, for $13,000 and renamed *(D) BEN FRANKLIN*, March, 1922.

OTTUMWA BELLE   #155273

Sternwheel rafter. Built 1895, Canton, Missouri. 81 tons, 81 tons, 104' x 22' x 4'. Had engines and some items from the *J. W. MILLS* and was built by Parmalee Brothers and then traded to S. and J. C. Atlee. In August 1915, under Captain Walter L. Hunter, she took the last lumber raft from Hudson, Wisconsin to the Atlee Mills at Fort Madison, Iowa—a fourteen-day trip with a single crew. Frank Okell was chief engineer, his brother Frank was president of the Atlee Lumber Company.

The *OTTUMWA BELLE* stopped en route to let Captain Stephen B. Hanks get on at Albany, Illinois, and he rode to Davenport on the historic trip. He was ninety-three. This last raft consisted of eight strings, thirty-six cribs long and twenty-eight courses deep. It was 128 feet wide and 1,150 feet long. The lumber, sawed at Hudson, Wisconsin, was about 3.5 million feet, and there was a deck load of 1.0 million feet consisting of large timbers, lumber and lath. *PATHFINDER* was the bowboat. The Interstate Materials Company of Davenport bought her and rebuilt her at the Kahlke yard in 1919 and renamed her *INTERSTATE* (new registry number).

P

PARK BLUFF   #150323

Sternwheel rafter. Built 1884, Rock Island. 96 tons, 96 tons, 107.3' x 22.7' x 3.5'. She had two double riveted steel boilers, 36" diameter by 18' in length; five 10" flues in each. Engines and boilers were from the McElroy Iron Works of Keokuk. *PARK BLUFF* was named for a noted summer resort at Montrose, Iowa. Owned in 1890 by the Des Moines Towing Company (R. S. Owen, Sam Speake, Frank A. Whitney and Thomas Peel, one-quarter each) of Montrose, Iowa. Captain Thomas Peel was master, Sam Speake was pilot, Frank Whitney was chief engineer and Captain R. S. Owen was clerk and business manager. She was used in the rafting business several years. She sank in Lake St. Croix, and an engineer, James Ferguson, was drowned. She was the bowboat to the rafter *GLENMONT.*

She was sold to Thomas Adams of Quincy who had her in the excursion business 1896 and 1897, perhaps later. Rebuilt at Wabasha, 1906, and renamed *HARRIET* when sold to Rock Island Sand Company.

PARK PAINTER   #20407

Sternwheel towboat. Built 1868, Pittsburgh, by George O. Ebermann and Company. 90 tons, 90 tons, 119' x 19.4' x 3.4'. Engines were 12" diameter cylinders, 4½' piston stroke. She had two boilers. Originally as an Allegheny River boat she towed coal barges. Sold to the Upper Mississippi in the 1870s (Hill Lemon and Company, a lumber firm in St. Louis) and placed in the rafting trade. She had debt problems in the fall of 1878 and was sold by a U.S. marshal at Dubuque and bought by Weyerhaeuser and Denkmann. Captain Al Duncan ran her in 1879, 1880. In 1881 she towed for Paige Dixon of Davenport. Dismantled at Clinton in 1881-1882, and her machinery was put in the *SILVER CRESCENT*, a rafter/packet.

PATHFINDER   #150773

Sternwheel rafter. Built 1898, Clinton. 62 tons, 62 tons, 85' x 20' x 3.6'. Engines were 8" diameter cylinders, 4' piston stroke and one boiler. Bowboat for George Winans' *SATURN* and was also the bowboat for *OTTUMWA BELLE* during the passage of the last raft. She had the boiler, engines and stacks of the *MAY LIBBY* built at Hastings and formerly owned by the Atlees. In 1916 she was sold to the Buchanan Sand and Supply Company, St. Joseph, Missouri. While moored in their fleet, a sand bar formed under her stern. She was caught on it and broke in two when the river fell.

PAULINE   #150147

Sternwheel rafter, wood. Built 1878 at Stillwater, Minnesota at the Durant and Wheeler yard, Josiah Batchelder assisting. 101 tons, 101 tons, 112' x 21' x 3.5'. Engines had 12" diameter cylinders, 6' piston stroke. She had two boilers, each 31" in diameter, 20' long, each having twenty 10-inch flues. She was named for Pauline Durant.

Durant and Wheeler used her in conjunction with their Stillwater lumber mills until 1880 when they sold her to Captains Al Hollingshead and D. C. Law. Captain D. C. Law relates, "A. F. Hollingshead and myself bought the *PAULINE* in the fall of 1880 from Durant and Wheeler . . . In the spring of 1881 we got a contract for running the Chippewa Lumber and Boom Company's lumber from Reads Landing (Minnesota). We also had a contract with the Daniel Shaw Lumber Co. and the Badger State Lumber Co. Hollingshead and myself went into partnership with J. M. Turner. He owned the steamer *NELLIE* and we owned the *PAULINE*. We pooled the boats— Turner did the work on the upper end and we did it below. Most of the lumber went to Hannibal, Mo.

"We ran that way for a couple of seasons. Then we got the contract of the Empire Lumber Company of Eau Claire (Wisconsin). They owned the sidewheel *CLYDE*, with iron hull. We took her with the contract, took her to Dubuque and made a stern wheeler out of her. I think that was in the fall of 1883. Then Turner sold the *NELLIE* and we built the *LILY TURNER* at Dubuque, about the same time, ran her in the rafting trade one season. I think that was in 1885. While so engaged she was run into by the *C. W. COWLES* of McGregor, just below Johnsonport, above McGregor on the 4th of July evening and sunk. One man was scalded to death by the bursting of a steam pipe.

"The next winter Hollingshead drew out of the company, taking the *LILY TURNER*, Captain Turner and myself keeping the *CLYDE* and *PAULINE*. The next fall I sold out to Turner and he sold the *CLYDE* to the Standard Lumber Company of Dubuque, retaining the *PAULINE* with the Empire contract and ran that one or two years."

In 1888, the *PAULINE* was sold to Tracy and Peel who put her into the packet trade between Burlington and Keithsburg (Iowa) for two seasons. F. A. Whitney was chief engineer. She was a good boat for the trade which soon built up so large that a bigger boat had to take her place and that one was the *MATT P. ALLEN*. In the spring of 1890 Tracy and Peel sold her to William Kratka of Lansing (Iowa) who ran her in the rafting business. Captain Walter L. Hunter was mate and second pilot in 1890 and Captain I. H. Short was master, Ira Fuller was chief engineer. In 1891 and 1892 Joseph Fuller was chief engineer and Charles Fess was assistant engineer. In 1894 she ran as a low water boat between LaCrosse and St. Paul for the Gateway City Packet Line. The Line was started in April 1894, and ceased operations in July primarily due to low water.

In 1898 she was sold to William Sauntry and Co. who rebuilt her and changed her name to *COLUMBIA*. They sold her to Van Sant and Blair who in turn sold her to Henry Flagler, head of the FEC railway, and she was used along with the *PHIL SCHECKEL* in building the Overseas Railroad to Key West. She was still in existence in 1915.

PEARL—(Number unknown)

Small sidewheel boat built at Hudson, Wisconsin in the late 1850s or early 1860s to run between Hudson and Stillwater. She went into the rafting business. In 1872 a Stillwater paper indicated, "The little steam *PEARL*, Capt. Jo Perro, leaves today with two log rafts of twelve strings each, 'destinated' for Keokuk and Burlington." She does not appear in LH.

PEARLIE DAVIS   #150902

Sternwheel towboat. Built Rock Island, 1901. 140 tons, 140 tons, 127' x 26' x 4'. Used machinery and some equipment from the *R. J. WHEELER*. Owned by William M. Davis of Clinton. Later went to Quachita River, towed oak staves from there to New Orleans. Burned while underway. Not in 1903 list.

PENGUIN   #150110

Sternwheel rafter/packet. Built at Burlington, 1877. 60 tons, 60 tons, 80' x 16.6' x 3.4'. Had one boiler, 42" diameter and 18' long. Engines were 10" diameter cylinders, 3½' piston stroke. Built by James L. and Silas Harris. In 1878 was in

Winona-Alton trade. She was built for the rafting trades, towing wood and rafting logs, and did this for two seasons. She was then sold to Captain Andrew J. Whitney of Rock Island in 1879 and used by him in towing from his dredges to river improvement work. Frank A. Whitney was engineer on her in 1882 and 1883. In 1883 she was on the Missouri River doing towing for the Wabash Railroad at Missouri City, Liberty and St. Charles. Through 1886, run by contractor Captain A. J. Whitney, sometimes on the Missouri. Captain Whitney sold her around 1886, and Captain E. Horace Hollingshead was master that season. The Specht Brothers may have bought her for their ferry business, H. Specht was master in 1887 with John Specht in 1888. In 1889 Thomas Pearson was master.

In 1886 under Captain Hollingshead, the PENGUIN hit a rock on the upper rapids and sank, but was soon raised. Later on by 1891, she was on the Ohio River, and by 1895, at Paducah. She was in Evansville by 1905. She was sunk there by the towboat PITTSBURGH on December 25, 1907, during high wind. PENGUIN burned August 28, 1908 at Evansville with two aboard, but no lives were lost.

PENN WRIGHT #150003

Sternwheel rafter. Built 1871, Cincinnati. 122 tons, 135' x 22' x 3.8'. Owned in 1882 by Captain H. L. Pevey [name also spelled Peavey] of Stillwater. Owned by Durant and Wheeler, Captain Henry L. Pevey, master. Two accidents marred her career. In July 1874 a steam pipe burst on the PENN WRIGHT as she lay to near Winona, scalding the chief engineer, Charles Patten, and a helper, Edward Parker, a brother-in-law of Captain Pevey. The latter [Parker] died from the injuries. On September 30, 1880 when near Bellevue, Iowa, she burst a steam pipe killing the chief engineer, Charles Tate, who was on watch and scalding his assistant, Albert Wish, and the water tender, Samuel Fowler. United States inspectors laid the accident on the dead engineer, "too much steam." Officers with Captain Pevey while he owned the vessel were Henry Whitmore, chief engineer, and John H. Fuller and Ira Fuller. Burned at Stillwater January 12, 1885.

PERCY SWAIN #91422

Sternwheel rafter. Built at Reads Landing in 1882 from MINNIE. 90 tons, 90 tons, 128' x 20' x 3.5'. In the fall of 1882 her upper works, machinery, etc., were removed and sent overland to Devils Lake, North Dakota. The remaining hull was bought by Captain David Swain, and he built PERCY SWAIN from it with the help of M. J. Godfrey. The vessel was named after a son of Captain David M. Swain. She was 139.8' x 19.7' x 3.5', engines were 12" diameter cylinders, 6' piston stroke, and were cross-compound, condensing of a type built by Swain. She was a rafter until sold in 1899 to E. H. Kirchner and Sons, Fountain City, Wisconsin, who used her in river contracting, building wing dams, etc. In 1904 she towed barges and house boats upriver from Clinton. James Steadman was engineer on her for a long time. Sold to Memphis parties and renamed (B) PROGRESS.

PETE KIRNS—(Number Not Known)

Sternwheel rafter. Built 1879 in St. Louis for Captain Peter Kirns, a floating raft pilot. 120 tons, 122' x 24' x 4'. The engines were 12" diameter cylinders, 4' piston stroke and were from the J. W. VAN SANT (#1). She was built for Captain Peter Kirns who put her in the rafting trade in charge of Captain I. H. Milliron towing lumber from the Chapman and Thorpe Mills at Eau Claire, Wisconsin, to St. Louis. Sold in the fall of 1879 to the Mississippi River Commission. Renamed (B) KIRNS in 1891, and sank near Belmont, Kentucky, 1893.

PETE WILSON #20060

Sidewheel vessel built 1864 in Menominee, Wisconsin. Originally 35 tons, 70' x 12' x 3'. She had a locomotive-type boiler, 36" diameter, 8' long, and had 2½" flues. When rebuilt, was 69 tons, 90' x 18.3' x 3.3' and was used as a bowboat. Knapp, Stout and Company used her mostly on the Chippewa. She was a single-engine geared boat. Master was Captain Phil Scheckel, pilots were Eli Minder, Michael Magill, and Marcellus Stevens. Engineers were Hiram Wilcox, Chuck Wilcox, Alvin E. Fuller, Sol S. Fuller, John Howard, and Ben Anderson. She had no cabin; her pilot house was on the main deck. Dismantled in 1888.

PHIL SCHAECKEL #150142

Also spelled SHECKEL, SCHECKEL, last used most often. Sternwheel towboat built in 1878 at Waubeck, Wisconsin for Knapp, Stout and Company. Originally 98' x 19' x 3.5'. Named for Captain Phil Scheckel, a fifteen-year employee. Used mostly on Chippewa River, touched at Menominee (on the Chippewa) and Reads Landing. Captain Phil Scheckel in command, 1883. Owned by Sam Van Sant and used as a bowboat for the B. HERSHEY. Rebuilt 1896-1897 at Wabasha and was given a new number, 150750.

PHIL SCHECKEL #150750

Rebuilt at Wabasha in 1896-97 from the former PHIL SCHECKEL. 99 tons, 111.5' x 24.8' x 4.2'. Guards were 2.8' wide. Wheel was 12' in diameter, had 14-foot long buckets, one steel boiler 3½' diameter and 16' long. Engines had 9" diameter cylinders, 42" piston stroke, 166 psi, 14" diameter smoke stacks. Dining room was 17' x 20'; engine room

RAFTING STEAMBOAT HISTORIES

was 18' x 20'; two staterooms, each 10' x 7½'; berths for sixteen in each. One stateroom was 7' x 7½', six berths; another was 7' x 7½' with eight berths. Office was 7' x 7½', two berths. Kitchen was 7½' x 10' (all on main deck). Pilothouse was 10' x 11' (outside). Pilotwheel, 6½' diameter to end of spokes. Cost was $6,633.57. She drew 11" light, used 2½ cords of wood in twenty-four hours, ran night and day six days every week during season. Sold 1901–02 to Captain Samuel R. Van Sant. Officers were: Phil Scheckel, captain, 1878 to 1901; pilots, Eli Minder, Marcellus Stevens, William Dustin, Henry Carlyle; and engineers were James McGuire, Ben Anderson, and Pearl Roundy.

In 1906, sold to Henry Flagler for work on Overseas Railway to Key West, registered, St. Augustine. On April 26, 1907, struck a rock near Johnson Key, Florida, and sank in 4½ feet of water, raised, Captain F. L. Moody. On June 11, 1907, collided with schooner *COLUMBIA* three miles from Pelican Key beach in Hawk Channel. The schooner was towed to Key West by the *PHIL SCHECKEL*. Not on list after 1918.

PILOT   #150242

Sternwheel rafter. Built 1882, LeClaire. 118 tons, 118 tons, 116.8' x 21.2' x 3.7'. Engines 10.5" diameter cylinders, 4¼' piston stroke. Machinery came from *WILD BOY*, a bowboat. Owned by Captains D. F. Dorrance and John McCaffrey of LeClaire. Used as bowboat. John McCaffrey was master, 1885. Captain Orrin Smith bought her for use as a bowboat. Owned in 1890 by Pilot Steamboat Company of LeClaire, Captain Orrin Smith, master. Sold in 1898 to the LeClaire Stone Company who used her in towing rock from its quarries. She sunk on the rapids in 1898 and was soon raised. Frank Long was chief engineer for some time. Rebuilt in 1903 and renamed *PEERLESS* (new registry number).

PIONEER   #20061

Sidewheel towboat rafter. Built 1866 in Osceola, Wisconsin. 115 tons. Dismantled 1874. Perhaps used in shifting logs around mills.

PRESCOTT   #150007

Sternwheel rafter. Built in Prescott, Wisconsin, 1870. 48 tons, 80' x 18' x 3'. One of the first bowboats. Owned by D. F. Dorrance and John Smith. The *PRESCOTT* was named after the place where she was built. She was constructed by Andrew Rader, Hap West and Robert Wilson. She was to carry passengers between Prescott and Hastings before the Chicago, Milwaukee, St. Paul and Pacific Railroad bridge was built at Hastings.

After the *PRESCOTT* was sold, the *ANNIE BARNES* was built to take her place. H. S. West was master and pilot, Robert Wilson was engineer, and Andrew Rader was clerk. The *PRESCOTT* was sold to Charley Gillespie and Herb Gerboth, and they ran her in the packet trade between Dallas City and Keokuk. They used corn cobs for fuel and even had special furnace grate bars. However, the arrangement proved unsuitable, and the use of corn cobs was discontinued after a few weeks. She was next sold to Vincent and Tom Peel and the Burlington Lumber Company. She worked for a few years as a rafter [circa 1874 and 1875], and Vincent Peel was captain, George Oman was chief engineer, and Tom Peel was second engineer. The Peels et al. sold the *PRESCOTT* to John Smith of LeClaire who used her as a helper craft over the Rock Island Rapids for four or five seasons. She was then sold to Vincent Peel and Andrew J. Whitney who ran her in government work for two years and then sold her to Sip Owens, Frank Whitney, Sam B. Owens, Sam Speake, and Tom Peel. They called themselves the Des Moines Rapids Towing Company. They also built the *PARK BLUFF* and ran the rapids from 1874 to 1893 and then sold both boats. The *PRESCOTT* was bought by Weyerhaeuser and Denkmann and used by them as a bowboat.

After the rafting business ceased, she was sold to the Davis Brothers of Rock Island. Captain Frank A. Whitney stated, "She was one of the most successful boats ever built, and it is said never lost a dollar for her owners. She had one steel boiler with engine cylinders 8½" bore and 3½' stroke . . . The boat . . . only had one serious accident when one of her firemen, W. Holmes, of Montrose, went out on a raft while in the canal above Keokuk to put a signal light on the corner of the raft, fell into the canal and was drowned. Every steamboat man [who lived] during the raft days will remember this faithful little steamboat."

PRINCE   #121018

Built as *(A) FRONTENAC*, 1896, at Wabasha. As *(B) PRINCE*, she was a passenger vessel, 146 tons, 146 tons, 138.9' x 29.8' x 5'. Crew of ten, 500 h.p., registered at St. Louis, 1917.

PROGRESS   #91422

Sternwheel towboat. Built *(A)* as *PERCY SWAIN*, a rafter, at Reads Landing in 1883. Engines were 12" diameter cylinders, 6' piston stroke. Named *(B) PROGRESS* circa 1921. Owned by the Tennessee Hoop Company of Memphis in 1925. Sank July 20, 1926 at Memphis.

PROVIDENCE   #77214

Built *(A)* as *JO LONG*. Sold to Vicksburg area, Captains Yerger and Morgan, circa 1898. Ran to Lake Providence and Davis Bend. Capsized and sank with loss of many lives.

Q

QUICKSTEP   #20607

Sternwheel rafter/towboat. Built 1893 at Dubuque as a rafter. 66 tons, 66 tons, 106′ x 20.5′ x 4′. Had engines of old rafter *ST. CROIX*, 12″ diameter cylinders, 4′ piston stroke. Owned by Volney A. Bigelow of LaCrosse. Used as bowboat for the *BART E. LINEHAN*. Master in 1893 was Captain A. Gallagher. By 1901 owned by the Kelly Lumber Company and operated on the White and Black rivers in Arkansas towing logs, etc. Burned on Lake Des Allemands on June 2, 1906, during a severe windstorm. The hull capsized after the fire.

R

R. D. KENDALL   #111105

Sternwheel rafter. 82 tons, 82 tons, 92′ x 23.5′ x 3.5′. Built 1896, Rock Island. Machinery came from the *SILAS WRIGHT*. The engines were 10″ diameter, 4′ piston stroke. She was used as a bowboat by Weyerhaeuser and Denkmann [of Rock Island] and served with the *F.C.A. DENKMANN* and *E. RUTLEDGE*. Circa 1906 she was bought by Jesse B. Hurl and P. J. Miller of Owensboro, Kentucky for towing in the sand and gravel business. In 1911 they sold her to Captain and Mrs. Frank T. Rounds of Cloverport, Kentucky. Much of her equipment was used in building the packet *GOLDEN GIRL*.

R. J. WHEELER   #110419

Sternwheel rafter. Built 1880 Baytown (South Stillwater), Minnesota. 140 tons, 140 tons, 126′ x 26.2′ x 3.9′. Used some machinery from the *ROBERT SEMPLE*. Owned by Durant, Wheeler and Company of Stillwater. Durant and Wheeler ran her until 1890 and then sold her to William Davis who continued in the towing trade until 1898, commanding her himself most of that time. His brother, George Davis, was pilot, Charles B. Roman was captain and pilot in 1897. Henry Fuller was also captain and pilot for a time. Ira Fuller, Alfred Fuller, and Clair C. Fuller were in charge of the engine room at various times and Orrin Fuller, then a youth, helped them for awhile. Bernard Rockwood was chief engineer for a number of seasons as was George Griffin. The *R. J. WHEELER* was commanded by R. J. Wheeler and William Whistler in 1890, by Ira Fuller in 1886 and by Ira DeCamp in 1889 and Charles B. Roman in 1890.

Sold to William M. Davis of Clinton, circa 1898–1900 and rebuilt and renamed *PEARLIE DAVIS* soon thereafter. She received a new registration number. In 1898, Captain Davis took her to the lower river and towed barges of staves to New Orleans.

Harry Dyer says this of her, "She was what I would call a model rafter. She was built low between decks so as not to catch the wind, was large and roomy in the deck room and fire box; had good power; (engines) fourteen inches by five feet, with three boilers and was light on fuel. Her engines were of the ROBERT SEMPLE, dismantled."

In 1890 the *Stillwater Gazette* mentions one trip of the *R. J. WHEELER*, "[She] left with a lumber raft . . . one of the finest ever constructed on Lake St. Croix [that] contained sixteen full strings of lumber aggregating 2,072,000 feet; 1,043,000 lath, 1,400,000 shingles and 4,000 pickets. The weight of the tow was nearly 6,672 tons which is considered a very good load for a tow boat to handle."

RAVENNA   #110823

Sternwheel rafter. Built 1889 at Stillwater by Bob Anderson and Jim O'Brien. 164 tons, 87 tons, 125.6′ x 23.0′ x 3.5′. Engines were 12″ diameter cylinders, 6′ piston stroke and came from the *G. B. KNAPP*. Anderson later sold his interest to Bronson and Folsom followed by O'Brien. Bronson and Folsom had John Hoy as master except for 1895 and 1896 when Captain C. H. Davison was in charge.

On June 2, 1902, the *RAVENNA* capsized in a storm at Maquoketa Chute near Dubuque and four were drowned including Captain Hoy and Clerk Byron Trask who were found locked in each other's arms. Two Muscatine lumbermen were also drowned. The vessel was raised and continued on in the lumber rafting trade.

In 1908 she was sold to Captains H. C. Wilcox and (son) Dwight who renamed her *(B) LACROSSE* and put in the packet trade between LaCrosse and Wabasha. Her last rafting masters were Charles Davidson and William Wier. Engineers were Sam Serene, J. H. Fuller, Charles Fisher and John Fuller, Jr.

An account of the 1902 tragedy follows:

Disaster at Maquoketa Chute Recalled: Captain Hunter Tells of Tragedy. (Adapted from the *Dubuque Telegraph Herald*, July 22, 1934)

Death stalked the entrance to Maquoketa Chute in June 1902 when the rafter *RAVENNA* was wrecked in a severe storm and went to the bottom of the river carrying with her Captain John Hoy and three other members of the crew. Captain W. L. Hunter who brought down the last raft, and who supervised the work of raising the *RAVENNA* recalled the accident.

The *RAVENNA* had her bowboat, *GYPSY*, ahead of her and was northbound after having delivered a raft to a Muscatine lumber company. Captain John Hoy of the *RAVENNA* had been advised by his pilot of the seriousness of the situation before the storm struck, but had ordered the boat to proceed.

Shortly after the boat had entered the Chute at about 4 P.M. on June 12, 1902, the storm broke from the direction of the Iowa shore and the steamboat, which was a narrow craft, only twenty-two feet wide, toppled over on its side and most of her crew were thrown into the water. Captain Hoy, however, and his clerk Byron Trask, who happened to be in the latter's cabin, were trapped and drowned. Two deckhands also lost their lives after their efforts to cling to floating wreckage failed. The bodies of the captain and clerk were not recovered for several days, while the other two were picked up in the vicinity of Eagle Point.

According to Mate Walker who was at the wheel when the storm struck, he had been hugging the Iowa shore which was lined with trees and which he expected would protect the boat from the strong wind. The accident occurred at a spot where the trees had been cleared, exposing the craft to the full force of the gale. "I rang for the captain as soon as I realized the situation" he said afterwards, "but it was too late. The next thing I remember the *RAVENNA* was on her starboard side and the water about us was a mass of struggling men, timbers, and effects from the boat."

Captain J. A. Hire of the *GYPSY* was in his stateroom at the time, but his craft, in some manner, escaped the fury of the storm, broke away from the *RAVENNA* and remained upright. There was no steam in her boilers, however, and the crew of the smaller boat were helpless to aid those struggling in the water because the wind had blown her almost directly to the Wisconsin shore line.

Many of the *RAVENNA*'s crew saved by clinging to the upturned hull and were rescued by a ferryboat which came down the river shortly after the accident occurred. Other were picked up by a watchman on the *RAVENNA* who swam to shore, jumped into a skiff that had been blown off the wrecked boat and returned to the scene of the tragedy, picking up men clinging to floating objects in the water.

Edward Johnson, one of the *RAVENNA*'s crew, described the death of Captain Hoy and Clerk Trask. Johnson was standing in the doorway of the Clerk's cabin when the storm struck and saw the Captain thrown to the floor and witnessed the efforts of the Clerk to get him to his feet. (A) wall of water, however, rushed into the cabin at this point and Johnson himself was hurled into the river. The Captain was found clasped in the arms of his clerk when the boat was raised and their bodies recovered.

Captain Hunter, who was serving on the rafter *ISAAC STAPLES* at the time, was notified to go to Maquoketa Chute to raise the sunken hull. In this work, he recalls, he resorted to the use of some 150 beer kegs furnished by a Dubuque brewery. (A) hole was cut in the side of the *RAVENNA* and the empty beer kegs, tightly sealed, were inserted. A series of ropes were placed about the hull, the ends being attached to trees on the shore. Buoyancy of the beer kegs righted the craft after Captain Hunter's boat pulled on other ropes. She was towed to Eagle Point, where she was remodeled and refitted. Later she ran between LaCrosse and Wabasha, her name being changed to *(B) LaCROSSE*.

RAY MOORE   #116224

Built as *(A) SCOTIA* in LaCrosse in 1889. 100.5' x 13.4' x 3'. Renamed *(B) RAY MOORE* in March 1929. Owned by George E. Breece Lumber Company, Monroe, Louisiana. Named for secretary of the firm. Lasted until circa 1937.

RED WING   #76793

Sternwheel rafter. Built as *(A) JUNIATA* in 1889 at Winona. 134' x 22.5' x 4.2'. Engines were 12" diameter cylinders, 6' piston stroke. Renamed *(B) RED WING* circa 1906-07. Captain Milt Newcomb of Pepin, Wisconsin ran her in the Wabasha-St. Paul packet trade and towed the excursion barge *MANITOU*.

In 1912 Captain Newcomb took *RED WING* and *MANITOU* to Durand, Wisconsin, on the Chippewa River—first boats there in twenty-six years. Captain Ralph Emerson Gaches bought both vessels and took them to Pittsburgh to run excursions on the Monongahela and Allegheny Rivers.

The *RED WING* burned while laid up at the Eichleay yard, Hays, Pennsylvania, December 24, 1926. The *MANITOU* was sold to J.S. Slyfield of McGregor, Iowa, and Lyman Howe of Prairie du Chien in April 1932.

REINDEER   #110765

Sternwheel rafter, packet. Built 1888, Dubuque (Diamond Jo yard). 124' x 23' x 3.3'. Engines were 12" diameter cylinders, 6½' piston stroke, two boilers, 32" diameter, 20' long, had a California cutoff. Owned 1890 by Alfred Hollinshead and D. C. Low of Lyons, Iowa, with Hollinshead serving as master. By 1893 owned by the Mississippi Towing Company, Lyons, Iowa, Captain Thomas C. Withrow serving as master. Snagged in Coon Slough, summer of 1893 or 1894. Believed to have hit wreckage from *LADY FRANKLIN* and *NOMINEE;* raised. She ran as a tri-weekly packet, Dubuque to Clinton, fall of 1897. She was rebuilt in 1901 at Quincy, Illinois, with a new hull and became the *ILLINOIS* of the Illinois Fish Commission. In 1895 Thomas C. Withrow was master; in 1896, John Pearson; in 1897, W. M. Moore; in 1898, J. Mather; and in 1900, for the Fish Commission, Thomas Williams.

RESCUE   #120982

Built as *(A) FRITZ*, Jeffersonville, 1894. 81 tons, 81 tons, 120' x 26' x 3.8'. In Pittsburgh as towboat after

1907. Twelve crew, 230 h.p. Still in 1924 LMV.

ROBERT DODDS #110543

Sternwheel rafter. Built 1882, South Stillwater. 93 tons, 80 tons, 83' x 22' x 1.4'. Engines 13" diameter cylinders, 5' piston stroke. Had engines of the rafter *M. WHITMORE*. Named for Captain Robert Dodds, a long time employee of Schulenburg, Boeckler. Owned by Schulenburg and Boeckler Lumber Company of St. Louis from 1882 to 1892. George Brasser was master all this time. In April 1893, she was sold to the Dodds Towing Company of Davenport who ran her in the rafting business for four or five seasons, towing for Schulenburg and Boeckler. Captain Hugh McCaffrey was master and one of the owners.

Owned in 1897 by John D. Pearson of Clinton and later by Mrs. Ida Moore Lachmund of Clinton. She rode and managed the vessel for six years. Mrs. Lachmund was well liked and respected by the rafters on the Upper Mississippi. Officers of the *ROBERT DODDS* at various times were: John D. Pearson, captain; Alfred R. Withrow, pilot; Henry A. Horton and Lewis Day, engineers; and Will Babatz, mate.

Captain Ralph Emerson Gaches bought *ROBERT DODDS* in January 1909 to tow his showboat. On September 11, 1909,. Captain E. A. Price bought the showboat *GRAND FLOATING PALACE* and the *ROBERT DODDS* from Gaches. She was rebuilt in 1911 at Vicksburg and documented as a new boat, 128.5' x 25' x 3'. Captain E. A. Price sold her to J. W. Menke in the spring of 1917. She then sunk at Newburgh, Indiana. Her new owners raised her in the fall of 1917, and she survived the ice of 1918 at Paducah. She towed corn out of the Cumberland River in the spring of 1918 and was sold to the Ripley Coal Company, Ripley, Ohio and dismantled thereafter (circa 1919). Her machinery was placed in the towboat *J. H. DONALD, JR.* built in 1920.

Under Captain George Brasser, Adophe Brasser (known as Don on the river) was mate, James Henry Harris was chief engineer of her for five seasons. Frank Whitney indicates that Mr. Harris had the finest engine room on the river. On February 19, 1918, Mr. James H. Harris wrote to George Merrick about Captain Brasser and the *ROBERT DODDS*. "I did not put the machinery on her, that having been done by the late W. B. Milligan of Davenport. I took her above LaCrosse on her first trip. Captain Brasser (pronounced as if spelled Brass-saw) commanded her and Geo. Tromley, Sr. was second pilot. . . . I remained on her until I resigned at the beginning of the season of 1887 to became Chicago manager of the Heine Safety Boiler Company. Previously to being chief on the *DODDS* I had been chief of the *M. WHITMORE*, out of which the *DODDS* was constructed. I took the *WHITMORE* single handed the fall prior to [when] the *DODDS* came out.

"As Capt. Brasser was entirely devoid of schooling, I was designated by the company to do the business of the boat, keeping the books, paying the bills, buying everything or at least supervising it, in fact was, in truth, commander in all things save the name, which is here recorded merely as an incident. With the authority here suggested, I created an engine room that was so prolific of art as to extend well into the realm of the studio, and it became famous from one end of the river to the other, as indeed it was the handsomest engine room that was ever on a steamboat.

"Hugh McCaffrey was pilot on the *DODDS* for two seasons before I left her, in place of Geo. Tromley. When I left the boat, I put H. C. Goodloe chief and the officers were George Brasser, Captain, Hugh McCaffrey, pilot, and S. C. Goodloe chief engineer.

"Finally the Schulenburg & Boeckler Co. sold their three boats to the late Captain John McCaffrey who took the towing by contract and continued until the failure of [the company]. His brother-in-law, George Tromley, Jr. commanded the *DODDS*."

ROBERT ROSS #110177

Sternwheel rafter. Built 1873, LaCrosse. Built from the wreck of the *JAMES MALBON*. 172 tons, 123' x 24.5' x 4.7'. Engines were 14" diameter cylinders, 6' piston stroke. Circa 1881, she was renamed *(B) J.S. KEATOR* and owned by J. S. Keator and Sons of Moline.

ROBERT SEMPLE #110217

Sternwheel towboat. Built 1871, Pittsburgh, Illinois. 111 gross tons, 58 net, 130' x 22' x 3'. Engines were 13" diameter cylinders, 5' piston stroke. She had three boilers, 36" diameter, 22' long, 110 h.p. Her cost was $10,000. Her wheel was 17' diameter with 17' long buckets. She could carry 200 tons, light draft of 30". Captain Thomas M. Rees, owner. Captain I. N. H. Carter, master. Durant and Wheeler brought her to Upper Mississippi circa 1875 or 1876. Ralph J. Wheeler was captain for a time; H. Pevey, captain and pilot also. Nelson Fuller was chief engineer for several seasons. Dismantled at South Stillwater in 1879; machinery put into new boat, the *R.J. WHEELER*.

RUBY #110470

Built as sidewheel rafter/towboat. First boat that Harry G. Dyer was on. Built at DeSoto, Wisconsin for Gardner and Wareham. 54 tons, 77' x 16.9' x 3.3' (perhaps later 105' x 23' x 4.2'). Inspected as a towboat at Stillwater, 1882. At Dubuque, 1895, L. A. Gardner was master and Wareham was engineer. She differed from the usual type of sidewheel craft of this period, as she had but one engine and was not geared as were the others. She was chartered in the spring of 1881 by Gillespie and Harper of Stillwater and used in towing logs from there to points

RAFTING STEAMBOAT HISTORIES

above the upper rapids. In 1884 she was put into the packet trade between Lansing, Iowa and LaCrosse for several seasons. Mr. Wareham sold his half interest to Captain H. Douglas of Wabasha, Gardner and Douglas dissolved their partnership and Gardner was killed soon thereafter in a street car accident in St. Paul in 1888. The *RUBY* was sold to John F. (Fisherman John) Jeremy in 1887 and not long after was sold to Captain H. A. Schroeder of Prairie du Chien who used her in the rafting trade and also as a short line packet. She burned in 1900, three miles below Glen Haven, Wisconsin, and her wreck then lay in Cassville Slough. George Herold was captain and pilot in 1881; L. A. Gardner, 1882; Silas G. Staples, 1882; J. J. Jeremy, 1888; Joseph Pierce, 1889; William Maikel, 1900; and H. A. Schroeder, date unknown.

RUTH #110967

Sternwheel rafter. Built 1892, Wabasha. 60 tons, 60 tons, 97.2' x 18' x 3.7'. Owned by Captain Sam Van Sant who ran her in 1892 and perhaps thereafter. Ran in rafting trade for several years. M. A. Davis, master, 1896. At Vicksburg, 1902.

S

ST. CROIX #115108

Sternwheel packet/rafter. Built 1870, Maiden Rock, Wisconsin. 98 tons, 115' x 20' x 4'. Originally run as a packet on St. Croix River by Lorenzo Schricker. Captain Isaac Grey ran her in the packet trade for two seasons between Prescott, Hudson, Stillwater and Taylors Falls and then sold her to Captain George Winans who ran her in the rafting trade for thirteen seasons. During this time, she was commanded by Winans, George Tromley, Jr., Joseph M. Hawthorne, and John O'Connor. By 1883 owned by Mueller Lumber Company, Davenport, Iowa; Captain George Tromley, Jr., master. Captain Walter Blair and Sam Van Sant bought her in 1887. By 1890 owned by Herbert O'Donnell of Dubuque. [Another source says Anthony Gallagher.] She towed logs and lumber for another three years. Hit a log and was lost while passing through the span at the Dubuque bridge in 1894. A log was pressed through her hull and she went to the bottom. Her owner fished her out and put her machinery into a new boat, the *QUICKSTEP*. Jacob Ressor was captain and pilot for a time on the *ST. CROIX*, and at one time, she was commanded by Henry Enders.

SAM ATLEE #115787

Sternwheel rafter. Built 1881, Rock Island, by S. and J. C. Atlee of Fort Madison, Iowa. 234 tons, 234 tons, 113.3' x 26.3' x 3'. Had engines from the old centerwheel ferry, *KEOKUK*. 10" diameter cylinders, 4½' piston stroke. First rafter to have an electric searchlight. James Huginin, first captain, followed by John McKenzie and Asa Woodward. Tom Wright was chief engineer; Harry Henderson, second engineer; Antoine LaRoque, second pilot; Asa Woodward and John Burns, masters. Sold to New Orleans circa 1898. Owned by Robert Cothell who took her to Jeffersonville in 1904. Much of her was used in building the *CONTROL*.

SATELLITE #116319

Sternwheel rafter. Built Rock Island, 1890. 60 tons, 60 tons, 76.5' x 15.9' x 3.9'. Built by George Winans. Used as a bowboat for the *JULIA*, later for the *NEPTUNE* and *SATURN*. After rafting, owned by Hannibal Material and Supply Company, Hannibal, Missouri. Sold to the Anderson-Tully Company, Memphis in September 1903. Rebuilt (hull) to 86' x 20' x 3.4'. Capsized in storm at Tamm's Landing on the Mississippi some one hundred miles from Memphis on February 4, 1917; no lives lost; value was $8,000.

SATURN (#1) #116476

Sternwheel rafter. Built 1892, Rock Island. 160 tons, 160 tons, 121.5' x 24.2' x 5'. Engines 16" diameter cylinders, 5' or 5½' piston stroke. She had two boilers, 20' long, 42" in diameter. Owned by Captain George Winans and later by A. B. Youmans of Winona. Burned at Kahlke Yard, Rock Island, April 4, 1900, along with the *VOLUNTEER* and *MASCOT*. Her pilothouse was located forward of the stacks. She was the only raft boat on the river to have steam-steering gear. In 1895, Captain Winans, while master, brought a raft of lumber into St. Louis from Stillwater that was 1,584 feet long and 272 feet wide containing 7,000,000 feet of lumber.

Harry Dyer states, "The *SATURN* was built according to the ideas of Capt. Winans based upon years of practical experience in towing logs and lumber and in many respects she was an improvement over the regular type of raft boat. She was full roofed fore and aft and her pilot house was placed forward of the smoke stacks, flush with the forward end of the hurricane roof. In hitching into a raft this made it very nice for the pilot as he could see the exact distance between the bow of his boat and the raft he was approaching. Her boilers were placed aft of forward making it much handier to get coal for the furnaces. Her pilot house being placed so far forward made her somewhat hard to handle when running light as the pilot was so near the jackstaff she would get the swing on him before he would notice it; but as she always towed her bow boat ahead, this fault was not material."

SATURN (#2) #117019

Sternwheel rafter. Built 1901, Rock Island, for Captain George Winans. 180 tons, 145.5' x 30' x 4'. Engines were 16½" diameter cylinders, 5' piston stroke. Crew in 1901 was Captain Winans, master; Peter O'Rourke, pilot; Levi King, chief engineer; Levi King, Jr., second engineer; Harry G. Dyer, mate; Earl Winans [son of George], clerk and captain of bowboat *PATHFINDER*. Mrs. Ella Tesson, steward; John Filty and Clarence King, engineers on the bowboat. Had three boilers, 42" diameter, 20' long. Built from the *JOHN H. DOUGLASS* at Kahlke's in Rock Island.

In June 1901, she left Stillwater with a lumber raft 1,480 feet long, 256 feet wide and 26 inches deep—had over 9,000,000 feet of lumber, covered over nine acres. The raft had 704 lumber cribs (32' x 16' x 26"). All but stern and bow cribs had deck loads of shingles, lath, pickets, dry lumber and timbers, adding another million feet. The *SATURN* delivered this raft to St. Louis in less than ten days. Owned next (1904) by Knapp Stout and Company and then Ledger and Morrissey. Sold to Missouri River and was an excursion boat at Omaha until 1914 or so.

In January 1914, Captain Booth Baughman of Kansas City, Missouri who owned her, sold her to the Rust-Swift Construction Company for use as a towboat in construction work on the Missouri, the price being $12,000. In 1916 she was still in service on the Missouri, hailing from Kansas City. George Williams was chief engineer in 1915.

Scotia #116224

Sidewheel rafter, initially. Built LaCrosse, 1889. 31 tons, 31 tons, 100.5' x 13.4' x 3'. Owned by McDonald Brothers who used her as a harbor boat and as a bowboat. She was rigged so the pilot could handle the engines from the pilothouse. Either wheel could be thrown out of gear by means of a lever. She had the engines of the *ZADA* (50 h.p.). Charles White was master in 1890; Henry Guyette also was captain on her. In 1906 she came to Paducah and was converted to a sternwheel vessel. Towed in this area for some time.

Sold to Pfaff and Smith, Charleston, West Virginia, about 1915. She towed sand on the Kanawha River until the spring of 1926; then sold to George E. Breece Lumber Company of Monroe, Louisiana. During Christmas season, 1928, she sank and was rebuilt in 1929 and renamed *(B) RAY MOORE*. Merrick says she and the rafter, *CARRIE*, were burned at LaCrosse on July 26, 1892, so she must have been rebuilt after the fire.

Sea Wing #116207

Sternwheel rafter. Built Diamond Bluff, Wisconsin, 1888. 110' x 20.8' x 4.5'. Engines were 10" diameter cylinders, 6' piston stroke. Owned by Captain David Wethern of Diamond Bluff. The *SEA WING* overturned and some ninety-eight excursion passengers and crew were drowned in a storm on Lake Pepin on July 13, 1890. The boat was raised and operated as a rafter out of St. Paul until circa 1900. Then the engines were remodeled and placed in the *TWIN CITY*. Although the SEA WING was primarily a rafting vessel, she occasionally engaged in chartering for excursions.

Lake Pepin was the scene of a great tragedy involving the *SEA WING* in July 1890. A Sunday excursion [a non-working day for the vessel] was planned. The First Regiment of the Minnesota National Guard was encamped at Camp Lakeview located about two miles below Lake City on Lake Pepin. Many of the Guard personnel were from nearby Red Wing, Minnesota, and the purpose of the excursion was to spend a pleasant day of visitation with families and friends. Captain David N. Wethern, a crew of ten, and eleven passengers (including his wife, son, and a brother) left Diamond Bluff, Wisconsin at 8 A.M. Sunday, July 13. The weather was very hot with low barometric conditions. The *SEA WING* had a barge alongside as she did not have enough capacity for the expected crowd. At Trenton, some twenty-two persons were embarked, and at Red Wing, some 165 souls.

The *SEA WING* and her barge reached Camp Lakeview safely and a good time was had by the Guard and the visitors. Towards the end of the afternoon around 5 P.M., storms were obvious to the north and northwest. Lake Pepin can be a treacherous body of water, providing little shelter to a bad storm. A tornado had destroyed several homes and killed five or six people near St. Paul that afternoon indicating the presence of bad weather (although Captain Wethern had no way of knowing this).

Around 8 P.M. when it had grown dark (and may have been quite dark due to storm clouds) the *SEA WING* set out for Red Wing. She had to go upstream to get back, a more difficult task than the easier downstream trip of the morning. Captain Wethern, perhaps despite his better judgment, deemed it safe to venture forth and so the excursionists and some others set out for Lake City. A storm was gathering very rapidly and the wind was clocked at 60 mph.

After going about 5–7 miles for perhaps an hour, it was realized that severe trouble might occur. Life preservers were recommended and the *SEA WING* suddenly and without obvious warning capsized. A cry was heard, "cut loose the barge" (probably to prevent her capsizing) and that was done. All those on the barge were saved but ninety-eight on the *SEA WING* perished, including Captain Wethern's wife, and Perley Wethern, his brother. The captain and Roy Wethern, his son, survived.

There were many heroic deeds performed the rest of the night as people struggled to save themselves and others. Floating portions of the vessel's equipment were helpful, such as life preservers, planks, chairs, etc. The dark night, illuminated only by flashes of lightning, made the task all the more formidable.

The barge grounded on the Minnesota side and survivors hurried to Lake City and Camp Lakeview to summon help. Skiffs were used to pick up swimmers and to visit the floating wreck to bring off any still alive on what had been the *SEA WING*. The Chicago Milwaukee St. Paul and Pacific Railroad dispatched a train about midnight from Red Wing to help.

On Monday morning at 6 A.M. the rafter *ETHEL HOWARD*, Captain J. G. Howard, arrived at Red Wing with forty-two bodies picked up during the night. The *NETTA DURANT*, also a rafter, arrived about noon with eight bodies. In the afternoon, the raft boat *LUELLA*, under Captain Antoine LaRoque, which had her raft with her, came upon the disaster scene. LaRoque tied his raft to the Wisconsin shore and his boat and crew, under the directions of others, helped search for those lost. Finally with the help of the *ETHEL HOWARD*, the *SEA WING* was pulled to shore and the cabin opened and the entire wreck searched. Some fifteen bodies were found in this fashion.

Another body was recovered on Tuesday and on Wednesday the rafter *MENOMONIE* passed over the wreck area and a body came to the surface. She continued cruising the area thereby agitating the water, and some thirty-one additional bodies were accordingly located. The ninty-eighth and last body was found on Thursday and the grim search was over.

Burials had started on Monday and continued through Tuesday, Wednesday, and Thursday. Red Wing was practically at a standstill during this time. Ten were interred in Diamond Bluff and ten at or near Trenton. Some seventy-one were interred in Red Wing at the Oakwood, German Lutheran and Catholic cemeteries.

A large, well-planned and attended memorial service was held on Friday afternoon, July 25. Prominent personages participated, clergy led forth in prayer and hymns were sung. A twenty-foot high marble obelisk with the ninety-eight names inscribed thereon was in place at the site of the service and wreathed in floral tributes to the deceased.

Red Wing today has commemorative material along its river front attesting to the grim happenings on July 13, 1890.

SILAS WRIGHT   #23247

Sternwheel rafter. Built 1866 at either Menominee or Eau Claire, Wisconsin. Built by Ingram and Kennedy. 91 tons, 91 tons, 106′ x 20.2′ x 3.8′. Owned by Porter and Moore [later Northwestern Lumber Company] who ran her as a packet between Reads Landing and LaCrosse. Captain J. M. Turner was her owner and master starting in 1877. In 1867 her officers were William Lee, captain; L. Fulton, pilot. In April 1868, she was sold to H. T. Rumsey of LaCrosse who ran her between LaCrosse and Chippewa Falls. William Lee was Captain the first part of the season and L. Fulton was pilot. Later in July 1868, Captain Chet Hall was in charge, and in September, he was succeeded by Captain L. Maynard. In April 1868, she came out in charge of Captain Louis Malin with L. Fulton and William Dustin, pilots. H. McMaster ran her as pilot when Captain Malin was absent. In 1870 she ran in the Chippewa River trade until July in charge of Captain Henry H. Herrick. On account of low water, she was taken off in July and put into the rafting trade.

She capsized and sank in twelve feet of water in Lake Pepin in July 1870. The steamboat inspectors indicated that the accident was caused by the pilot leaving his wheel in a panic when the storm struck, and had he stuck to his position and handled the craft as he ought to have done, she would not have turned turtle. The boat was promptly raised and ran for many years as a bowboat in charge of Captain Jack Walker. Dan Davison and John Rook and James Hugunin were in command at times. In 1890 she was sold to Captains Isaac C. Wasson and J. W. Rambo who used her as a helper on the upper rapids.

Her end came on September 8, 1892, when she was run over by her own raft on the upper rapids and completely demolished. While handling the raft as a bowboat, she struck a ring bolt on a buoy amidships, cutting her hull in two and sinking her instantly at Winnebago Landing about nine miles above Rock Island. The raft kept coming on in that swift water and went over her, completely stripping her upper works and machinery. Her engines were later recovered and placed in the *R. D. KENDALL*. No lives were lost, but the crew had a lively thirty seconds in climbing aboard the raft. She was valued at $3,500 at that time.

SILVER CRESCENT   #115834

Sternwheel rafter. Built 1881, Clinton, Iowa by McMahon and Duncan. Used engines of rafter, *PARK PAINTER* (12″ diameter cylinders, 4½′ piston stroke). Built by Captains O. P. McMahon and A. E. Duncan. She was 123.3′ x 22′ x 2.9′ and was of 221 h.p. In the season of 1882 she was in command of Captain A. E. Duncan and towed for the Paige-Dixon Company, Davenport. In the fall of 1882 Captain Duncan sold his half interest to his partner, Captain McMahon, who ran her until 1890. She was sold by him in 1890 for $7,000 and owned equally (one-third each) by LeClaire Navigation Company, Van Sant and Musser Transportation Company, and W. S. Mitchell. Master in 1890 was W. S. Mitchell; George Tromley, pilot. Captain Walter Blair bought her in 1892 for $7,000 and remodeled her for the short packet trade (Burlington and Davenport). Dismantled at Winona in 1909.

SILVER LAKE　　#115667

Sternwheel vessel. Built 1877, Chippewa Falls, Wisconsin for service on the Chippewa River. [Another source says she was built in 1879, LaCrosse.] 31 tons. Run for a number of years by Captain William M. Smith of Reads Landing. Sold to Captain Charles Martin of LaCrosse; his son, Melvin, ran the engines [in rafting trade]. In 1880 she was a ferry between Lansing, Iowa and DeSoto, Wisconsin. In St. Croix River trade in 1882, and at the end of that season, sold south to Arkansas and put into the packet trade on the St. Frances River. Finally dismantled at Helena, Arkansas. Captain William Smith was known as "Noisy Bill" as he seldom spoke except for necessary commands.

SILVER WAVE　　#115667

Sternwheel rafter. Built in 1872 as *(A) D. A. MCDONALD*, LeClaire. 120' x 24' x 4'. Engines were 14" diameter cylinders, 4' piston stroke. Renamed *(B) SILVER WAVE* in 1879 when purchased by Van Sant and Musser Transportation Company, Muscatine. Jerome Short, captain, 1881 and 1882. Captain John McKenzie, master, 1883. Walter A. Blair was clerk and cub pilot on her in 1879-81. Dismantled at LeClaire, 1890. Once went from LeClaire to Beef Slough in 29 hours, 37 minutes, 300 miles; not beaten by any other raft boat.

Because of her bad luck when she was the *D. A. MCDONALD*, Captain Van Sant changed her name to *SILVER WAVE* and under this name she was successful and made money for her owners. She was also a popular excursion boat from Dubuque, Clinton, LeClaire, Moline, Davenport and Rock Island. Some of her pilots were Sam Hitchcock, J. Hugunin, George Rutherford, I. H. Short, Lome Short, Jas. Whistler, Stephen Withrow, William M. Smith and last by George Trombley, who landed her for the last time after one of the best seasons for profit she ever made. She ended her days where she started, at LeClaire at the end of the 1889 season and was replaced by the *J. W. VAN SANT* (second). James Steadman was chief engineer in 1882, John Burns was mate in 1881 and 1882. After dismantling, her machinery was put into the *VERNIE MAC* and her hull was built over into a coal barge.

STERLING　　#22680

Sternwheel rafter. Built Maquoketa, Iowa, 1864. 63 tons. Built by George Allen and others, including Flugel Simonton who commanded her for several seasons. She was bought by the CB&Q railroad who used her to tow barges in transporting rock from LeClaire to Burlington. She was unsuited to the work and was sold to Captain Paul Kerz in 1867 who ran her as a rafter until 1875 and then sold her to W. J. Young and Company, Clinton, but stayed on as captain of the boat. Captain Kerz ran her from 1867 until 1875, serving as captain part of the time. Adam Younker also commanded her part of the time—Captain Kerz had married his daughter. Conrad Kraus was second engineer of the *STERLING* in 1869. James Whistler was captain and Nelson Whistler was mate when the Youngs owned her. Dismantled at Hastings circa 1884 and her engines went into the *LUELLA*.

STILLWATER　　#115161

Sternwheel rafter. Built 1872, LeClaire. 146 tons, 146 tons, 125.4' x 24.4' x 3.8'. Owned by Durant and Wheeler. Commanded by Austin J. Jenks when she first came out; Albert E. Duncan was mate to Captain Jenks in 1872. Sold to Weyerhaeuser and Denkmann circa 1880. Captain Al Carpenter was in charge until he talked himself out of a job [1874 and thereafter]. Captain James Huginin was in charge, 1881-83. Captain Whistler and Isaac Wasson were also masters on her when owned by Weyerhaeuser and Denkmann. Her machinery was from the *LACON* and before that, the *CHALLENGE*. Dismantled at Rock Island, 1891, and some elements placed in the *E. RUTLEDGE*.

T

TABER　　#141525

Sternwheel rafter, towboat. Built LeClaire, 1898 as the *LYDIA VAN SANT* [*TABER* was assigned a different registry number]. Engines were 12" diameter cylinders, 6' piston stroke. The Van Sant Company towed logs for the Taber Lumber Company of Keokuk from 1900 to 1910. The Van Sants refused to renew the towing contract so E. Carroll Taber bought the *LYDIA VAN SANT*, renaming her *TABER* and operated her for three years until their mill had finished sawing. They then sold *TABER* to Captain Tom Williams of Evansville, and she was rebuilt and renamed *SANCO* (given a new registry number).

TEN BROECK　　#145306

Sternwheel rafter. Built at South Stillwater, 1882, for Gillespie and Harper. One hundred forty-eight tons, 148 tons, 130' x 26' x 3.9'. Engines, 17" diameter cylinders, 4½' piston stroke, came from the *MARK BRADLEY*. She was sold to Van Sant and Walter Blair. Blair was master for six years. Later sold to Captain John McCaffrey and sons, and also towed ties on Tennessee River. Burned at Cairo, November 1904.

THISTLE　　#145508

Sternwheel rafter, towboat. Built at LaCrosse, 1889. 103 tons, 103 tons, 150.1' x 28.4' x 4.7'. Engines were 18" diameter cylinders, 5' piston stroke and came from the towboat

BLUE LODGE. Owned in 1890 by McDonald Brothers, N. B. Lucas, master. In 1893 owned by Kratka Towing Company, Lansing, Iowa. Also operated for Carnival City Packet Company (St. Paul-LaCrosse) in 1894 along with *LIZZIE GARDNER.* Captain Morrell Looney had ownership in her in 1894. Found to be too heavy on fuel and had too much draft. Sold to the Three States Lumber Company, Cairo, Illinois, towed ties and lumber, Captain Bud Smedley, master in 1897. In the fall of 1900 she was taken to Higginsport, Ohio, for dismantling. Her engines went to a new towboat being built there called the *HERMANN PAEPCKE.*

The New Idea   #145502

Sternwheel. Built 1889 Jeffersonville by Howard. 146 tons, 146 tons, 125' x 26' x 4'. Engines were 14" diameter cylinders, 5' piston stroke. She had two boilers, each 40" in diameter, 24' long. Renamed *(B) KATHERINE* circa 1895.

The Purchase   #90374

Sternwheel rafter. Built 1869 Pittsburgh as *(A) MOUNTAIN BELLE.* Renamed *(B) THE PURCHASE* when operating at St. Paul, owned by William McCraney, Captain Roy Wethern. Condemned and dismantled at Wabasha, 1917.

Tiber   #24504

Sternwheel towboat/rafter. Built 1862, Pittsburgh. 135 tons, 135 tons, 141' x 32' x 4'. Delivered oil on the Allegheny River. During Civil War, 1864, she served in Federal service, handling barges carrying military supplies between St. Louis and Arkansas. Bought by John Tobson of Winona who used her in towing grain barges in 1869 with John Killeen as master. Sold to Green City Lumber Company who had Captain William Blakeslee in charge; Vitel Burrow, second pilot. In 1883 owned by Quincy Lumber Company, Captain William Kratka, master. Frank Looney was also a captain. Dismantled in 1888 at LeClaire, Iowa, and boilers placed in *IRENE D.,* built by Dorrance Brothers of LeClaire.

Twin City   #145853

Sternwheel. Built 1900, Diamond Bluff, Wisconsin. 144 tons, 144 tons, 134.3' x 26.0' x 4.0'. Built by George Wethern. Sold to Cumberland River and renamed *(B) WARRENN,* circa 1903. Had machinery of the *SEA WING.* Had two boilers, 18' long. Engines had 10" diameter cylinders, 6' piston stroke.

U

Union   #2547

Sidewheel rafter. Built 1863, Durand, Wisconsin. 28 tons. Owned by Seth Scott, built for Chippewa River service. Chartered by Captain George Winans in September 1863 ($7.00 per day) to tow a raft to the mill. First attempt was unsuccessful, but in 1864 Captain Cyrus Bradley with W. J. Young's encouragement chartered her to run a raft of logs from Reads Landing to Clinton, Iowa, for W. J. Young and Company. The venture was successful, and most agreed it was the first trip using a steamboat. Winans then ran her three or four more seasons in rafting. She then did occasional towing around Reads Landing. Rebuilt in 1869 after being cut down by ice at Chippewa Falls, Wisconsin; changed to thirty-seven tons. Dismantled 1881.

Captain E. E. Heerman relates this about the *UNION.* "In 1862 I happened to furnish something towards building this boat. She was built at Durand, Wisconsin by Captain S. C. Scott and Captain J. W. Harding who were largely interested in getting out stove bolts. At this time there was plenty of good timber for this purpose nearby.

"Her length was about one hundred feet, in breadth, beam [was] 12.9 feet, I think, and less than three feet depth of hold. She was a sidewheel geared boat, similar to the steamer *MONITOR.* Her boiler was manufactured in Chicago by P. W. Gates & Co., before 1857, and sold to W. H. Gates of Alma, for a sawmill where it was used for a year or two. After the great financial crash of 1858 the mill quit business. Both Scott and Harding told that they had bought this boiler for their boat but it was not used in the boat as it had been in the mill. The balance wheel and pulley had been removed and a pinion and core wheel installed instead. The boiler was about eight feet long and less than three feet in diameter. The firebox was built with copper flues very close together. The pillow blocks were bolted on the boiler and so was the engine. The shaft on the boiler pillow blocks held the pinion and this was about eight by ten. This pinion meshed into the cog wheel which was about three or four feet in diameter, and I think geared four to one, giving great power for the size of the boiler.

"Scott and Harding used her on the Chippewa for a time. Scott finally sold his interest to Harding. Several years later Scott was agent for my boats at Durand and I think died there after I left the river. Captain Harding continued to operate her, finally selling her I suppose to the Eau Claire Lumber Company, as Mr. Kemp of that firm told me that the *UNION* was their boat.

"About this time the lumbering firm of E. Pound & Co. of Chippewa Falls, was complaining that their freight charges were too high, and that the boats should deliver their freight to the Falls and there were some trips made with the steamer *CHIPPEWA* to demonstrate that it was safe. This part of the river being situated above the mills, and the river being full of floating logs made it a dangerous business.

"I understood that A. E. Pound & Co. finally bought the UNION, whether for rafting or for use on the Chippewa I never knew. Capt. Winans may have owned her. He had charge of her as I know up to the time [she] was cut down by the ice at Chippewa Falls.

"The first I saw of her after she was sunk was in the spring of 1863. Later on, after considerable dickering I bought her as she lay, paying for the hull $75, and for the boiler, $1,000. I wish to add that by law the boiler could not be used on the same bottom that it had been on before, hence my reason for buying the hull of the UNION. I rebuilt her, bring her out in the latter part of August 1869, and used her as a passenger and freight boat and in towing lumber up to the year 1880. I then dismantled her at Reads Landing, taking the boiler on board the Missouri River steamer MINNIE H., bringing it back to Bismarck, N.D., where I sold it for use in the coal mines.

"Captain Geo. Winans had charge of the UNION during the balance of the season of 1869, I think, from August, when she came out until close of navigation, but it may have been his brother, Aaron Winans. Other captains who served for a time on the UNION were John and Henry Walker, William Dobler, William Woodward, Noisy Bill Smith, Alex Gordon, Michael McCall, Eli Minder, Sol Crosby, L.C. Malin, William Dustin and other I do not call to mind. Among the engineers were E. Peck, Joe Myers, Louie Dusher, Pat Gregan, Alex Stokes and Oliver Stokes.

"The first bell in use on the steamboat UNION is now used to call the audiences to the auditorium at the Devils Lake Chatauqua, North Dakota.

"I cannot bid farewell to her without relating the story of a bloody fight that took place in 1870 between the crews of the UNION and the MINNIE WILL. It took place at my boat yard in LaCrosse, located between Colemans and Fall Mills. I was to meet the UNION there, and happened to be on time. I had been in the warehouse getting out material for repair, and had just stopped on board the UNION. The cook on the UNION was a colored man named Andy. He came to me and said that the cook on the other boat had taken his buck saw, and would not return it. I told him to let it go and I would get him another saw. I went on with my business; but almost immediately Andy returned and said he had his saw. At the same instant the crew of the other boat came rushing on to the forecastle of the UNION, apparently in a great rage, and the knockdown commenced without any parley. Clubs, wrenches, and anything else that could be reached were in use. At one time, in the fiercest part of the fracas the only two of my crew that I saw standing were the engineer at his engine, and Andy, the cook near him with his saw in his hand. The other boat backed out while I was engaged in getting on shore some of those who had been knocked overboard. I immediately sent for doctors Arthur and Chamberlin. Dr. Arthur arrived first and at once pressed me into service to assist in dressing the wounds of the injured. The first three were dressed and ended up as they lay in the sand on shore. After getting thru the medical attendance, I found that the UNION had seven men short, all of whom we found in the wheelhouse, all more or less injured. They said that some had been knocked overboard, while others had jumped overboard to save their lives. Some of them had cuts in their head four to eleven inches long and knowing that Andy had not been able to distinguish friend from foe in the fight in which he took an active part (I suspected him). Two raft crews on one boat was putting them in pretty thick. In early days many of the floating crews were pretty rough, and there was plenty of material alongside to make them worse, but in time the steam vessels that finally monopolized the rafting business on the great river were civilizers and a great blessing to humanity. The bad element could not get jobs on the towboats."

V

VERNIE MAC   #161681

Sternwheel rafter, towboat. Built 1892, Wabasha by Samuel Peters and Son. 91 tons, 91 tons, 124.3′ x 22′ x 3.8′. Engines were 14″ diameter cylinders, 4′ piston stroke,. The engines came out of the SILVER WAVE and before that, were in the steam boat GUIDON and were in use some sixty years. Originally owned by Captain Duncan J. McKenzie of Alma, Wisconsin; Captain William Weir, master. Ran in rafting trade until 1898 and then sold to Captain John Kent and others of Osceola, Wisconsin, who put her in the St. Croix River and lake passenger and freight service in the short-lived Interstate Park Navigation Company. She served there for two seasons, and in 1900 was sold to the Anderson Tully Towing Company of Memphis. Silas Alexander was second pilot in 1895 and 1896. John Fuller, Jr. and Pearl Roundy were chief engineers for a time.

She also towed showboats. She sank in September 1904, near Vicksburg. Towed WONDERLAND showboat in 1917 and sank it on a rock below Lock #20, Ohio River. Did charter work, became more decrepit, and at the end towed a garbage barge, renamed (B) BESSIE KATZ.

VIOLA   #25717

Sidewheel rafter. Built 1865, Franconia, Minnesota. 36 tons. Blair says she was successful but gave way to the sternwheel rafters. While backing out of Richland Slough (between LaCrosse and Winona) May 9, 1876, hit a snag and sank. The machinery was salvaged.

An 1890 photo of the *ALFRED TOLL* as sunk and wrecked near Dubuque. Built at LaCrosse in 1880, owned at times by Captain P. S. Davison, G. L. Short, and Volney Bigelow. Some masters on her were Albert M. Short, Abe Looney and Lyman Short.
Photo courtesy of Murphy Library Special Collections, University of Wisconsin-LaCrosse and Winona County (Minnesota) Historical Society.

Another 1890 photo of the sunk and wrecked *ALFRED TOLL*.
Photo courtesy of Murphy Library Special Collections, University of Wisconsin-LaCrosse.

The vessel at right is the *BERNICE* of 1899, at one time a bowboat for the *CHANCY LAMB*. The *ELLEN R.* is at the left.
Photo courtesy of the J. W. Rutter Collection.

A side view of *BERNICE* when she was engaged in towing after her rafting career was over.
Photo courtesy of Edward A. Mueller Collection.

PROGRESS was originally the rafter (A) *PERCY SWAIN* built at Reads Landing in 1883. Lost in July 1926 at Memphis. Shown here rigged for towing.
Photo courtesy of the J. W. Rutter Collection.

The *COMMANDER*'s rafting career was brief as the (A) *NORTH STAR* (built in Dubuque in 1906). As (B) *EUGENIA TULLY* and (C) *COMMANDER* she saw service on the Missouri River. Lost in April 1929.
Photo courtesy of the J. W. Rutter Collection.

The *CHANCY LAMB* was named after the founder of the firm. She was built at Clinton in 1872.
Photo courtesy of Murphy Library Special Collections, University of Wisconsin-LaCrosse.

The *CHANCY LAMB* ran as a packet out of Nashville after her rafting career was over. Sank in February 1911 at Clarksville, Tennessee. Two crew members were drowned.
Photo courtesy of Murphy Library Special Collections, University of Wisconsin-LaCrosse and Winona County (Minnesota) Historical Society.

The *CLYDE* was a long-lived rafter and was the first iron-hulled steamboat on the upper river. Her usual bowboat was the *MARY B*.
Photo courtesy of Murphy Library Special Collections, University of Wisconsin-LaCrosse.

Another view of the *CLYDE*. From 1900 on she was used as a towboat on the Tennessee River. She last served in 1941, at that time being seventy-one years old!
Photo courtesy of Murphy Library Special Collections, University of Wisconsin-LaCrosse.

The towboat *CONQUEST* had a brief career as the rafter (A) *J. M. RICHTMAN*. She was used in 1905 and thereafter to tow the showboat *SUNNY SOUTH*. In September 1909 she was lost in Bayou Sara, Louisiana, along with other vessels, in a storm.
Photo courtesy of the J. W. Rutter Collection.

The *R. D. KENDALL*, shown here with the *F. WEYERHAEUSER*, was a bowboat for most of her rafting life. After 1906 she served in Kentucky in the sand and gravel business.
Photo courtesy of Murphy Library Special Collections, University of Wisconsin-LaCrosse.

The *CYCLONE* was an 1891 rafter built at Stillwater for Durant and Wheeler. Her capstan today can be found in Fountain City, Wisconsin.
Photo courtesy of Murphy Library Special Collections, University of Wisconsin-LaCrosse.

From 1900 to 1907 the *CYCLONE* ran as a packet between Wabasha and St. Paul.
Photo courtesy of Murphy Library Special Collections, University of Wisconsin-LaCrosse.

The *ELLEN* started life as a wooden rafter and steam yacht. The U.S. Army Corps of Engineers at Rock Island acquired her around 1930 and put a steel hull under her.
Photo courtesy of the J. W. Rutter Collection.

Another view of the *ELLEN*. She was sold at public auction in 1943 and later was converted to a diesel propeller vessel.
Photo courtesy of the J. W. Rutter Collection.

HELEN MAR, built in 1872 at Osceola, Wisconsin, was originally in the packet trade on the St. Croix River. Sold to Knapp, Stout in 1880. Ten years later she was with McDonald Brothers and was dismantled in 1904.
Photo courtesy of Murphy Library Special Collections, University of Wisconsin-LaCrosse.

A view of the *HELEN MAR* pushing a raft under a steel bridge under construction.
Photo courtesy of Murphy Library Special Collections, University of Wisconsin-LaCrosse and Winona County (Minnesota) Historical Society.

This is the sternwheel rafter *IOWA* which was rebuilt in 1877 at Bellevue, Iowa, having been a sidewheel ferry for twelve years before that. Owned by Knapp, Stout for a few years and later owned by William Davis, Samuel Van Sant and Walter Blair. Subsequently engaged in towing. This photo shows raftsmen roping up lumber raft.
Photo courtesy of Murphy Library Special Collections, University of Wisconsin-LaCrosse.

This photo shows the *IOWA CITY* and a rafting crew in the foreground preparing a raft for its southerly journey.
Photo courtesy of Murphy Library Special Collections, University of Wisconsin-LaCrosse.

JOHN M. DOUGLASS was built from the *DAN THAYER* at LaCrosse in 1884. Rebuilt at Rock Island in 1899 and given a new registry number. In September 1900 she pushed a raft 128 feet wide and 1,400 feet long past Rock Island.
Photo courtesy of the J. W. Rutter Collection.

A pair of "Davises." The *PEARLIE DAVIS* being pushed by the *ZALUS DAVIS*.
Photo courtesy of the J. W. Rutter Collection.

Built at Prescott, Wisconsin in 1884, the *LUELLA* used the engines of the *STERLING*. Shown here with an excursion party.
Photo courtesy of the J. W. Rutter Collection.

The *SATURN* (2nd) was built in 1901 at Rock Island for Captain George Winans. In June 1901 she left Stillwater with a lumber raft 1,980 feet long and 256 feet wide, with over nine million feet of lumber and covering nine acres. Sold to Missouri River parties as an excursion boat and was still there in 1915.
Photo courtesy of the J. W. Rutter Collection.

The *SEA WING* as new. Used as a rafter.
Photo courtesy of Edward A. Mueller Collection.

The *SEA WING* a few days after her loss of ninety-eight passengers and crew on July 13, 1890. (See account of the disaster under *SEA WING* in boat listing section.)
Photo courtesy of Murphy Library Special Collections, University of Wisconsin-LaCrosse.

The modern riverfront at Red Wing, Minnesota and plaques that commemorate the 1890 *SEA WING* disaster and pay tribute to her dead.
Photos courtesy of Edward A. Mueller Collection.

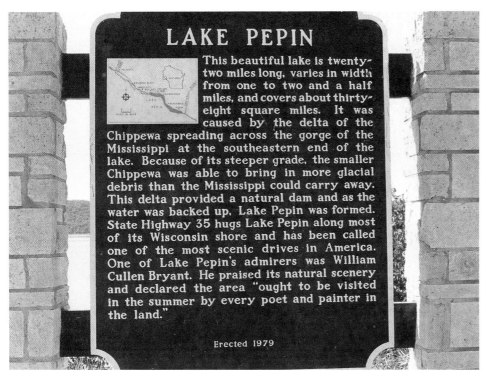

Lake Pepin at times can be a treacherous body of water to a steamboat. It is deceptively beautiful. This marker on Wisconsin Route 35 takes note.
Photo courtesy of Edward A. Mueller Collection.

Another reminder of the rafting days, a roadside plaque on Wisconsin Highway 35 near Lynxville.
Photo courtesy of Edward A. Mueller Collection.

Steamboat memories at the Depot Museum, Pepin, Wisconsin.
Photos courtesy of Edward A. Mueller Collection.

The rafter *PERCY SWAIN*. Note empty coal boxes along the bank and plank used as a gangway for access to the vessel.
Photo courtesy of Edward A. Mueller Collection.

A view of the powerful *KIT CARSON*.
Photo courtesy of the Historical Society of McGregor, Iowa.

Rafting memorabilia in Florida. The bell of the *WABASH* (A) *F. C. A. DENKMANN* at a Coral Gables estate owned by a Denkmann family descendant.
Photos courtesy of Denise Birmingham.

The *GARDIE EASTMAN* was an 1882 rafter owned by Gardiner, Batchelder, and Wells of Lyons, Iowa. Joseph Buisson was her captain for seven years and Joseph Hawthorne for three years.
Photo courtesy of Edward A. Mueller Collection.

The *GLENMONT* was built at Dubuque in 1885 using engines from the *IDA FULTON*. In 1905 her cabin, engines and boilers were transferred to a new hull. The combination that resulted was the *NORTH STAR*.
Photo courtesy of Edward A. Mueller Collection.

The *COLUMBIA* was built from the *PAULINE* circa 1900 in Stillwater. She was used to help build the Overseas Railroad to Key West from 1906 until 1911.
Photo courtesy of Edward A. Mueller Collection.

Below: the *BUN HERSEY* was a small bowboat and is portrayed on a post card of the day with a raft. She was built in 1883 at Stillwater.
Photo courtesy of Edward A. Mueller Collection.

This 1895 scene is of rafts lying-to at McGregor, Iowa awaiting towing vessels to take them downriver.
Photo courtesy of Edward A. Mueller Collection.

Harry Dyer was mate on the *ISAAC STAPLES* in 1898. She was sold to the Van Sant Towing Company in 1907 and burned in December of that year.
Photo courtesy of Edward A. Mueller Collection.

The *J. W. VAN SANT* was named for John Van Sant, father of Samuel. She was owned by the Van Sant and Musser Towing Company.
Photo courtesy of Edward A. Mueller Collection.

The *PEERLESS*, although not a rafter, was one of the upper Mississippi vessels that went south and worked in the Florida Keys, helping to build the Overseas Railroad. Shown here pushing a barge of water tanks; all fresh water had to be brought in by steamboat.
Photo courtesy of the State of Florida Archives.

The *HELENE SCHULENBURG* was a rafter built in 1874; she cost $16,000. Captain Robert Dodds was her usual master. She was later in excursion work and was dismantled in Rock Island circa 1897.
Photo courtesy of Winona County (Minnesota) Historical Society.

The private pleasure craft of the Mayo Brothers was their *ORONOCO,* which had started life as the rafter (A) *E. RUTLEDGE* in 1892. She reverted to a towboat circa 1914.
Photo courtesy of Winona County (Minnesota) Historical Society.

The *LUELLA* is shown passing a Diamond Jo Warehouse along the river.
Photo courtesy of the Putnam Museum of History and Natural Science, Davenport, Iowa.

The *LINE HANSON* is the middle vessel between two barges circa 1885. As an occasional rafter, she was employed around Dubuque and rebuilt as (B) *GEORGIE S.*
Photo courtesy of the Putnam Museum of History and Natural Science, Davenport, Iowa.

The *IDA FULTON* is seen here between two barges. She served in the Civil War and was also a freighter. This photo probably shows her on an excursion.
Photo courtesy of the Putnam Museum of History and Natural Science, Davenport, Iowa.

RUBY was Harry G. Dyer's first steamboat. This photo shows her early in life and perhaps rigged as a ferry?
Photo courtesy of the Putnam Museum of History and Natural Science, Davenport, Iowa.

The *CLIMAX* was built in 1893 in Burlington and used as a bowboat with the *NEPTUNE*. She went to Memphis in 1903 and was dismantled in 1907.
Photo courtesy of the Putnam Museum of History and Natural Science, Davenport, Iowa.

Two rafters, the *WYMAN X* of 1867 at left and the *TIBER* of 1862 at right, from an old stereo photo.
Photo courtesy of the Putnam Museum of History and Natural Science, Davenport, Iowa.

A side view of the 1881 *SAM ATLEE* with a barge alongside. She was the first rafter to be equipped with an electric searchlight.
Photo courtesy of the Putnam Museum of History and Natural Science, Davenport, Iowa.

The *LITTLE HODDIE* certainly lived up to her name as she was only 83.7 feet long. She worked around Beef Slough and as a bowboat for the *LUELLA*.
Photo courtesy of the Putnam Museum of History and Natural Science, Davenport, Iowa.

The *F. WEYERHAEUSER* was a first-class rafter built at Rock Island for Weyerhaeuser and Denkmann. She had large engines and three boilers and was also used as a pleasure craft. About 1913 she went to the U.S. Lighthouse Service and was renamed *DANDELION*.
Photo courtesy of the Putnam Museum of History and Natural Science, Davenport, Iowa.

The *EUGENIA TULLY* started as the rafter *NORTH STAR* and was renamed (B) *EUGENIA TULLY* in 1917, and was later named (C) *COMMANDER* circa 1928.
Photo courtesy of the Putnam Museum of History and Natural Science, Davenport, Iowa.

The rafter *LADY GRACE* was a Chancy Lamb and Sons vessel. Harry Dyer stated, "she was one of the finest and most powerful raft boats."
Photo courtesy of Edward A. Mueller Collection.

The *L. W. CRANE* at Reads Landing. The *HIRAM PRICE* is at left. Both were sidewheelers built in the 1860s.
Photo courtesy of the Joe Dobler Collection.

The *ETHEL HOWARD* (left) assisting in salvage of the partially sunken *BART E. LINEHAN* suspended between two barges. She was originally a ferry at Red Wing. McDonald Brothers owned her after 1896.
Photo courtesy of Murphy Library Special Collections, University of Wisconsin-LaCrosse.

The *HELENE SCHULENBURG*, owned by Schulenburg and Boeckler, alongside a raft.
Photo courtesy of the Winona County (Minnesota) Historical Society.

The *ISAAC STAPLES,* shown bow-on.
Photo courtesy of Murphy Library Special Collections, University of Wisconsin-LaCrosse and Winona County (Minnesota) Historical Society.

The *LECLAIRE BELLE* was built in 1873 at LeClaire. She was the first craft Captain Walter Blair worked on. Blair said, "she practically paid for herself every season she ran." She was dismantled at LeClaire after seventeen years of service with the Van Sants and Blair.
Photo courtesy of Murphy Library Special Collections, University of Wisconsin-LaCrosse.

The *MASCOT* shown next to a log raft.
Photo courtesy of Murphy Library Special Collections, University of Wisconsin-LaCrosse.

The *PERCY SWAIN*, an 1882 Reads Landing-built rafter. She was built on the hull of the *MINNIE* by Captain David Swain. She was a rafter until 1899 and was then used in contracting and towboating.
Photo courtesy of Murphy Library Special Collections, University of Wisconsin-LaCrosse.

The *ROBERT ROSS* was built in 1873 from the wreck of the *JAMES MALBON*. She was renamed (B) *J. S. KEATOR* circa 1881. Shown here with empty and full boxes for coal.
Photo courtesy of Murphy Library Special Collections, University of Wisconsin-LaCrosse.

The *STILLWATER* was an 1873 LeClaire-built sternwheel rafter. Dismantled at Rock Island in 1891. Shown here assembling a raft.
Photo courtesy of Murphy Library Special Collections, University of Wisconsin-LaCrosse.

Two rafters in winter quarters. The *PRESCOTT* is at the right; the steamboat at the bank is unknown.
Photo courtesy of Murphy Library Special Collections, University of Wisconsin-LaCrosse and Winona County (Minnesota) Historical Society.

The 1889 Stillwater built *RAVENNA*
Photo courtesy of Murphy Library Special Collections, University of Wisconsin-LaCrosse and Winona County (Minnesota) Historical Society.

The RAVENNA capsized in a storm in June 1902. Captain John Hoy and three crewmen were drowned. She was raised and continued in the lumber trade until 1908 when she was a packet between LaCrosse and Wabasha.
Photo courtesy of Murphy Library Special Collections, University of Wisconsin-LaCrosse.

This SATURN (1st) was Captain Winan's idea of what a raftboat should be. In 1895 Captain Winans used this vessel in taking a lumber raft from Stillwater to St. Louis, 1,584 feet long and 272 feet wide, containing seven million feet of lumber. *Photo courtesy of Murphy Library Special Collections, University of Wisconsin-LaCrosse.*

The SCOTIA was an odd-looking sidewheel bowboat. Shown here with the KIT CARSON in the background. Also went to Paducah and then to the Kanawha River. Probably renamed (B) RAY MOORE in 1929. Photo courtesy of Murphy Library Special Collections, University of Wisconsin-LaCrosse.

Reads Landing on the right and the *SILAS WRIGHT*, an 1866 craft, at left. Originally a packet on the Chippewa River and later a bowboat. Sank in September 1892, being run over by her own raft. Engines salvaged and placed in the *R. D. KENDALL*.
Photo courtesy of Murphy Library Special Collections, University of Wisconsin-LaCrosse.

The sternwheel *SILVER CRESCENT* of 1881. Remodeled in 1892 by Captain Walter Blair for the short packet trade (Burlington-Davenport) in 1892. Dismantled at Winona in 1909. *Photo courtesy of Murphy Library Special Collections, University of Wisconsin-LaCrosse.*

The SILVER WAVE was originally (A) D. A. MCDONALD. Renamed (B) SILVER WAVE in 1879 when purchased by Van Sant and Musser. Once went from LeClaire to Beef Slough in 29 hours, 37 minutes, a distance of 300 miles, not beaten by any other rafting steamboat. Dismantled at LeClaire in 1896. *Photo courtesy of Murphy Library Special Collections, University of Wisconsin-LaCrosse and Winona County (Minnesota) Historical Society.*

The *TABER* was purchased from the Van Sants (where she was the *LYDIA VAN SANT*) and towed logs until 1913. She was then sold and rebuilt as *SANCO*. Photo courtesy of Murphy Library Special Collections, University of Wisconsin-LaCrosse.

A striking view of the rafter *TEN BROECK* of 1882 pushing a log raft. Sold later to Van Sant and Blair. Burned at Cairo, November 1904. *Photo courtesy of Murphy Library Special Collections, University of Wisconsin-LaCrosse.*

The *THISTLE* rafted for three years for the McDonald Brothers and later was a towboat until she was dismantled in 1900. Built in 1889 at LeClaire. *Photo courtesy of Murphy Library Special Collections, University of Wisconsin-LaCrosse.*

The machinery of the ill-fated SEA WING ended up in this vessel, TWIN CITY, which was built in 1900 at Diamond Bluff, Wisconsin. Renamed (B) WARRENN circa 1903.
Photo courtesy of Murphy Library Special Collections, University of Wisconsin-LaCrosse.

This 1892, Wabasha-built rafter/towboat, the *VERNIE MAC*, had William Wier as her first master. Ran in the rafting trade for six years and then was in towing. She towed the *WONDERLAND* showboat in 1917. In her old age she was renamed (B) *BESSIE KATZ* and towed a garbage barge. *Photo courtesy of Murphy Library Special Collections, University of Wisconsin-LaCrosse.*

The ninety foot VIVIAN was built in 1896 at Lyons, Iowa. She was in rafting until 1902 and then went into towing. Towed coal barges for at least three years. *Photo courtesy of Murphy Library Special Collections, University of Wisconsin-LaCrosse.*

The *VOLUNTEER* was a rafter from 1891 to 1899 when she was remodeled for the Carnival City Packet Company. Burned at Kahlke's yard in April 1900 along with the *MASCOT* and *SATURN*. Photo courtesy of Murphy Library Special Collections, University of Wisconsin-LaCrosse.

The W. J. YOUNG, JR. was built at Dubuque in 1882 for the W. J. Young Company of Clinton. Captain Paul Kerz was her master for thirteen years. At the time of her construction she was the most up-to-date rafter afloat. In 1885 Captain Walter Blair operated her as a packet for eight years between Davenport and Burlington.
Photo courtesy of Murphy Library Special Collections, University of Wisconsin-LaCrosse.

WABASH was the former rafter (A) F. C. A. DENKMANN. Shown here pushing the showboat THE GRAND FLOATING THEATRE. She was in service over fifty years! Photo courtesy of Murphy Library Special Collections, University of Wisconsin-LaCrosse.

The WANDERER was built for Chancy Lamb and Sons. The Lamb family's houseboat was named IDLER and is shown here towed by WANDERER. She went to Florida in 1906 and helped to build the Overseas Railroad to Key West. Lost in 1909 in Florida. *Photo courtesy of Murphy Library Special Collections, University of Wisconsin-LaCrosse.*

WEST RAMBO was a rafter built at LeClaire in 1884 and lasted until 1905 when she was dismantled. Worked as a rafting pilot boat for the Rock Island-LeClaire Rapids pilots. *Photo courtesy of Murphy Library Special Collections, University of Wisconsin-LaCrosse.*

The ZALUS DAVIS was a single-deck bowboat built at Dubuque in 1894. George Winans owned her from 1909 until 1911. She was dismantled in 1912 and her engines were placed in the SAMUEL PETERS. Shown here with the R. J. WHEELER. Photo courtesy of Murphy Library Special Collections, University of Wisconsin-LaCrosse.

A log raft is in the channel with a bowboat clearly shown (center left) and another log raft is at the bank (right). *Photo courtesy of Murphy Library Special Collections, University of Wisconsin-LaCrosse.*

A log raft in the center is being floated into position and a lumber raft is in the foreground. Alma, Wisconsin is in the background. *Photo courtesy of Murphy Library Special Collections, University of Wisconsin-LaCrosse.*

A group poses on the rafter ECLIPSE. Pilot is at top center in the pilot house.
Photo courtesy of *Murphy Library Special Collections, University of Wisconsin-LaCrosse.*

An old-time print of a floating raft (and steamboat) at the junction of the Wisconsin River with the Mississippi. *Photo courtesy of the Edward A. Mueller Collection.*

A well-known view of the varied sidewheel and sternwheel rafting vessels at Reads Landing. Left to right they are: *HIRAM PRICE, L. W. CRANE, ANNIE GIRDON, BUCKEYE, L. W. BARDEN, CLYDE, ST. CROIX, WM. HYDE CLARK,* and *SILAS WRIGHT. Photo courtesy of the Joe Dobler Collection.*

A combined log and lumber raft going through a railroad swing bridge on the Mississippi. *Photo courtesy of Murphy Library Special Collections, University of Wisconsin-LaCrosse.*

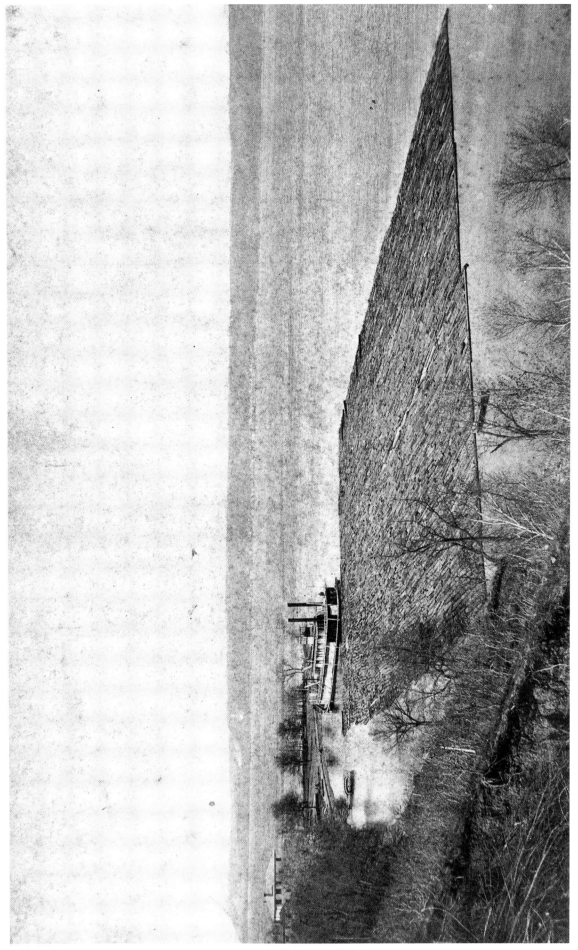

A wide raft and her steamboat in a cove along the Mississippi.
Photo courtesy of Murphy Library Special Collections, University of Wisconsin-LaCrosse.

A small "clean-up" raft going through the Marquette (North McGregor) pontoon bridge circa 1920. *Photo courtesy of Murphy Library Special Collections, University of Wisconsin-LaCrosse.*

VIOLA   #25617

Sidewheel rafter. Built Maquoketa, Iowa, in 1865 and her machinery was put in at LaCrosse. Named for a daughter of Oscar Knapp, one of her owners. 39 tons. She was intended for the LaCrosse and St. Croix Falls trade, but she was too slow and her owners disagreed. Her first master was Oscar Knapp; then L. D. Bartlett and then Cornelius Knapp, a cousin of Oscar. She was later engaged in rafting and about 1876 was owned by Isaac Staples, James Anderson and Edward T. Root. Burned at Rock Island, November 14, 1882, no loss of life.

VIRGINIA   #202591

Sternwheel towboat. Built Wabasha, 1905. 79 tons, 79 tons, 104.5' x 23.5' x 4'. Engines were 11" diameter cylinders, 3½' piston stroke; 125 h.p. The VIRGINIA was named after Samuel R. Van Sant's granddaughter. Built from rafter WEST RAMBO and sold shortly after building sold to the Florida East Coast Railroad and was used on construction of the overseas railroad to Key West. Was caught in hurricane at Boot Key Harbor, October 11, 1909 and lost one stack overboard. Sank in Moser Channel December 2, 1909, was raised. Foundered October 17, 1910 at Boca Chica, Florida in a hurricane, abandoned, Captain J. R. Blair master at the time.

VIVIAN   #161763

Sternwheel rafter. Built 1896, Lyons, Iowa by Chancy Lamb and Sons. 75 tons, 75 tons, 90' x 21' x 3.5'. In rafting trade until 1902; Captain Abe Mitchell in charge; George Rockwood was engineer for a spell. In 1902 sold to Moir Brothers, pearl button manufacturers of Burlington, towed shells to Moir Brothers pearl button factory in Burlington. Captain Tom Peel in charge. She was sold in 1903 for $8,000 and Captain Peel delivered her to Louisville.

The Marmet Coal Company used her to tow between the Kanawha River and Cincinnati in 1904 and 1905. Supposedly in February 1906, she was renamed or rebuilt as SALLIE MARMET (#1) in West Virginia and her name was later changed back to VIVIAN when the second SALLIE MARMET was built. This cannot be verified in the Lists of Merchant Vessels for the appropriate years. Dismantled and hull used as a freight barge at Madison, Indiana and was owned by Turner and Mason; the gas boat HELEN M. towed her.

VOLUNTEER   #161649

Sternwheel rafter/packet. Built 1891, LeClaire. 168 tons, 168 tons, 137.8' x 24.3' x 4.0'. Engines were 13" diameter cylinders, 4½' piston stroke. Had machinery of EVANSVILLE. Nicknamed "Old Soldier" by raftsmen. Owned by LeClaire Navigation Company and sold to Carnival City Packet Company in the summer of 1899 for $7,000 and remodeled. Lysander Darling was master and pilot and James Stedman was engineer for a time. While in the Davenport-Burlington trade in 1899, she ran "herself through" in July, losing a pitman overboard. Converted to a true packet, fall, 1899, with sixteen staterooms and a swinging stage. Burned at Kahlke Shipyard, April 20, 1900, along with the MASCOT and SATURN, valued at $12,000.

W. W.   #126010

Built as (A) CITY OF WINONA at Dubuque, 1882. Rebuilt as (B) W.W. in spring, 1905 by Captain John Streckfus and named for his associate, Captain Walter Wisherd. 212 tons, 178 tons, 137' x 29.1' x 4.6', 305 h.p. with thirteen crew. Bought in April, 1917 by Captain Frank Rounds, Owensboro, Kentucky, to replace GOLDEN GIRL. Bought by John F. Klein circa 1920 and towed pipe-laden barges from the Upper Ohio to the Lower Mississippi. Bought by Captain Ralph Emerson Gaches in spring 1921, who used her to tow a showboat. Sank spring 1922, at Brush Creek Island, Ohio River.

WABASH   #120445

Built as rafter, (A) F.C.A. DENKMANN in Dubuque in 1881. 120' x 22' x 3.7'. Engines were 14" diameter cylinders, 6' piston stroke. Renamed (B) WABASH, 1899 by Mrs. Marge Shelby who bought her to tow corn out of the Wabash River. Showboat entrepreneur Captain W. R. Markle bought her in May 1909 to tow a showboat. She was towing the showboat HIPPODROME in 1911. In 1913, handled the Cooley showboat, SUNNY SOUTH. Owned by Captain J. W. Menke in 1914, was foreclosed and bid in at sale in June 1915 for $700. Sold through John F. Klein to the Chicago Mill and Lumber Company in March 1917. Briefly named (C) ALICE H for a short period and then changed back to WABASH. Then went to Greenville, Mississippi and towed logs until March 1933. Captain Chess Wilcox bought her and renamed her (D) HALLIE (for his wife).

WANDERER   #81590

Sternwheel rafter. Built 1897 in Clinton for Chancy Lamb and Sons. 84 tons, 84 tons, 100' x 21' x 3.6'. John Whistler was master for several years and George Rockwood was engineer. A houseboat, IDLER, was built (120' x 20") and could accommodate 20 people. The IDLER was towed ahead of WANDERER as far as New Orleans for the Lamb family. Captain John Whistler was her usual master. In 1906 she was sold to the Florida East Coast Railroad for overseas railroad work. Sank in Jewfish Creek near Miami, October 14, 1906. Lost March 24,

1909, Money Key, Florida with eighteen aboard; no lives lost, crew removed by COLUMBIA.

WANETTA   #81712

Sternwheel towboat or bowboat. Built 1900, Muscatine, Iowa. 40 tons, 40 tons, 71' x 14' x 4'. Sank November 1913, in the Missouri River.

WARRENN   #145853

Sternwheel built 1900, Diamond Bluff, Wisconsin as *(A) TWIN CITY*. 134' x 26' x 4'. Was at Vicksburg, 1903, at Louisville, 1905. Ran on upper Cumberland River. Beached and dismantled at Burnside, Kentucky, October 9, 1907.

WEST RAMBO   #81044

Sternwheel rafter. Built 1884, LeClaire. 105 tons, 105 tons, 107' x 22' x 3.6'. Owned by Upper Rapids Transportation Company of LeClaire; Captain J. W. Rambo, master. Was a rafting pilot boat for the Rock Island-LeClaire rapids. Dismantled in 1905, and machinery went into the *VIRGINIA*, which later went to Florida for the FEC Railway.

WILL DAVIS   #81502

Sternwheel towboat. Built 1895, Lyons, Iowa, 150 tons, 75 tons, 100.8' x 23.6' x 3.6'. Off records by late 1908.

W. J. YOUNG, JR.*   #80888

Sternwheel rafter. Built at Dubuque in 1882 for W. J. Young and Company of Clinton. 146' x 32' x 5.5'. Engines were 14" diameter cylinders, 6' piston stroke. Captain Paul Kerz, master for thirteen years; Conrad Kraus, chief engineer for some time. She was a very fine and successful boat, and at the time of her construction, was considered the most up-to-date rafter afloat. In 1885 sold to Walter Blair for packet trade between Davenport and Burlington and ran there for eight years. In 1903 sold to Kentucky and Indiana Bridge Company of Louisville. Overhauled at Rock Island for excursion trade and given a new registry number as *HIAWATHA* circa 1903. Burned near Louisville, no lives lost. *Found also as *WM. J. YOUNG, JR*.

W. M. HYDE CLARK   #80071

Sidewheel rafter. Built 1870, Dubuque, launched April, 1870, foot of 7th Street. 14 h.p., 38 tons. Off records by 1882.

WYMAN X   #80145

Sidewheel rafter. Built 1867, Taylors Falls, Wisconsin. 141 tons. Built by W. H. C. Folsom of Taylors Falls and named for Wyman X. Folsom, his son. George Winans was master at one time. When the hull was completed, it was towed to Minneapolis where the machinery, which was built by the North Star Iron Works, was put in. This was the first machinery built in Minnesota for a Mississippi river steamboat. Much of the time she ran with the *NELLIE KENT*; the two steamers formed a daily line between the two cities. During 1869 and 1870, E. Y. Seevy was master.

Captain Folsom sold the vessel in the fall of 1872 to Butler and Gray of Stillwater who put her to towing logs. While in this service, she was commanded at one time by Captain C. Knapp and Captain Edward T. Root. Under Captain Root, she had the *JENNIE GILCHRIST* as a bowboat in going over the rapids, the first time a boat was so used. In 1875, the *IDA FULTON* and the *WYMAN X*, taking advantage of high water, went up the Minnesota River. In 1878 she was dismantled and the machinery placed in the *I. E. STAPLES* which later saw her name changed to *(B) DAVID BRONSON*.

Z

ZADA   #28093

Sidewheel harbor boat (towboat). Built LaCrosse, 1880 for McDonald Brothers. 37 tons, 37 tons, 96' x 30' x 3.4'. W. W. Gordon, master for several seasons. In 1889 engines used in *SCOTIA*.

ZALUS DAVIS   #28126

Sternwheel rafter. Built 1894, Dubuque. 46 tons, 46 tons, 90' x 18.6' x 3.4'. Engines 9" diameter cylinders, 4' piston stroke built by the Iowa Iron Works. Boiler of locomotive firebox type. Built by Captain William F. Davison of Clinton. Single deck, bowboat. Dismantled 1912; engines went to the *SAMUEL PETERS*. Owned by Captain R. J. Wheeler and Captain Will Davis. She was used as a bowboat for the *R. J. WHEELER* until she was sold to H. S. Rand of Burlington about 1900, Captain William Davis still remained command. During one or two winters, she went to the lower river where Captain Davis used her in the stave trade. In 1902, while under tow of the *CHANCY LAMB* upstream, a hog chain brace slipped from its mounting and went through the bottom of the *ZALUS DAVIS*, sinking her. She was raised at a cost of $1,500.

In 1909, she was sold to Captain George Winans who took out the old firebox boiler and installed a new one, sixteen feet long, forty-two inches in diameter with ten six-inch flues which improved her greatly. Captain Winans used her until the close of the season of 1911 when he sold her to Samuel Peters and Sons at Wabasha. They rebuilt her as the *SAMUEL PETERS* and sold her to the Moline Sand Company. Later she was transformed into a pleasure boat called the *MARQUETTE* and was still in service in 1916. Captain Winans rated her as one of the best small boats he ever owned.

Lists

Listing of Rafting Steamboats

This list has all of the names of the rafting vessels that were found. There were frequent name changes of these steamboats. In order to keep track of the vessels as they changed names, a numbering system is used. Thus, *(A)* means the initial name, *(B)* is the second name, etc.

A. REILING
A. T. JENKS, *(B)* ED DURANT, JR., *(C)* JOSEPHINE LOVIZA
ABNER GILE
ACTIVE
ALBANY
ALFRED TOLL
ALICE D.
ALICE WILD
ALVINA
ALVIRA
ANNIE H., *(A)* F. C. A. DENKMANN, *(B)* WABASH, *(D)* HALLIE
ANNIE GIRDON
ARTEMUS GATES
ARTEMUS LAMB, *(B)* CONDOR

B. F. WEAVER
B. HERSHEY
BART E. LINEHAN
BELLA MAC
BEN FRANKLIN, *(A)* E. RUTLEDGE, *(B)* JOHN M. RICH, *(C)* ORONOCO
BERNICE
BESSIE KATZ, *(A)* VERNIE MAC, *(C)* JEFFERSON
BLUE LODGE
BOREALIS REX
BROTHER JONATHAN
BUCKEYE
BUN HERSEY
BURDETTE

C. J. CAFFREY, *(A)* J. H. BALDWIN
C. W. COWLES
CARRIE

CHAMPION
CHANCY LAMB
CHARLOTTE BOECKLER
CITY OF WINONA, *(B)* W. W.
CLERIMOND, *(A)* GAZELLE
CLIMAX
CLYDE
COMMANDER, *(A)* NORTH STAR, *(B)* EUGENIA TULLY
CONDOR, *(A)* ARTEMUS LAMB
CONQUEST, *(A)* J. M. RICHTMAN
CYCLONE

D. A. McDONALD, *(B)* SILVER WAVE
D. C. FOGEL
DAISY
DAN HINE
DANDELION, *(A)* F. WEYERHAEUSER
DAN THAYER, *(B)* JOHN DOUGLASS
DAVID BRONSON, *(A)* I. E. STAPLES, *(C)* HENRIETTA
DEXTER
DISPATCH
DOUGLAS BOARDMAN

E. DOUGLAS
E. RUTLEDGE, *(B)* JOHN H. RICH, *(C)* ORONOCO, *(D)* BEN FRANKLIN
ED DURANT, JR., *(A)* A. T. JENKS, *(C)* JOSEPHINE LOVIZA
ELLEN
EMERSON, *(A)* MOLINE
EMMA
ETHEL HOWARD, *(B)* MARY B.

EUGENIA TULLY, *(A)* NORTH STAR,
   (C) COMMANDER
EVANSVILLE
EVERETT

F. C. A. DENKMANN, *(B)* WABASH, *(C)* ANNIE H.,
   (D) HALLIE
F. WEYERHAEUSER, *(B)* DANDELION
FLYING EAGLE, *(A)* IRENE D.
FRANK
FRITZ, *(B)* RESCUE
FRONTENAC, *(B)* PRINCE

GARDIE EASTMAN
GAZELLE, *(B)* CLERIMOND
GEORGIE S., *(A)* LINE HANSON
GLENMONT
GOLDEN GATE
GYPSEY, *(A)* LUMBER BOY
GUSSIE GIRDON

H. C. BROCKMAN
HALLIE, *(A)* F. C. A. DENKMANN, *(B)* WABASH,
   (C) ANNIE H.
HARDWOOD, *(A)* NEPTUNE
HARTFORD
HELEN MAR
HELENE SCHULENBURG
HENRIETTA, *(A)* I. E. STAPLES, *(B)* DAVID
   BRONSON
HIRAM PRICE
HORACE H., *(A)* LITTLE HODDIE

I. E. STAPLES, *(B)* DAVID BRONSON,
   (C) HENRIETTA
IDA FULTON, *(A)* CONVOY No. 2
INTERSTATE
INVERNESS
IOWA (1)
IOWA (2)
IOWA CITY
IRENE D., *(B)* FLYING EAGLE
ISAAC STAPLES

J. C. ATLEE
J. G. CHAPMAN
J. H. BALDWIN, *(B)* C. J. CAFFREY
J. K. GRAVES
J. M.
J. M. RICHTMAN, *(B)* CONQUEST
J. S. KEATOR, *(A)* ROBERT ROSS
J. W. MILLS
J. W. VAN SANT (1)
J. W. VAN SANT (2)
JAMES FISK, JR.
JAMES MALBON
JAMES MEANS

JENNIE HAYES
JEFFERSON, *(A)* VERNIE MAC, *(B)* BESSIE KATZ
JESSIE B.
JESSIE BILL
JOHN H. RICH, *(A)* E. RUTLEDGE,
   (C) ORONOCO, *(D)* BEN FRANKLIN
JO. LONG, *(B)* PROVIDENCE
JOHN H. DOUGLASS, *(A)* DAN THAYER
JOHN RUMSEY
JOHNNY SCHMOKER
JOSEPHINE LOVIZA, *(A)* T. JENKS, *(B)* ED.
   DURANT, JR.
JULIA
JULIA HADLEY
JUNIATA, *(B)* RED WING

KATHERINE, *(A)* THE NEW IDEA
KIRNS, *(A)* PETE KIRNS
KIT CARSON

L. W. BARDEN
L. W. CRANE
LACROSSE, *(A)* RAVENNA
LADY GRACE
LAFAYETTE LAMB
LAST CHANCE
LECLAIRE
LECLAIRE BELLE
LILY TURNER
LINE HANSON, *(B)* GEORGIE S.
LION
LITTLE EAGLE
LITTLE HODDIE, *(B)* HORACE H.
LIZZIE GARDNER
LONE STAR
LOTUS
LOUISVILLE
LUELLA
LUMBER BOY, *(B)* GYPSEY
LUMBERMAN
LYDIA VAN SANT

M. WHITMORE
MARK BRADLEY
MARS
MARY B.
MASCOT
MAUD
MAY LIBBY
MENOMONIE
MINNESOTA
MINNIETTA
MINNIE WILL
MOLINE, *(B)* EMERSON
MOLLIE MOHLER
MONITOR
MOONSTONE

MOUNTAIN BELLE, *(B)* THE PURCHASE
MUSSER

NATRONA
NELLIE
NELLIE THOMAS
NEPTUNE, *(B)* HARDWOOD
NETTA DURANT
NINA
NORTH STAR, *(B)* EUGENIA TULLY,
  (C) COMMANDER
NOVELTY

ORONOCO, *(A)* E. RUTLEDGE, *(B)* JOHN H.
  RICH, *(D)* BEN FRANKLIN
OTTUMWA BELLE

PARK BLUFF
PARK PAINTER
PATHFINDER
PAULINE
PEARL
PEARLIE DAVIS
PENGUIN
PENN WRIGHT
PERCY SWAIN, *(B)* PROGRESS
PETE KIRNS, *(B)* KIRNS
PETE WILSON
PHIL SCHECKEL
PILOT
PIONEER
PRESCOTT
PRINCE, *(A)* FRONTENAC
PROGRESS, *(A)* PERCY SWAIN
PROVIDENCE, *(A)* JO LONG

QUICKSTEP

R. D. KENDALL
R. J. WHEELER
RAVENNA, *(B)* LACROSSE
RAY MOORE, *(A)* SCOTIA
RED WING, *(A)* JUNIATA
REINDEER
ROBERT DODDS
ROBERT ROSS, *(B)* J. S. KEATOR
ROBERT SEMPLE

RUBY
RUTH

ST. CROIX
SALLIE MARMET, *(A)* VIVIAN, *(C)* VIVIAN
SATELLITE
SATURN (1)
SATURN (2)
SCOTIA, *(B)* RAY MOORE
SEA WING
SILAS WRIGHT
SILVER CRESCENT
SILVER LAKE
SILVER WAVE
STERLING
STILLWATER

TABER
TEN BROECK
THE NEW IDEA, *(B)* KATHERINE
TIBER
THE PURCHASE, *(A)* MOUNTAIN BELLE
THISTLE
TWIN CITY, *(B)* WARRENN

UNION

VERNIE MAC, *(B)* BESSIE KATZ, *(C)* JEFFERSON
VIOLA (1)
VIOLA (2)
VIRGINIA
VIVIAN, *(B)* SALLIE MARMET, *(C)* VIVIAN
VOLUNTEER

WABASH, *(A)* F. C. A. DENKMANN, *(C)* ANNIE H.,
  (D) HALLIE
WANDERER
WANETTA
WARRENN, *(A)* TWIN CITY
WEST RAMBO
WILL DAVIS
WM. HYDE CLARK
W. (Wm.) J. YOUNG, JR.
WYMAN X.

ZADA
ZALUS DAVIS

Steamboat Nicknames According to Harry Dyer

Steamboat Name	Nickname	Remarks
BELLA MAC	"Bella Danger"	Always in trouble
B. HERSHEY	"Bow and Arrow Boat"	Had half breed captain, Cyp Buisson
BOREALIS REX	"Carbolic acid"	
DOUGLAS BOARDMAN	"Other of the twins"	She and the *F. C. A. DENKMANN* were both built at Eagle Point, Dubuque, Iowa at the same time
F. WEYERHAEUSER	"Big Fred"	
F. C. A. DENKMANN	"One of the twins"	She and the *DOUGLAS BOARDMAN* were both built at Eagle Point, Dubuque, Iowa at the same time
CYCLONE	"Hurricane"	
CLYDE	"Come hither, go hence"	Very fast boat
DEXTER	"Old Faithful"	She was the oldest McDonald boat
HELENE SCHULENBURG	"Dutch girl"	
INVERNESS	"Scotty"	McDonald boat
JENNIE HAYES	"Jane Snake"	Long and narrow, built for use as a packet
JO. LONG	"Daily News"	Named after Newt Long
KIT CARSON	"The Scout"	
MOLLIE WHITMORE	"Papa's Darling"	Her captain was George Brasser. He talked to her as if she was a person.
ST. CROIX	"Drunken Dutchman"	Chris Schricker, superintendant of the Schricker Mueller Company was always drunk
TIBER	"Mason"	Had Masonic device between smokestacks

Rafting Pilots and Masters

The following list of steamboat pilots and masters on rafting vessels is largely derived from Captain Walter Blair's enumeration of such pilots. Many of these pilots were also masters of their vessels.

Christ Adolph
Silas Alexander
Nelson Allen
Washington Allen

Russ Baldwin
Aug. Barlow
Charles Barnes
Frank Bernard
Volney A. Bigelow
Walter Blair
W. H. Blair
Joseph Blow
John Bradley
C. G. Bradley
George Brasser
Hiram Brazee
Sherman Brown
Surveyor Bruce
William Buchanan
Cyprian Buisson
Henry Buisson
Joseph Buisson
Vetal Burrow
James Butts

Peter Carlton
Alf. Carpenter
Chris Carpenter
George Carpenter
Robert N. Cassidy
I. L. Chacey
A. J. Chapman
John Cheshire
James Coleman
Hiram Cobb
John Cormack

Lysander Darling
Gordon Davis

William Davis
Charles Davidson (or Davison)
Daniel Davison
A. O. Day
L. A. Day
Ira DeCamp
Gary Denberg
Joe Denvier
Frank Diamond
E. W. Dixon
William Dobler
Robert Dodds
Thomas Dolson
William Dorr
A. E. Duncan
Thomas Duncan
Edward W. Durant

Edwin Efuir
Lafe Egan
William Elliott

Daniel Flynn
Thomas Forbush
Patrick Fox
Henry Fuller
Ira Fuller
John Fuller
James Fullmer

John Gabriel
John Gainer
Patrick Gainer
William Ganley
Paul Gerlach
John Gilbert
James Gleason
John Goodnow
W. W. Gordon

Ed Grant
Joe Guardapee

James Haggerty
Sherman Hallam
John Hampton
John Hanford
David Hanks
Samuel Hanks
Stephen B. Hanks
Joseph Hawthorne
George Herold
Pembroke Herold
Albert J. Hill
Peter Hire
Samuel Hitchcock
Al. Hollingshead
Horace Hollingshead
John Hoy
Thomas Hoy
Harry Huginin
James Huginin
John Huginin
Walter Hunter
Ed Huttenhorn

Robert Irvin

A. T. Jenks
I. B. Jenks
Hugh Johnson
Sam Johnson

Adam Kerz
Paul Kerz
Cyrus King
Peter Kirns
Cornelius Knapp
Al Knippenberg
William Kratka

David Lamb
Andrew Lambert
John Lancaster
S. E. Lancaster
John Langford
Perry Langford
Peter Larivere
Andrew Larkin
Antoine LaRoque
D. C. Law
Phileas O. Lawrence
John Laycock
John Leach
Frank LePoint
J. T. R. Lindley
Carl Looney
Frank Looney
Morrell Looney
Napoleon B. Lucas

Samuel Macey
Al Martin
Frank Martin
George Martin
Hugh McCaffrey
John McCaffrey
William McCaffrey
R. B. McCall
John B. McCarty (Mushrat)
D. A. McDonald
John McDonald
Toliver McDonald
O. F. McGinley
Frank McIntyre
John McKane
John McKinge
Robert McClarney
Daniel McLean
O. P. McMahon
Sandy McPhail
Herbert Miliron
Edward Miller
Abram Mitchel
Brainerd Mitchel
W. S. Mitchel
John Monroe
J. G. Moore

Boyd Newcomb
Frank Newcomb

Isaac Newcomb
James Newcomb
Rufus Newcomb
W. B. Newcomb
George S. Nichols

John O'Connor
Peter O'Rourke
Thomas O'Rourke
Rueben Owens

David Parmalee
John Parker
W. A. Payne
John Pearson
H. L. Peavey
Thomas Peel
Vincent Peel
George Penney
Wiley Penney
Joseph (Big Jo) Perro
David Philamulee
Caleb Philbrook

John Quinlan

Samuel Register
James Rellis
Jacob Ressor
Charles Rhoads
Dan Rice
C. B. Robman
John Rook
Ed Root
Robert Roundy
George Rutherford
H. L. Ryder

St. Germain
William Savage
John Schmidt
C. W. Schricker
John Seabring
Christ Seeford
Albert Shaw
Daniel Shea
A. M. Short
Charles Short
G. C. Short
Harry Short
I. H. Short

J. E. Short
Joseph Short
William Simmons
Joseph Sloan
Charles Slocumb
William Slocumb
Harvey Smith
Peter Smith
Russell Smith
William Smith
Harry Stafford

O. J. Thompson
George Trombley (Tromley)
George Trombley, Jr. (Tromley)
R. H. Trombley (Tromley)
Jerry Turner

George Wallace
Henry Walker
Jack Walker
Isaiah Wasson
William Weir
Frank Wetenhall
Harry Wheeler
R. J. Wheeler
James Whistler
Nelson Whistler
William H. Whistler
Charles White
Edward Whitney
Alfred Withrow
Steven Withrow
Thomas C. Withrow
Edward Whitney
Frank Wild
Thomas Wilson
Aaron Winans
George Winans
Mahan Winans
William Wooden
Asa Woodward
David Wray

Adam Younker
William York
A. R. Young
Jack Young
Joseph H. Young
William Young

Rock Island Rapids Pilots
1840–1915

This information is derived from a listing by Captain Walter Blair in his book, "A Raft Pilot's Log."

Rock Island Rapids Pilots

Philip Suiter
John Suiter, son of Philip
William Suiter, son of Philip
John Suiter, son of John
Zach Suiter, son of John
Harvey Goldsmith
Silas Lancaster
William Rambo
DeForest Dorrance
J. W. Rambo, son of William
Oliver P. White
J. N. Long
Dana Dorrance
Durbin Dorrance
Orrin Smith

Des Moines Rapids Pilots

William West (at Price's Creek, 1928)
Valentine Speak, died at Montrose, 1880
R. S. Owen, died at Montrose, 1915
Sam Speak, died at Montrose, 1900
Charles Speak, died at Mt. Pleasant, 1895
Sam Williams, died in California, 1878
Charles H. Farris, living at Montrose, 1928, seventy-eight years old

Engineers

This listing of rafting steamboat engineers was derived from Captain Walter Blair's enumeration as found in his book, "A Raft Pilot's Log."

William Adamson
Lon Ames
Herman Anding

John Baer
Gus Bailes
E. P. Bartlett
Harry Beesley
John Beard
George Bee
Edward Bergen
Henry Bingham
John Bromley
A. H. Bryan
James Burgess
William Burns

Charles Burrell
S. T. Burtnett
Spencer Burtnett
Thomas Burtnett

Alex Campbell
Robert Carter
J. L. Carver
James Cary
Thomas C. Chambers
Charles Chaplin
Sam Critchfield
L. B. Culbertson

George Dansbury
Enoch Davies

Bert Davis
Marion Davison
Daniel Dawley
Thomas DeCamp
Charles Dillon
Frank Dillon
William Dodge
Bud Dolson
Thomas Doughty
James Duncan
Mart Dustin

William Eckler
William Edwards
Charles Evans
Sam Evans

A. C. Fairweather
James Fearn
William Feis
Charles Fest
Charles Fisher
William Fisher
Sam Fowler
Alfred Fuller
Alvin Fuller
Clair Fuller
Eugene Fuller
Hiram Fuller
John Fuller
Joseph Fuller
Milton Fuller
Sol Fuller

George Galloway
Henry Gerboth
William Gibson
William Glynn
F. E. Goldsmith
George Gray
George Griffith

George Haikes
B. C. Hanks
D. R. Hanley
M. L. Hanley
James H. Harris
Charles Harvey
Edward Hollingshead
Henry Horton
Fred Hufman
James Hunt
G. W. Hunter
Edward Huttleby

T. G. Isherwood

Levi King
Manny King

Conrad Kraus
William Krause

Fred Mack
P. M. Maines
Joe Manwaring
P. H. Martin
Lem Maxfield
Elmer McCraney
William McCraney
James McGuire
John McKeever
Sam Mikesell
James Miller
William P. Milligan
Zach Morgan
Oliver Murray
A. L. Mussey
William Myers

Milt Newcomb
Samuel Nimrich
Wilbur Norris
David Nugent

Charles O'Hara
Frank O'Kell

Dee Patton
J. W. Perry
John Pickety
O. G. Potter

Peter Quinn

B. B. Rockwood
George Rockwood
Tyler Roe
Milton Roundy
Oren Roundy
Pearl Roundy
Robert Roundy

William Schoels
Thomas Scullum
S. E. Serene
Peter Servus
Hugh Shannon
Robert Shannon
George Sherman
James L. Sherman
Thomas Slade
James Smith
Robert Solomon
James Stedman
Earl Steele
Lyman Stewart
Edward Stokes
Oliver Stokes

Henry Tully
James Tully
Frank Utter

John Van Alstine
A. C. Van Bebber
Charles Voight

John Walker
Sam Walker
David Westcott
Henry Whitemore
F. A. Whitney
George Wilcox
John Wiley
Ben Wilson
John Wright
Thomas Write

A. R. Young
Hub Young
Jesse Young

Mates

This listing of rafting steamboat mates was largely derived from information set forth by Captain Walter A. Blair in his book, "A Raft Pilot's Log."

Harry Adamson	Louis Freneau	John McCarty
Albert Babatz	Edward Johnson	John McMahon
Louis Babatz	Herman Johnson	Peter Reese
William Babatz	Thomas Kennedy	Charles Rook
John Bailey	William Kerrigan	C. W. Schricker
William Boldt	Joe LaReveire	George Senthouse
Don Buckingham	John Lund	James Shannon
George Budde	James Lyons	Del Shaw
Harry G. Dyer	Thomas Maley	John Suiter
John Elliott	Henry Massman	Henry Tweisel

Appendix

How the Watch is Changed on a Steamboat

Harry G. Dyer
1945

There are three watches on a Mississippi River rafting steamboat: the forward watch, the after watch, and the dog watch.

The forward watch runs from six o'clock A.M. until noon, the after watch from noon until six o'clock P.M. At night the forward watch runs from six o'clock P.M. until eleven o'clock P.M., the after watch from eleven o'clock P.M. until three o'clock A.M. and the dog watch from three o'clock A.M. to six o'clock A.M. This changes the watch every twenty-four hours.

On day a man is on the forward watch and the next day on the after watch. In the summer on a steamboat it is always hot and it is much easier to sleep in the forenoon as it is generally cooler than in the afternoon. On a raft boat there are a pilot, engineer, fireman, 'helper,' and two fuel passers on watch at a time, the rest of the crew are off watch.

Let's see how the day starts. At 5:45 A.M. the first breakfast bell rings and at six o'clock sharp, the second bell and the 'off-watch boys' get their breakfast. That important business being finished, the pilot goes to the pilot house, the engineer to the engine room and the fireman to the fire box, each man relieving his partner, pulling him 'off watch.' The latter get their breakfast and are 'in the hay' soon afterwards to sleep until noon when they become the 'on watch' again until supper time.

Meals are served promptly at 6 A.M., noon, and 6 P.M. At night a lunch is set in the cabin for the officers and in the mess room for the deck crew and firemen. No bells are rung at night and it is up to the watchman to call the watch.

The deck crew of a raft boat consists of eight raftsmen and two linesmen and on some boats, a 'handyman.' Two of the raftsmen act as fuel passers on their watch so each two men get six hours out of each twenty-four as fuel passers. It is not easy on a raft boat to arrange a dining table large enough for the full crew; for that reason one table is set in the cabin and one in the messroom. The kitchen and pantry were located between them but the food and the service was just the same on each table and lots of it.

On the *JUNIATA* in 1899 the kitchen bill was fifty-seven cents a day and that did not include the cook's wages. There were eighteen men on the boat and that meant fifty-seven cents for each man or $10.26 for stores. Captain George Winans used to say, "I want to pay them well, feed them well, and I want them to work like hell!"

United States Steamboat Inspectors' Examination for Chief Mate's License

The following information was furnished by Harry G. Dyer. He states that this exam was in use on the Mississippi River in 1905.

1. How long have you served as deck hand or lamp trimmer and on what boats?
2. Have you ever served as second mate or watchman and on what boats?
3. Which is the larboard and which the starboard side of the boat?
4. What are the duties of the mate on watch?
5. How would you load freight in the deck room of a stern wheel boat?
6. Are you reasonably familiar with Marine Law?
7. How are signal lights carried and what is their use?
8. What is the required diameter and length of a signal light globe?
9. What pressure is required on a hose?
10. On going aboard a vessel as mate, what would you consult to find the necessary equipment of the vessel? What are the equipments of a vessel?
11. How should the equipment be marked?
12. What are the davits and what is their use?
13. How would you rive up a set of double and triple blocks?
14. What are the dimensions of a wood float?
15. How many pounds of cork must a life preserver contain?
16. What is dunnage?
17. Is it the duty of the mate to examine all packages brought aboard for shipment?
18. What is a station bill?
19. Prepare a station bill.
20. How often should the captain or the mate drill the crew?
21. What are life lines, how attached, and their use?
22. Where would you store dangerous liquids and explosives?
23. To whom would you report a serious accident?
24. What would be the mate's duty in laying a boat up?
25. How many square feet would you allow each deck passenger?
26. What is the load line of a vessel?
27. Where and how should your license be carried?
28. What is the certificate of inspection? How often used?
29. What are spars?
30. Explain how you proceed to get your vessel afloat by the use of spars.
31. What lines are used in towing barges?
32. Can you make and mark a lead line up to 24 feet?
33. What does quarter less twain mean? (10 feet)
34. What does mark twain mean? (12 feet)
35. What does quarter twain mean? (13½ feet)
36. What does half twain mean? (15 feet)
37. What does mark three mean? (18 feet)
38. What does quarter less three mean? (16½ feet)
39. What does quarter three mean? (19½ feet)
40. What does quarter less four mean? (21½ feet)
41. What does mark four mean? (24 feet)
42. What is the next sounding? (deep four, 25 or more)

Upper Mississippi River Ferries and Ferry Boats

This is a listing developed by Harry G. Dyer of the vessels that plied ferry routes between St. Paul, Minnesota and St. Louis, Missouri from 1866 to about 1902 when Mr. Dyer left the river.

Cities	Name of Vessel(s)	Kind of Boat
Hudson, Wis.-Lakeland, MN	J. O. BENNING	Sidewheel
Hastings, MN-Prescott, Wis.	PLOWBOY	screw
	ANNIE BARNES	screw
Red Wing, MN	unnamed	cable boat
Pepin, Wis.-Reads Landing, MN	BELLE OF PEPIN	sidewheel
Pepin, Wis.-Lake City, MN	MERLE SPAULDING	screw
Stockholm, Wis.-Lake City, MN	ETHEL HOWARD	sidewheel
Wabasha, MN-Wisconsin shore	CITY OF WABASHA	centerwheel
Fountain City, Wis.-Winona, MN	ROBERT HARRIS	screw
LaCrosse, Wis.-LaCrescent, MN	WARSAW	centerwheel
DeSoto, Wis.-Lansing, Iowa	COMET	screw
	SILVER LAKE	sternwheel
	J. A. RHOMBERG	centerwheel
	POTOWOUOC	sternwheel
	J. C. THOMPSON	screw
	MERTIC	sidewheel
	HAZEL	screw (st)
	DORAN	screw (gas)
Prairie du Chien, Wis.-McGregor, Iowa	MILWAUKEE	sidewheel
	CITY OF MCGREGOR	centerwheel
Cassville, Wis.-Turkey River Junction, Iowa	CITY OF CASSVILLE	tread-power (horse(s))
Dubuque, Iowa-Dunleith, Ill.	KEY CITY	screw
Savanna, Ill.-Sabula, Iowa	CITY OF SABULA	sidewheel
Clinton, Iowa-Garden Plain, Ill.	AUGUSTA	sidewheel
Lyons, Iowa-Fulton, Ill.	J. P. GAGE	sidewheel
LeClaire, Iowa-Port Byron, Ill.	PORT BYRON	sidewheel
Rock Island, Ill.-Davenport, Iowa	J. W. SPENCER	sidewheel
Burlington, Iowa-East Burlington, Ill.	FLINT HILLS	sidewheel
	JOHN TAYLOR	sidewheel
Quincy, Ill.-West Quincy, Iowa	FRANK SHERMAN	sternwheel
Nauvoo, Ill.-Montrose, Iowa	CITY OF NAUVOO	sidewheel
Canton, Mo.-east shore, Ill.	CANTONIA	sidewheel
Warsaw, Mo.-Alexandria, Ill.	CITY OF WARSAW	sidewheel
Hannibal, Mo.-Kinderhook, Ill.	A. T. DAVIS	centerwheel

APPENDIX

Upper Mississippi River Bridges

This information was compiled by Harry G. Dyer in 1943 and represents the bridges encountered by rafters during their time on the river.

Location	Bridge Owned by	Bridge Channel Span
Fort Snelling, Mn.	Omaha Railroad	100 foot draw opening
St. Paul, Mn.	Chicago, Great Western R. R.	142 foot draw opening
St. Paul Park, Mn.	Chicago, Rock Island and Pacific R. R.	125 foot E, 158 foot W draw openings
Hastings, Mn.	Chicago, Milwaukee and St. Paul R. R.	130 foot E, 100 foot W; draw openings
Red Wing, Mn.	High bridge	416 foot channel span, 55.3 foot elevation above high water
Reads Landing, Mn.	Chicago, Milwaukee and St. Paul R. R.	315 foot center span pontoon bridge
Winona, Mn.	Chicago and Northwestern R. R.	154 foot draw openings
Winona, Mn.	High bridge	352 foot channel span, 72 foot elevation above high water
Winona, Mn.	Chicago, Burlington and Quincy R. R.	200 foot draw openings
LaCrosse, Wis.	Chicago, Milwaukee and St. Paul R. R.	160 foot draw openings
LaCrosse, Wis.	High bridge (wagons)	Elevation above high water unknown
Prairie du Chien, Wis.	Chicago, Milwaukee and St. Paul R. R.	315 foot center span pontoon bridge
Eagle Point, Iowa	High bridge (wagons)	345 foot channel span, 56.7 feet above high water
Dubuque, Iowa	Illinois Central and Chicago, Burlington and Quincy R. R.	156 foot draw openings
Dubuque, Iowa	High bridge (wagons)	355 foot channel span, 55 feet above high water
Sabula, Iowa	Chicago, Milwaukee and St. Paul R. R.	160 foot draw openings
Lyons, Iowa	High bridge (wagons)	356 foot channel span, 55 feet above high water
Clinton, Iowa	Chicago and North-western R. R.	200 foot east draw span, west closed
Rock Island, Ill.	Chicago, Rock Island and Pacific R. R. and wagon bridge	162 foot draw openings
Rock Island, Ill.	Crescent R. R. draw bridge	200 foot draw openings
Muscatine, Iowa	High bridge (wagons)	428 foot channel span, 55 feet above high water
Keithsburg, Ill.	Central of Iowa R. R. draw bridge	222 foot open spans, 55 foot elevation above high water
Burlington, Iowa	Chicago, Burlington and Quincy R. R.	153 foot draw openings
Fort Madison, Iowa	Atchinson, Topeka and Santa Fe R. R.	163 foot draw openings
Keokuk, Iowa	Wabash and Western R.R. and wagon bridge	167 foot draw openings
Quincy, Ill.	St. Louis, Keokuk and Northwestern R. R. and wagon bridge	152 foot draw openings
Hannibal, Mo.	Hannibal and St. Joseph R. R. and wagon bridge	160 foot draw openings

Location	Bridge Owned by	Bridge Channel Span
Louisiana, Mo.	Chicago and Alton R. R.	197 foot draw openings
Alton, Ill.	Chicago, Burlington and Quincy R. R.	200 foot draw openings
St. Louis, Mo.	Merchants high bridge for railroads, stages	84.5 foot center span, 500 foot side spans (2) 81.5 feet high
St. Louis, Mo.	Eads high bridge, railroad on lower level, street cars, wagons, trucks and pedestrians, upper level	520 foot center span, 502 foot spans (2), 85 feet high at center
St. Louis, Mo.	Municipal Free Bridge	645 foot side spans (2), 647 foot center span, 106 foot height, all spans

(Note: the Eads bridge was the first one built at St. Louis, the McKinley next and the Municipal was the last one built, circa 1914–15).

The term "draw" usually indicates a swing bridge that rotated horizontally around a support in the river. Later on these bridges were replaced by high bridges, that is, bridges that did not have to be opened for navigation purposes or by draw bridges as we know them today, i. e., bridges that rotate vertically to allow for navigation. The height of fifty-five feet was evidently established on the Mississippi River as the minimum underclearance height for fixed bridges.

Station Bill on a Rafting Steamboat

Harry G. Dyer

1938

Crew Member	Duties
Master	In general charge
Pilot	On watch at the wheel
First Engineer	In charge of the engine room
Second Engineer	Starts fire pump
Mate and four men	At life boats
Watchman and four men	At hose and fire buckets
Steward or cook	Works cabin crew
Clerk	Attends to passengers

The station bill designates the place for each member of the crew in case of fire or a serious accident. Five short blasts of the steam whistle call the crew to quarters.

Steamboats and Masters that Harry G. Dyer Worked on or Served

Year	Steamboat	Master
1881	RUBY	George Harrell
	ALFRED TOLL	Abe Looney
1882	SILVER WAVE	J. E. Short
	JIM WATSON	George Harrell
	MOLINE	Isaiah Wasson
	ISAAC STAPLES	James Ressor
1883	BELLA MAC	Charles Short
	A. T. JENKS	James Newcomb
	MENOMONIE	S. B. Withrow
1884	MENOMONIE	S. B. Withrow
	HELEN MAR	John Wooders
	ED. DURANT, JR.	A. R. Withrow
1885	BART E. LINEHAN	William Slocumb
	DAN THAYER	I. H. Short
	DEXTER	John O'Conner
1886	LILY TURNER	Al Hollingshead
1887	HELENE SCHULENBURG	E. Chacy
1888	LOUISVILLE	Henry C. Walker
	NETTA DURANT	Al Duncan
	IOWA	Thomas Duncan
	KIT CARSON	Robert N. Cassidy
1889	LOUISVILLE	Henry C. Walker
1890	MOUNTAIN BELLE*	Henry C. Walker
	ABNER GILE	John Wooders
	PAULINE	Jerry M. Turner
1891	PAULINE	William Kratka
1892	ISAAC STAPLES	Charles B. Roman
	CYCLONE	Robert N. Cassidy
	DAISY	Ira Fuller
	BELLA MAC	N. B. Lucas
	CLYDE*	Morrell Looney
1893	CLYDE*	Morrell Looney
1894	CLYDE*	John Hoy
	J. K. GRAVES*	John O'Connor
1895	J. K. GRAVES*	John O'Connor
1896	C. W. COWLES	Joseph Buisson
	INVERNESS	John O'Connor
	J. W. VAN SANT	George Tromley, Jr.
1897	C. W. COWLES	Joseph Buisson
	BART E. LINEHAN	William Dobler
1898	ISAAC STAPLES*	William Wier
	LADY GRACE	Charles B. Roman
	R. J. WHEELER	William Wier

Year	Steamboat	Master
1899	JUNIATA*	William Wier
1900	MUSSER*	S. B. Withrow
	NEPTUNE*	Robert Mitchell
	JOHN H. DOUGLASS	George Winans
1901	SATURN*	George Winans
	KIT CARSON	William Dobler
1902	JUNIATA*	S. B. Withrow

*Dyer was mate on these vessels

Rhyming on the River

Many tales of the Mississippi River cite so-called "poetry" about the names of vessels as set to rhyme by river personnel. All of these indicate that the author is unknown but it undoubtedly was Harry G. Dyer. Mr. Dyer states in an October 4, 1917 letter to the *Burlington (Iowa) Saturday Evening Post* that was published on October 6 that he had compiled the "poetry."

"I am sending you a list of the old rafters and old packets of other days set to rhyme as they used to be sung by the deck hands and lumber jacks.

"This does not mean to be a complete list of the raft boats. The 'BLUE LODGE' was the largest boat of this character on the Mississippi and the 'MINNIE WILL' was the smallest."

"The F. WEYERHAEUSER and the FRONTENAC
The F. C. A. DENKMANN and the BELLA MAC
The MENOMONIE and the LOUISVILLE
The R. J. WHEELER and the JESSIE BILL
The ROBERT SEMPLE and the GOLDEN GATE
The C. J. CAFFREY and the SUCKER STATE
The CHARLOTTE BOECKLER and the SILVER WAVE
The JOHN H. DOUGLASS and the J. K. GRAVES
The ISAAC STAPLES and the HELEN MAR
The HENRIETTA and the NORTH STAR
The DAVID BRONSON and the NETTA DURANT
The KIT CARSON and the J. W. VAN SANT
The CHANCY LAMB and the EVANSVILLE
The BLUE LODGE and the MINNIE WILL
The SATURN and the SATELLITE
The LECLAIRE BELLE and the SILAS WRIGHT
The ARTEMUS LAMB and the PAULINE
The DOUGLAS BOARDMAN and the KATE KEEN
The I. E. STAPLES and the MARK BRADLEY
The J. G. CHAPMAN and the JULIA HADLEY
The MOLLIE WHITMORE and the C. K. PECK
The ROBERT DODDS and the BOREALIS REX
The PETE KIRNS and the WILD BOY
The INVERNESS and the L. W. BARDEN
The NELLIE THOMAS and the ENTERPRISE
The PARK PAINTER and the HIRAM PRICE
The DAN HINE and the CITY OF WINONA
The HELENE SCHULENBURG and the NATRONA
The FLYING EAGLE and the MOLINE
The E. RUTLEDGE and the JOSEPHINE
The TIBER and IRENE D.
The D. A. MCDONALD and the JESSIE B.
The GARDIE EASTMAN and the VERNE SWAIN
The JAMES MALBON and the L. W. CRANE
The SAM ATLEE and the WILLIAM WHITE
The LUMBERMAN and the PENN WRIGHT
The STILLWATER and the VOLUNTEER
The JAMES FISKE, JR. and the REINDEER
The THISTLE and the MOUNTAIN BELLE
The LITTLE EAGLE and the GAZELLE
The MOLLIE MOHLER and the JAMES MEANS
The SILVER CRESCENT and MUSCATINE
The JIM WATSON and the LAST CHANCE
The KATE WATERS and the ED. DURANT
The DAN THAYER and the FLORA CLARK
The ROBERT ROSS and the J. G. PARKE
The ECLIPSE and the J. W. MILLS
The J. S. KEATOR and the J. J. HILL
The LADY GRACE and the ABNER GILE
The JOHNNIE SCHMOKER and the GEORGE LYSLE
The LAFAYETTE LAMB and the CLYDE
The B. HERSHEY and the TIME AND TIDE"

Dyer indicates that a similar song was sung by the negro deck hands.

Later on, Dyer mentions the same "poetry" in an article written for the LaCrosse, Wisconsin Historical Society., In it he states, "The Old Boats Set to Rhyme.

"On June 8, 1888, I was standing on the levee at Paducah, Kentucky when a Cincinnati and New Orleans packet, the NEW MARY HOUSTON, landed to take on one thousand barrels of flour.

"The flour was to be loaded in the hold, and I went aboard the craft and was standing at the hatchway watching the colored deck hand send the barrels down the chute. A number of the roustabouts were in the hold taking the flour away and storing it.

"It was necessary for those on the deck to warn their companions in the hold when a barrel was started down the chute. The deck hand warned them by singing, or rather chanting, the names of the boats on the lower river, such as . . .

"The *NATCHEZ* and the *GOLDEN CROWN*
The *U. R. SCHENCK* and the *PARIS C. BROWN*.

"At the end of every line he would send a barrel down the chute.

"A few years ago I thought I would see how many names of boats on the upper river I could make rhyme. My efforts follow:"

[And then the "poetry" previously cited was set forth].

One author says that the poem was 'kept alive by oral tradition' and the poem again reached print in the *Burlington Saturday Evening Post* in 1927 [but no author was stated] and was copied by Charles Edward Russell in his book published in 1928, *"A Rafting on the Mississippi."*

In all the versions, there is some misspelling of the vessel names. The version set forth here has been corrected for this. Also in the later versions, there are a few vessel names substituted. For example, *PARK PAINTER* for *LECLAIRE BELLE*, *LECLAIRE BELLE* for *PARK PAINTER* and *STERLING* for *TIBER* and *TABER* for *TIBER*.

Mississippi River Distances (1880)

These mileages are from a U. S. government survey of 1880. They represent the distances rafting steamboats had to travel in the era before river improvements had been made.

Place	Mileage (Descending)	Place	Mileage (Descending)
Minneapolis, Mn.	—	Lynxville, Wis.	224
St. Paul, Mn.	12	Prairie Du Chien, Wis.	241
New Port, Mn.	21	McGregor, Ia.	244
Hastings, Mn.	39	Wisconsin River mouth, Wis.	248
Prescott, Wis.	42	Clayton, Ia.	255
Diamond Bluff, Wis.	55	Glen Haven, Wis.	262
Trenton, Wis.	61	Cassville, Wis.	273
Red Wing, Mn.	65	Wells Landing, Ia.	289
Maiden Rock, Mn.	76	East Dubuque, Ill.	302
Stockholm, Wis.	83	Dubuque, Ia.	303
Lake City, Mn.	89	Bellevue, Ia.	327
North Pepin, Wis.	92	Savanna, Ill.	348
Reads Landing, Mn.	96	Sabula, Ia.	350
Wabasha, Mn.	99	Lyons, Ia.	367
Alma, Wis.	108	Fulton, Ill.	368
Minnieska, Mn.	118	Clinton, Ia.	370
Mt. Vernon, Mn.	121	Albany, Ill.	375
Fountain City, Wis.	130	Camanche, Ia.	377
Winona, Mn.	137	Cordova, Ill.	386
Trempealeau, Wis.	150	Princeton, Ia.	387
Dresbach, Mn.	161	Port Byron, Ill.	393
LaCrosse, Wis.	169	LeClaire, Ia.	393
Brownsville, Mn.	179	Hampton, Ill.	399
Warner's Landing, Wis.	187	Davenport, Ia.	409
Bad Axe, Wis.	192	Rock Island, Ill.	410
Victory, Wis.	200	Buffalo, Ia.	420
DeSoto, Wis.	207	Muscatine, Ia.	439
Lansing, Ia.	212	Port Louisa, Ia.	453

Place	Mileage (Descending)	Place	Mileage (Descending)
New Boston, Ill.	462	Alexandria, Mo.	544
Keithsburg, Ill.	468	Canton, Mo.	563
Oquawka, Ill.	480	LaGrange, Mo.	570
Burlington, Ia.	493	Quincy, Ill.	580
Dallas, Ill.	507	Hannibal, Mo.	600
Pontoosac, Ill.	509	Cap Au Gris, Mo.	675
Ft. Madison, Ia.	516	Grafton, Ill.	702
Nauvoo, Ill.	524	Alton, Ill.	718
Montrose, Ia.	527	St. Louis, Mo.	741
Warsaw, Ill.	544		

Mississippi River Distances (1940)

This mileage table is for the 1940s after locks and dams had been constructed on the Upper Mississippi and distances accordingly shortened.

Place	Mileage	Place	Mileage
Minneapolis, Mn.	0	Victory, Wis.	180
Minneapolis, Lock No. 1	5	Lansing, Iowa	190
Farmer's Grain Elevator	13	Lynxville, Wis.	202
St. Paul—Sibley Street	14	Lynxville, Lock No. 9	205
St. Paul Terminal	16	Prairie du Chien, Wis.	218
Newport, Mn.	22	Marquette, Iowa	218
Hastings, Lock No. 2	38	McGregor, Iowa	219
Hastings, Mn.	39	Clayton, Iowa	228
Point Douglas, Mn.	41	Guttenburg, Lock No. 10	238
Prescott, Wis.	42	Cassville, Wis.	246
Smith's Landing, Wis.	49	Dubuque, Lock No. 11	270
Diamond Bluff, Wis.	53	East Dubuque, Ill.	273
Red Wing, Lock No. 3	56	Dubuque, Iowa	274
Red Wing, Mn.	62	Bellevue, Lock No. 12	296
Frontenac, Mn.	74	Bellevue, Iowa	296
Stockholm, Wis.	79	Savanna, Ill.	316
Lake City, Mn.	80	Sabula, Iowa	318
Pepin, Wis.	86	Fulton, Lock No. 13	331
Reads Landing, Mn.	90	Lyons, Iowa	333
Wabasha, Mn.	93	Fulton, Ill.	333
Alma, Lock No. 4	100	Albany, Ill.	339
Alma, Wis.	100	Camanche, Iowa	341
Minnieska, Mn.	111	Cordova, Ill.	350
Whitman Mn., Lock No. 5	114	Port Byron, Ill.	355
Fountain City, Wis.	120	LeClaire, Iowa	356
Winona Lock No. 5A	124	LeClaire, Lock No. 14	360
Winona, Mn.	127	Moline, Ill.	367
Homer, Mn.	132	Rock Island, Lock No. 15	370
Trempealeau, Wis.	138	Davenport, Iowa	371
Trempealeau, Lock No. 6	139	Buffalo, Iowa	380
Dresbach, Mn., Lock No. 7	150	Andalusia, Ill.	380
LaCrosse, Wis.	155	Montpelier, Iowa	384
Brownsville, Mn.	164	Fairport, Iowa	390
Genoa, Wis., Lock No. 8	174	Illinois City Landing, Ill.	391

APPENDIX

Place	Mileage
Muscatine, Lock No. 16	396
Muscatine, Iowa	398
New Boston Lock No. 17	416
Keithsburg, Ill.	425
Oquawka, Ill.	437
Burlington Lock No. 18	443
Burlington, Iowa	449
Dallas, Ill.	462
Pontoosac, Ill.	464
Fort Madison, Iowa	470
Nauvoo, Ill.	478
Montrose, Iowa	479
Keokuk, Iowa, Lock No. 19	489
Warsaw, Ill.	493
Alexandria, Mo.	494
Canton Lock No. 20	510
Canton, Mo.	511
LaGrange, Mo.	517
Quincy, Ill.	526
Quincy, Ill., Lock No. 21	528
Hannibal, Mo.	544
Saverton, Mo., Lock No. 22	562
Louisiana, Mo.	580
Clarksville, Mo., Lock No. 24	590
Mozier Landing, Ill.	603
Hamburg, Ill.	604
Cap Au Gris Lock No. 25	622
Grafton, Ill.	635
Jersey Landing, Ill.	639
Portage, Mo.	641
Alton, Ill., Lock No. 26	650
Mouth of Missouri River	658
St. Louis, Mo., (North Market Street Terminal)	673

Index

Note: This index covers the first forty-four pages of text only.

A lines, 12
A. T. JENKS, 14, 15, 31
ABNER GILE, 19
ACTIVE, 9
ADMIRAL, 10
after table, 39
after table cooks, 38
Albany, Illinois, 6, 9
Alexander, Silas, engineer, 27
Alexandria, 8
ALFRED TOLL, 13
ALICE BROWN, 16
Allen, William, engineer, 22
Alma, Wisconsin, 2, 14, 33
Alton, Illinois, 6, 17
Alton Slough, 6, 17
ALVIRA, 10
AMARANTH, 7
anchor, 29
ANNIE GIRDON, 4, 31
anvil, 17
ARTEMUS LAMB, 5, 13, 31, 37
ascending boat whistle signal, 43
Assembly, legislative body in Wisconsin, 10
auger, 2, 14, 34
auger hole, 2

B. HERSHEY, 5, 13, 14, 31, 36
backed her out, 19
backing bell, 43
backing bell pull, 44
backing strong, 43
backing slow, 43
backing bell, sternwheel steamboat, 43
Bad Axe Bend, 24
baker, 39
barges of logs, 14
bark marks, 2, 33
Barnes, Silas, cook, LaCrosse, 25, 39
Barnes, Silas, steward, 27
Barrow, Fred, cook, 39
BART E. LINEHAN, 6, 12, 18, 20, 21, 25, 26, 27, 31
Battle Island, 24

Bear, John, engineer, 18
Beef Slough, 2, 3, 10, 33
Belcher sawmill, Red Wing, Minnesota, 12
bell and whistle signals, 43
bell pull, 44
Bell, Harry "Shorty," mate, 14
BELLA DANGER, nickname for *BELLA MAC*, 15
BELLA MAC, 14, 15, 21, 22, 23, 31
Bellevue, Iowa, 41
berries, 39
best raft pilot, 25
Big Eyed George, hobo, 41
Big Nick Hargett, hobo, 41
bight of line, 16
Bill, E. C., captain, 9
Bill, Fred A., clerk, 9, 10
Bill and Champion, 9
Bingham, Henry, chief engineer, 25
Black River, Wisconsin, 20, 23
Black, Mr. and Mrs. Harvey, cooks, 16
Black Dailey, hobo, 41
Black Andy, hobo, 40
Black, Harvey, cook, Read's Landing, 39
Black Haley, hobo, 41
blacksmith, 3, 4, 34
blacksmith shop, 17, 33
Blair, Walter, captain and pilot, 36
Blondie Joe, hobo, 41
BLUE LODGE, 4, 31
boarding camps, 33
Boating magazine, 1
boiler maker, 22
boom, 2, 33, 34
boom men, 3
boom chain, 3, 33, 34
boom end, 3
boom, definition, 12
boom logs, 34
boomers, 3, 34
boring holes, 34
bow oars, 9
bow boat, 5, 6, 10, 11, 27

Bradley, Jack, pilot, 18
Bradley, Cyrus, captain and pilot, 4, 8, 9
brail, 2, 3, 27, 33, 34
brail droppers, 34
brailers, 3, 34
brailing crew, 3
brails, 40
Brasser, George, pilot, 29, 36
"Break and water line," 15
breaking a boom, 36
breast line, 18
bridge draw spans, 3
Brockie Shang, hobo, 40
Bronson and Folsom, 23, 24, 28, 29, 31, 35
Bronson and Folsom whistle signals, 43
Bronson, 24
Brown, Charles, E., Curator, State Historical Society of Wis., 30
Brownsville, Minnesota, 13, 15, 28
Bruce, Severe, pilot, 1
Buchanan, Tom, mate, 23
BUCKEYE, 4, 9, 10, 32
Buehler, Charles, cook, Read's Landing, 20, 25, 39
Buena Vista, Iowa, 26
Buffalo, Wisconsin, 41
Buffalo John, hobo, 41
Buffalo Dutch, hobo, 41
Buisson, Joseph, captain and pilot, 25
Buisson, Cyprian, captain and pilot, 4, 5, 13, 25, 30, 36
Buisson, Henry, 25
Bulger, "floating" hobo, 41
bulkhead, 26
bull pen, 17, 18
Bullet Chute, 15
Burlington, Iowa, 7, 9, 20, 22, 23, 27, 29, 39
Burlington, Iowa bridge, 17
Burlington Lumber company, 32
Burlington, Iowa Saturday Evening Post newspaper, 1, 10
Burns, John, mate, 13
Burrell, Charles, chief engineer, 19

Burrow, Fred, cook, LaCrosse, 27, 39
Butts, Jim, pilot, 14

C. J. CAFFREY, 31
C. L. Coleman Lumber Company, 27
C. Lamb and Sons, 10, 31, 37, 35, 39
C. W. COWLES, 10, 25, 31
C. Lamb and Sons whistle signals, 43
cabin, 39
cabin fare, 15
Cairo, Illinois, 8, 15, 40, 42
California, 10
call to quarters whistle, 43
cam rods, 16, 29
Camanche, Iowa, 7, 9
Canton, Missouri, 19
CAPITOL, 27
capstan, 16
captain's wages, 35
card tricks, 41
Carondelet, Missouri, 15
CARRIE, 31
Carson and Rand, 7
Cassidy, Robert, N., captain and pilot, 16, 17, 21, 23
Cassville, Wisconsin, 42
Catfish Tom, cook, Davenport, Iowa, 28, 39
chains, 26, 34
Chambers, Tom, chief engineer, 21
CHAMPION, 4, 31
Chancy, Ezra, captain and pilot, 36
CHANCY LAMB, 31
Chapman, Jack, captain, 10
CHARLOTTE BOECKLER, 31
check line, 12, 16, 18, 28, 29
check works, 16
Chicago Fatty, hobo, 40
Chicago Simpson, hobo, 41
Chicago, Illinois, 15, 24, 28
Chief Higbey, hobo, 41
Chimney Rock, 21, 28, 29
Chippewa River logs, 33
Chippewa Falls, Wisconsin, 3, 7, 9
Chippewa River, 2, 6, 7, 8, 16, 17, 33
Chippewa rafts, 17
CHIPPEWA FALLS, 10
Chiser, Jack, pilot, 14
Christine (a Dane), cook, Lyons, Iowa, 38, 39
CITY OF WINONA, 10, 32
Clayton, Iowa, 19
cleanliness, 39
Clearey, Jo, hobo, 41
Clemmons, Frank, mate, 15, 18
clerks' wages, 35
Clever Willie Young, hobo, 41
Clinton Lumber Company, 20
Clinton bridge, 17
Clinton, Iowa, 1, 5, 9, 13, 20, 40, 41
CLYDE, 18, 19, 22, 23, 24, 31
coal passer, 14

coal, 13, 25
coal trade, 16
Cody, Tom, mate, 14
Columbus, Kentucky, 14
cook shanty, 2
cooks, 38
cooks' wages, 35
Coon Slough, 13
Cooper Jack, hobo, 41
Corbett, James, captain, 15
Corcoran, Owen, mate, 16, 21
core wheel, 4, 8
corner lines, 12
cornfield sailors, 21
Costello, "Big Handed Mike," hobo, 41
craft stuff, 5
crank windlass, 3
crockery barge, 13
Cronin, Dennis, raftsman, 27
Cronin, John, linesman, 27
Crooked Slough, 15
cross lines, 12
crossing, river, 13
Crystal City, Missouri, 18
CYCLONE, 23, 27, 30, 31, 38

D. A. McDONALD, 41
D. C. FOGERL, 32
DAISY, 23, 31
DAN THAYER, 9, 18, 19, 29, 37
Daniel Shaw Lumber Company, 32
Davenport, Iowa, 25
Davenport, Otto, engineer, 28
Davidson, captain and pilot, 24
Davidson, Charles, engineer, 20
Davis, William, captain and pilot, 27
Dawley, Dan, engineer, 14
Day, Al, captain, inspector of hulls, 36
Decamp, Ira, pilot, 25
Decamp, Thomas, chief engineer, 25
Decamp, Mrs. Thomas, cook, 25
deck crew, 16
deck load, 2, 4, 9
deckhands, 40
Denkmann, William, Weyerhaeuser and Denkmann Company, 36
Des Moines rapids, 8
descending boat whistle signal, 43
Deschman, Isaac, watchman, 27
DeSoto, Wisconsin, 12, 13, 14, 18, 25
Devil's Elbow (river bend), 13
DEXTER, 20, 31
Diamond Jo Line boats whistle signals, 43
Diamond Jo Line, 15
Diamond Jo Company, Dubuque, Iowa, 26
Dillon, Frank, engineer, 20
Dillon, Joseph, engineer, 20
Dimmock, Gould and Co., Moline, Illinois, 14, 32
Dirty Shorty No. 1, hobo, 41

Dirty Shorty No. 2, hobo, 41
Dirty Shorty No. 3, hobo, 41
distress signal, 44
diver, 26
Dixon, Decker, captain and pilot, 21
Dobler, William, captain and pilot, 21, 25, 26, 27, 30, 36
Dobler, William, pilot, 4, 6, 16, 20
doctor, (boiler feed pump), 19
Dodds, Robert, captain and pilot, 36
Dorrance, D. J., 17
Dorrance, D. F., rapids pilot, 6
double crew, 8, 13
double header, 6
double headed, 5, 17
double tripping a bridge, 16
double trip, 15
double-decker, 27
Douglas, John H, secretary, Knapp, Stout Company, 19
DOUGLAS BOARDMAN, 31, 38
driving plugs, 34
dropping line, 34
Drury and Kirns, 32
dry lumber, 11,
Dubuque, Iowa, 41
Dubuque, Iowa, 7, 10, 17, 18, 19, 23, 24, 25, 26, 27, 28, 29
DUBUQUE riot, 14
Duck's Nest, 18
ducks, 39
Dude Wilson, fisherman and hobo, 41
Dumont, John C., U. S. Steamboat Inspector, 10
Duncan, Al, captain and pilot, 20
Duncan, Al, pilot, 36
Dunn, captain and pilot, 24
Durand, Wisconsin, 7
Durant, Billy, cook, Stillwater, 38, 39
Durant and Wheeler, Stillwater, Minnesota, 15, 16, 18, 23, 31, 37, 38
Dyer, Harry G.'s mother, death of, 24
Dyer, Harry G., mate, 5, 7, 9, 10, 12, 19, 20, 21, 22, 23, 24, 27, 28, 29, 30, 31, 33, 35, 36, 39, 40
Dyer, Harry G., linesman, 27
dynamo, 13

E. RUTLEDGE, 31
Eagan, William, chief engineer, 18
Eagle Island, 29
EAGLE, 8
Eau Claire, Wisconsin, 11
ECLIPSE, 32
ED DURANT, JR., 18, 31, 38
electric searchlight, 5, 13
electric searchlight, (first), 13
EMMA, 10,
end mark, 3, 33
engine room, 43
Ervine, Bob, pilot, 23
Erwin, Robert, pilot, 4, 21, 22

INDEX

ETHEL HOWARD, 26
Evansville, Indiana, 14
EVANSVILLE, 31
EVERETT, 14, 39
EXCELSIOR, 7

F. WEYERHAEUSER, 4, 31
F. C. A. DENKMANN, 5, 31
Fairport, Iowa ("Jugtown"), 14
fastest floating raft trip, 10
fastest raft trip, 16
Fayerwether, Arthur, engineer, 28
Ferguson, James, engineer, 19, 21
ferry boat, 41
Fess, Charles, engineer, 22
fid, 41
filling up, 34
fin boom (sheer), 3, 33
Finley, Tom, cook, Brownsville, Minnesota, 39
fire, 43
fire box, 11, 27
fireman, firemen, 14, 21, 26, 27, 40, 41
firemen's wages, 35
fish, 39
fishermen, 39
fishing, 41
Fleming Brothers, 12
floating raft, 2, 8, 36
floating pilots, 4
Flopeared Shang, hobo, 41
Flopper Murphy, hobo, 40
"fly," 5
fly split, 17
Forbush, Thomas, captain and pilot, 4, 10
Forepaugh Billy, hobo, 41
forge, 17,
Fort Madison, Iowa, 6, 42
forward table, 39
forward table cooks, 38
Fountain City bay, 21
FRANK, 9
Frazier, Ed, raftsman, 27
Frommel, Louis, mate, 27
Frontenac, 44
fuel, 35
fuel costs, 35
Fuller, Ira, captain and pilot, 4, 23, 36
Fuller, Joseph, chief engineer, 22
Fulton, Illinois, 26, 41, 42

Galloway, George, chief engineer, 28
Ganley, William, pilot, 1, 4
GARDIE EASTMAN, 32
Gardiner, Batchelder, and Wells, 32
Gardner, Henry, engineer, 12
gate boom, 34
Gault, Ladd, engineer, 20, 25
Gem City Lumber Company, Quincy, Illinois, 26, 32
GEM CITY, packet, 5, 13

Genoa, Wisconsin, 13, 15
Gentle Willy, hobo, 41
Gillespie and Harper, 31
Gillespie and Hayes, Stillwater men, 12
glass factory, 18
Glen Haven, Wisconsin, 19
GLENMONT, 31
Goff, John, cook, Stillwater, 23, 39
Graham, Fred, engineer, 25, 27
Griffin, George, chief engineer, 18
Grits Miller, hobo, 41
grub pins, 1
Guttenburg, Iowa, 28, 42

half raft, 3, 27, 34
Handsome Charlie, hobo, 41
handyman, 34
Hanely, Gene, clerk, captain of bow boat, 28
Hanks, Stephen B., captain and pilot, 1, 4, 6
Hanks, David, 4
Hanks, Ben, chief engineer, 28
Hannibal, Missouri, 4, 8, 10, 18, 20, 21, 22, 23
Hannibal, Missouri bridge, 17
Harding and Scott, 8
Harding, Jos. W., 7
Harms, Fred, cook, Read's Landing, 39
Harrell, George, captain and pilot, 12, 13, 14, 15
HARTFORD, 31
hatchway, 26
Hawes, James, 12
Hawthorne, Joe, captain and pilot, 28, 29
head block, 2
head cook, 39
header, 33, 34
Heerman, E. E., captain, 9
Heider, Conrad, "Coon," 22
HELEN MAR, 18, 21, 31
Helena, Arkansas, 14, 15
HELENE SCHULENBURG, 20, 31
hemlock logs, 33
Herold, George, 4
Herold, Pembroke, 4
Hershey Lumber Company, Muscatine, Iowa, 13
Hershey Slough, 25
"hitching in," 11
hobo drinking party, 41
Hobo Kelley, hobo, 41
hoboes, 38
hog chain, 16
Holmes, Mr., 20
Holmes, Billy, cook, LaCrosse, 39
Homer, 27
Horse Creek, Missouri, 15
Horton, Henry, chief engineer, 20
Howard, George, cook, Burlington, Iowa, 14, 39

Hoy, John, captain and pilot, 24, 36
Hoy, John, pilot, 4
Hudson, Charles, clerk, 15
Hultz, Arthur, raftsman, 27
Hunter, Walter, pilot and mate, 22
Hunter, Walter, captain and pilot, 6, 27, 36
hurricane roof, 11, 44
Hurricane Island, 19
Huttenhow, Edward, pilot, 28

IDA FULTON, 12, 31
Illinois Chute, 27
International Harvester Company, 15
INVERNESS, 31
IOWA, 32
IOWA CITY, 9
ISAAC STAPLES, 13, 14, 22, 23, 24, 27, 28, 31

J. W. VAN SANT, 4, 10, 25, 27, 31
J. W. MILLS, 31
J. W. WHITNEY, 10
J. G. CHAPMAN, 32
J. S. KEATOR, 31
J. H. WILSON, 10
J. K. GRAVES, 24, 31
J. M. RICHTMAN, 28
"Jambolaya," 39
"jambolya" (jambolye), 38
JAMES MEANS, 10, 32
JAMES FISK, JR. 31
JAMES MALBON, 31
Jefferson City, Missouri, 14
JIM WATSON, 13, 14, 15, 31
Jimmy The Section Boss, roustabout, 41
Jo, Jo the Dog-faced Boy, 41
Jobin, Leroy, diver, 26
John H. Douglas, 20
John Paul Lumber Company, 12, 27
JOHN H. DOUGLASS, 9, 28, 29, 32
JOHNNIE SCHMOKER, 31
Judge Cady, 9
Judson, Dave, mate, 19
JULIA HADLEY, 4
JULIA, 5, 9, 32
JUNIATA, 23, 27, 28, 29, 30, 35, 39, 40

Keator Lumber Company, 31
Keithsburg Clark, hobo, 41
Keithsburg, Illinois, 41
Kelley, 19
Keokuk Shang, hobo, 40
Keokuk, Iowa, 8, 19, 41, 42
ketch marker, 34
ketch mark, 34
Kewanee, Illinois, 42
Kid Dailey, hobo, 41
King, Levi, Sr., engineer, 5
King, Levi, Jr., engineer, 5, 29
King, Levi, Sr., chief engineer, 29
KIT CARSON, 4, 20, 31

kitchen expenses, 35
kitchen, 39
kiwah (wooden fan), 41
Kiwah Billy, hobo, 41
Knapp, Cornell, captain and pilot, 37
Knapp, Stout and Company, 4, 5, 6, 7, 16, 18, 19, 20, 21, 22, 29, 31, 37
Knapp, George, captain, 44
Kratka, William, pilot, 36

L. W. BARDEN, 4, 32
L. W. CRANE, 4
LaCrosse, Wisconsin, 12, 14, 15, 19, 20, 21, 22, 23, 24, 26, 27, 28, 29, 39, 42
LaCrosse, Wisconsin highway bridge, 23
LaCrosse Kid, thief, hobo, 41
LaCrosse French, hobo, 41
LaDuke, Pete, raftsman, 27
LADY GRACE, 27, 31, 35
LAFAYETTE LAMB, 31
Laird and Norton dock, Winona, Minnesota, 28
Lake Pepin, 4, 8, 20, 41, 44
Lake City, Minnesota, 8, 38
Lakeland, Minnesota, 12
Lamb, Chancy, 39
Lambert, Andy, pilot, 20
Lancaster, Sam, pilot, 22
Lancaster, John, 36
Langdon, George, mate, 18, 19
Lansing Bay, 6, 22
Lansing, Iowa, 10, 13, 22, 42
lanterns, 13
LaPointe, Frank, mate, 25
larboard side, 19
LaRogue, Antoine, pilot, 14
Larrivere, Joe, mate, 25
LAST CHANCE, 31
lath, 2, 4, 5, 9, 11
Lawson, William, watchman, 27
Lawson, Herman, clerk, 27
leadsmen, 44
LeClaire Navigation Company, 31
LeClaire rapids, 17
LeClaire, Iowa, 14, 25
LECLAIRE BELLE, 31
levee, LaCrosse, Wisconsin, 15
levee, 23, 25
levers, 26, 43
Leyhe Bros., 8
LIBBIE CONGER, 15
LILY TURNER, 19, 20
Lincoln, Abraham, 1, 6
linesman, 12, 16
linesmen wages, 35
LITTLE EAGLE, 31
Liverpool, England, 14
log rafts, 1, 5, 26, 29, 33
log loss, 34
log books, 27

log raft (last), 6
log marks, 2
Loken, Andrew, pilot, 36
LONE STAR, 10, 32
Long, Bert, engineer, 28
Looney, Morrell, captain and pilot, 23, 24, 36
Looney, Abe, captain, 13
LOTUS, 10
Louisiana, Missouri bridge, 17
LOUISVILLE, 18, 20, 21, 31
Lubey, Ed, fireman, 26, 27
Lucas, Napoleon Bonaparte, "Bony," captain and pilot, 20, 23, 36
Luken, Andrew, pilot, 4
Luker, Jimmy, hobo cook, 39
lumber cribs, 1, 2, 4, 5, 7, 8, 9, 16, 17, 29
lumber raft, 1, 2, 5, 9, 16, 19
lumber raft (last), 6
lumber raft (largest), 29
LUMBERMAN, 31
Lumberman's Bank, Stillwater, Minnesota, 24
Lynxville, Wisconsin, 15, 24
Lynxville Bay, 6
Lyons, Iowa, 20, 28

machinist, 28
MAGGIE REANEY, 32
Make a fly, 17
manila rope, 34
Maquoketa Slough, 24
Marcham, Albert H, captain, 12
Marine Mills, Wisconsin, 2
MARK TWAIN, government boat, 27
MARK BRADLEY, 12, 31
MARS, 10, 32
Martin, Ross, cook, Wabasha, Minnesota, 27, 28, 39
mates' wages, 35
mates' stores, 35
MAY LIBBY, 9
McAloon, Mable, cook, 29, 30
McAloon, Tom, cook, 29
McAloon, Smiler, cook, Stillwater, 39
McCaffery, Kate, 25
McCann, John, mate, 23
McCaroll, Illinois, 7
McCaroll Academy, 7
McCarty, John, "Mushrat," hobo, 41
McCraney, Elmer, 10
McDonald, Dan, captain, 22, 23
McDonald Brothers, 15, 20, 21, 22, 24, 25, 26, 27, 31, 38
McGinley, Otis, mate, pilot, 4, 14, 36
McGregor, Iowa, 12, 18, 19
McKerrow, George, Prohibitionist candidate, 10
McPhail, James, (Big Sandy), pilot, 1, 4
meat cook, 39

Memphis, Tennessee, 14, 15, 27
MENOMOMIE, 6, 14, 16, 18, 24, 28, 31
Merrick, George, 10
mess room, 39
Metzer, Ben, mate, 25
Mickey the Singer, hobo, 42
Mills, John, mate, 20
Minneapolis, Minnesota, 10
MINNESOTA, 8
MINNIE WILL, 4, 9
Mississippi River rafts, 17
Mississippi River Logging Company, 34
Mitchell, Bob, captain and pilot, 28
model raft boat, 30
Moline chain, 17
Moline, Illinois, 23
MOLINE, 13, 31
Mollie Two-Head, wife of Robert Moulton, 40
MOLLIE WHITMORE, 31
MOLLIE MOHLER, 31
monkey wrench, 18
Montrose, Iowa, 14
morale, 38
Morgan, Monk (Monkey), hobo, 41
MORNING STAR, packet, 25
Moulton, Molly, cook, 39
Moulton, Bob, "Double-headed Bob," cook, LaCrosse, 23, 39, 40
MOUNTAIN BELLE, 9, 10, 21, 31
Mrs. Rhodes, cook, LeClaire, Iowa, 39
Muscatine, Iowa, 13, 16, 21, 25, 28
Mush Head Ryan, river boat bum, 41
Musser Lumber Company, Muscatine, Iowa, 13
MUSSER, 28, 31

NATRONA, 31
NEPTUNE, 9, 28, 29, 32, 40
Nesbitt, Newton, fireman, 27
NETTA DURANT, 20, 31, 38, 41
New Hampshire, 40
New Boston Bay, 16, 29
New Orleans, Louisiana, 14, 16, 18
New Boston, Illinois, 16, 27
Newcomb, Milton, chief engineer, 23, 24
Newcomb, Rufus, clerk, 23, 24
Newcomb, Milton, captain and pilot, 28, 30
Newcomb, John, 9
Newcomb, James, captain, 15, 20, 36
Newton, George, cook, Lynxville, Wisconsin, 21, 39
Newton, Mrs. George, cook, 21
Nichols, George, pilot, 20
Nimrick, Sam, engineer, 14
NINA, 12, 31
Nine Mile Island, 19
North Dakota, 21, 22
NORTH STAR, 31

INDEX

Norton, Harry, "Foxy Norton," hobo deckhand, 41

O'Brien, Jim, cook, LaCrosse, 39
O'Conner, John, captain and pilot, 20
O'Connor, John, pilot, 36
O'Donnell, Steve, riverman, 14
O'Rourke, Peter, pilot, 4, 20, 29, 36
oar blade, 17
oar stem, 17
oars, 17
OCEAN WAVE, 44
Ohio River, 8, 16, 28
Old Jerry Lanigan, 41
Oliver, Ora, chief engineer, 29
Oquaka, Illinois, 14, 29
Oquawaka, 29
Orait, John, chief engineer, 20
Orait, James, engineer, 20
Osceola, Wisconsin, 20
OTTUMWA BELLE, 27
Overcoat Johnny, hobo, 41

P. S. Davidson Lumber Company, LaCrosse, Wisconsin, 19, 37
P. T. Barnum's Chinese giant, 40
"Pack Slabs Damn Lively Come On," 37
packet cook, 19
packet trade, 28
Paducah, Kentucky, 16, 18
Paige Dixon and Company, 32
Pan Line, 27
pantry, 39
PARK PAINTER, 32
pastry cook, 39
patented, 34
PATHFINDER, 5, 6, 9, 11, 29, 32
PAULINE, 21, 22, 31
PEARL, 10
peavies, 14
Peel, Mary, (captain Peel's daughter), 14
Peel, Vincent, captain, 14
PENN WRIGHT, 32
Pepin, Wisconsin, 28
Perro, Big Joe, captain, 4
PETE KIRNS, 32
PHIL SCHECKEL, 31
Piasa Island, 6, 17
pickets, 2, 4, 5, 9
pike poles, 14
piling, 33, 34
pilot house, 36, 37, 44
pilots' wages, 35
pine logs, 33
pinion, 8
Pittsburg Crutch, hobo, 41
Pittsburgh, Pennsylvania, 16, 18, 41
Plaquemine, Louisiana, 27
plug and lockdown method, 2
plug mill, 33

POLAR STAR, 14
POLAR STAR disaster, 14
Polis, Henry, mate, 23
Port Byron, Illinois, 13, 20
potteries, 14
Pound, Halbert & Co., 7
Prairie Home cemetery, Waukesha, Wisconsin, 11
Prescott, Wisconsin, 2, 11, 26, 29, 30
Prommel, Louis, mate, 25, 27
pulley, 44
pump (boat), 26

QUICKSTEP, 26
Quincy, Illinois, 6, 20, 21, 25, 26, 42
Quincy, Illinois bridge, 17

R. J. WHEELER, 27, 30, 31
race, 33
raft channel, 12
raft kit, 35
rafting shed, 1
rafting kit, 12, 14
rafting works, 33, 34
rafting boat meals, 38
rafting crews, 38
raftsman 13, 16, 26
raftsmen wages, 35
ratlines, 35
RAVENNA, 24, 31
re-rafting, 1
Read's Landing, Minnesota, 4, 5, 6, 7, 8, 9, 10, 16, 17, 20, 29, 41, 42
ready whistle, 44
Red Wing, Minnesota, 12, 42
Red McCarty, hobo, 41
Red Wing, Minnesota bridge, 40
Red Murphy, hobo, 41
RED WING, 28
Reddick, John, "Smokestack Billy," hobo, 41
Redwing Dutch, hobo, 42
Reed, George, captain and pilot, 36
Reese, Charles, engineer, 14
Reeser, Gene, 21
Republican, 10,
Ressor, Jacob, pilot, 14
Rhoades, Charles, 4
Richtman Slough, 28
ROBERT DODDS, 31
ROBERT ROSS, 31
ROBERT SEMPLE, 31
Rock Island jail, 27
Rock Island, Illinois, 6, 14, 22, 27, 29, 42
Rock Island rapids, 8
Rock Island bridge, 6, 17
rolling mills, 18, 19
Roman, Charles B., captain and pilot, 22, 24, 27, 28, 36
roof bells, 44
rotary pump, 26

Round Hill, 2, 33
Roundy, Milton, engineer, 25
Roundy, Tom, builder, 10
roustabouts, 40, 41
Rowe, Tyler, chief engineer, 16, 18
royalty, 4
Ruby, Jerome, engineer, 14
RUBY, 12, 13, 14, 15, 30
rudder, 43
Rudiver, Joe, "Minneapolis Shang," captain and pilot, 41
Rumsey Landing, 7
running line, 14
running bridges, 5
Rutledge, 34

Sabula bridge, 17
Sabula, Iowa, 12, 13
saloons, 40
SAM ATLEE, 5, 10, 13, 32
SAM ROBERTS, 14, 15
sand pump, 26
sand bar, 27, 34
SATELLITE, 32
SATELLITE (1st), 5, 9
SATURN (1st), 5, 9, 11
SATURN, 29, 32
SATURN (2nd), 9
Sawed Off Kelley, hobo, 41
sawmill, 29
scale sheet, 34
scaler, 34
Schmidt, John, pilot, 25, 27
Schulenburg Company, 35
Schulenburg and Boeckler Company, 31, 36
SCOTIA, 31
Scott, Seth, 7, 8
Scotty the Singer, hobo, 40, 42
Scritchfield, Bob, engineer, 18
Seeger, Mrs., cook, 22
Seestrom, Fred, "Redwing Dutch," hobo, 40
Seneca, hobo, 41
Serene, Sam, engineer, 23, 24
Seyford, Henry, mate, 16
Seymour Hotel, St. Paul, Minnesota, 11
Shang, 41
Shang McCann, hobo, 41
Shang Nolan, hobo and fireman, 41
Shang, definition, 40
Shannon, Robert, chief engineer, 25, 27
Shaw, Billy, engineer, 16
Shaw, David, engineer, 21
sheer (fin boom), 3
shelled corn, 14
shingles, 2, 4, 5, 9, 11
Shohokan Chute, 21
shore lines, 34
shore marks, 13
Shore, Allen, M., pilot, 20

Short, Charles M., pilot, 19, 20
Short, George C., pilot, 20
Short, Ira H., "Windy," captain and pilot, 9, 19, 20, 28
Short, Jerome, E. "Lome," captain and pilot, 4, 13, 20, 36
shoulder, 13
showboat, 28
Shuttleworth, Mrs. Ruth, State Historical Society of Wis., 30
sidewheel steamboat, 43
SILAS WRIGHT, 9, 32
Silent Nine, LaCrosse, Wisconsin drinkers club, 41
SILVER WAVE, 13, 31
SILVER CRESCENT, 32
Simmons, Billy, "Billy Irish," hobo, 41
single crew, 13
skiff, 3, 6, 13, 16, 18, 20
Slocumb, Bill, captain and pilot, 37
Slocumb, William, captain and pilot, 18, 19
Smith, "Noisy" Bill, hobo and pilot, 41
smoke stacks, 11
SMOKY CITY, 18
snag, 26
snow and ice, 10
Snow Gallagher, fireman and hobo, 41
sound water, 44
spike, 41
Spike Ike, hobo, 41
split on the pier, 5
square lumber, 11
St. Louis, Missouri, 1, 2, 4, 5, 6, 9, 10, 14, 15, 16, 17, 18, 19, 20, 23, 29, 36, 44
St. Croix River, 2, 6
St. Croix Falls, Wisconsin, 1
St. Paul, Minnesota, 24, 25, 29, 44
St. Paul to Wabasha packet trade, 28
St. Louis Slim, hobo, 41
St. Paul boom, 11
St. Paul, Minnesota boom, 30
St. Louis-St. Paul trade, 13
ST. CROIX, 9
stamping hammer, 3
Standard Lumber Company, Dubuque, Iowa, 23, 24, 29
Stanton, Billy, raftsman, 24
star pilot, 5, 13, 16, 36
steamboat hoboes, 40
steamboat inspection law, 44
STERLING, 31
stern, 16
stern oars, 4, 8
sternwheel steamboat, 43
Steubenville Jim, cook, Steubenville, Ohio, 39
steward, 39
stewards' wages, 35
Stewart and Company, contractors, 27
Stillwater, Minnesota, 2, 4, 7, 9, 10, 11, 12, 14, 18, 20, 23, 25, 28, 29, 30, 36, 38

STILLWATER, 31
stock boards, 5
Stokes, Edward, chief engineer, 27
Stokes, Elmer, engineer, 27
Stombs, Joe, chief engineer, 21
Stone, Al, mate, 20
stop and back, 43
stopping bell, 43
stopping and starting bell, sternwheel steamboat, 43
stopping bell pull, 44
stops the engines, 43
strings, 2, 5, 29
suction line, 26
Surveyor General, 33
Surveyor General (St. Paul, Minnesota), 3, 6
Swain, D. M., 28
Sweeney, James, cook, LeClaire, Iowa, 28, 39
Synder, M. L., Republican candidate, 10

TABER, 32
Tattered Jack Welch, hobo, 41
TEN BROECK, 31
Tennessee River, 18
Tepeotee, 8
Tesson, Mrs. Ella, cook, LeClaire, Iowa, 29, 39
Tesson, Ella, steward, 5
The Camel, hobo, 40
The Fox, hobo, 40
The Owl, hobo, 40
The Squirrel, hobo, 40
THISTLE, 4, 24, 31
Thomas, Herman, cook, LaCrosse, 23, 39
Thompson, Orrin, 18
three brail piece, 3
Three Brail Billy, hobo, 40
throttle valve, 43
TIGER, 10
towing grain, 14
towing logs, 20, 25, 28
tramps, 40
treadle, 44
Trempealeau, Wisconsin, 39
Tromley, Charles, pilot, 25
Tromley (Trombley), George Jr., pilot, 5, 25, 36
Tromley, George, Sr., captain and pilot, 25
Tully, Henry, engineer, 20
Tully, James, chief engineer, 23
Turner, Jerry, captain and pilot, 4, 19, 22
Turner and Hollingshead, 19
Tuttle, Fred, cook, Wabasha, Minnesota, 39
Tuttle, Reed, engineer, 29
Twin Islands, Minnesota, 15

U. S. Steamboat Inspection Service, 10
U. S. Treasury Department, 10
U. S. Department of Commerce, 10
U. S. marshal, 14, 15, 16, 18, 25
ultimate rafter, 11
UNION, 4, 7, 8, 9, 10, 28

Valley Navigation Company, 31
Van Bebber, George, chief engineer, 22
Van Sant, Sam, captain and pilot (also Governor of Minnesota), 28
Van Sant and Musser Transportation Company, 13, 31
Van Sant Company, 35
VERNIE MAC, 27, 40
VIVIAN, 31
VOLUNTEER, 31

W. J. YOUNG, JR., 31
W. J. Young and Company, Clinton, Iowa, 4, 31, 35
W. W. O'NEIL, 16
Wabasha, Minnesota, 8, 25, 27
wages, 35
Walker, Hank C., captain and pilot, 20, 21, 22, 37
WANDERER, 31
Warren, John, enginer, 16
Warsaw, 8
Wasson, Isaiah, captain, 14
watchman, 21
watchmen's wages, 35
water power sawmill, 1
Waukesha, Wisconsin, 10, 11
Waukon Bay, 24
ways, 26
Webber, Louie, cook, 8
well-being, 38
went to the bank, 13, 16
West Newton rafting works, 6, 26, 27
West Newton-LaCrosse trade, 27, 29
West Newton, Minnesota, 5, 15, 24, 25, 27, 28, 34
West Newton Slough, 3, 33
Wetenhall, Frank, pilot, 23, 24
Weyerhaeuser and Denkmann, 31
Weyerhaeuser Company, 35
Whalen, George, cook, LaCrosse, 23, 24, 38, 39
wheel shaft, 4, 28
Wheeler, R. J., captain, 18
Whiskey Farrell, hobo, 41
whistle, blowing, 44
Whistler, William, captain and pilot, 36
Whistling Charley, hobo, 41
white ash lumber, 15
White, Dick, 18, 19
Whitey Tate, hobo, 41
Wier, William, captain and pilot, 27, 28, 30

INDEX

Wild, Frank, pilot, 21
WILD BOY, 32
Willard, Joe "Nosey," hobo, 41
Wilson, T. B., 9
Winans, Earl, clerk and captain of bow boat, 29
Winans, Earl Francis (son of George), clerk, 5, 9, 11
Winans, Francis (son of George), 9
Winans, George, captain and pilot, 1, 4, 5, 6, 7, 9, 10, 13, 28, 29, 30, 36
Winans, Winifred (daughter of George), 9, 11
windlass, 3
windlass poles, 19
Winona, Minnesota, 8, 17, 27, 28, 42
Winona bridge, 17
wire bell pulls, 44
Wisconsin state legislature, 10
"witch" tool, 1, 17
Withrow, Stephen B., captain and pilot, 4, 6, 16, 17, 28, 36, 37
Withrow, A. R., captain, 18
Womacks, 14
wood plugs, 33, 34
Woods, Andy, cook, Stillwater, 39
Woodward, Asa, 4
Wright, George, cook, LaCrosse, 23, 39
WYMAN X, 10, 32

Youmans Brothers and Hodgins, 32
Youmans, A. B., 10

ZADA, 31
ZALUS DAVIS, 9, 27
zero mark, 8
Zimmerman and Ives, Guttenburg, Iowa, 27
Zuckever, John, chief engineer, 28

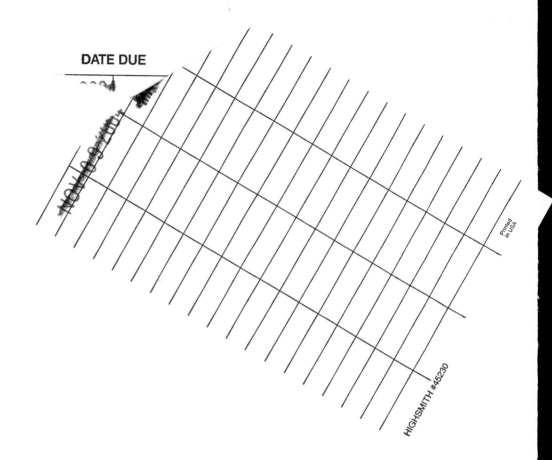